SURF NATION

Also by Alex Wade

WRECKING MACHINE

SURF NATION

IN SEARCH OF THE FAST LEFTS AND HOLLOW RIGHTS OF BRITAIN AND IRELAND

ALEX WADE

SIMON &
SCHUSTER

London · New York · Sydney · Toronto

A CBS COMPANY

First published in Great Britain in 2007
by Simon & Schuster UK Ltd
A CBS COMPANY

1 3 5 7 9 10 8 6 4 2

Simon & Schuster UK Ltd
Africa House
64–78 Kingsway
London WC2B 6AH

www.simonsays.co.uk

Simon & Schuster Australia
Sydney

A CIP catalogue for this book
is available from the British Library.

ISBN-10: 0-7432-8598-0
ISBN-13: 978-0-7432-8598-8

Typeset in Caslon by M Rules
Printed and bound in Great Britain by
CPI Mackays

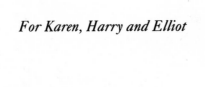

For Karen, Harry and Elliot

CONTENTS

PART ONE

Zed Layson – off the top re-entry at the Soup Bowl, Barbados.

1

ZED'S PLACE

It all started in Barbados. I was visiting the former British colony on a press trip and would be writing a travel piece for the *Independent on Sunday*. It was work, admittedly of the more miraculous kind that comes but once in a freelance hack's life. I leapt at the opportunity with the dignity of a starving man let loose in a pizzeria, pausing only to wonder whether there was any surf in Barbados.

A quick look at volume one of the bible of overseas surfing travel, the *World Stormrider* guide, told me of breaks with names such as the Soup Bowl, Duppies, Maycocks and Freights. There were waves in Barbados, for sure – the Soup Bowl was 'a powerful, hollow wave', with conditions almost always at least head high. 'Respect the locals,' warned the *Stormrider* guide, 'and be careful of the rocks and urchins on the inside.' That sounded out of my league, as did Tropicana – 'a treacherous left for experts only'. Worse still was Duppies, which was not merely 'a consistent, powerful right that suffers from strong currents', but also a break 'some distance offshore, reputed to be sharkey', whose name 'refers to malevolent spirits and ghosts'. It was not, said the writer of this section of the guide, for the faint-hearted: 'the vibe is heavy', was the wholly discouraging conclusion.

I was not convinced that I would be riding any Bajan waves on this particular press trip. I grew up in Exmouth, in south-east Devon, where there are often perfect windsurfing conditions but very little by way of surfing waves. I learnt to windsurf to a reasonable level, until the dislocation of my right shoulder out at sea in a force six, 4 ft swell off the Canary Island of Fuerteventura made me think that being closer to the shore might be wiser, were the shoulder ever to pop out again. In truth, it had already escaped from its socket five times, each thanks to the addictive but highly painful pursuit of skateboarding. From around the age of twenty-two, therefore, I eschewed windsurfing and skateboarding in favour of surfing. The only trouble was that by then I lived inland. My surfing would come on whenever I got a chance to practise, only for such ability as I mustered to recede as if it were of no more value than a piece of flotsam or jetsam, ambivalently bobbing in the shallows. There was, in short, no way that I would be paddling out at the Soup Bowl or Tropicana. As for Duppies, the malevolent spirits and ghosts would have to pick on someone their own size.

But the thing about surfing is that however impoverished one's ability, the desire to surf, for the sport's ever growing band of aficionados, is irresistible. The sight of a perfect wave, or of magnificent lines of swell sweeping inexorably to the shore, will make anyone who has ever experienced the sensation of surfing go weak at the knees, forget conventional notions of responsibility and obliterate knowledge of their own less-than-impressive ability. They will, unless conditions are clearly only for the insane, do everything possible to get into the water. And so it was that when I visited the Soup Bowl, and duly watched around twelve surfers performing a succession of superb moves on sizeable 6–8 ft waves under a grey sky, I couldn't wait to hire a board and give it a go myself.

Not, that is, at the Soup Bowl. Even if I made the paddle-out I would be deadwood in the water, too terrified to take the vertical drop on the right-hand waves and in the way of those who knew what they were doing. No, what I needed was a mellower break.

I asked one of the surfers hanging around drinking coconut juice if there was such a thing on Barbados. 'Yeah, man,' he drawled. 'Half an hour down the coast. Zed's place at Surfer's Point. Nice and easy there.'

I set off in my hire car and with relatively few unintended detours into sugar-cane fields found Surfer's Point, whose resident surf god is Zed Layson. Zed is a white Bajan in his mid-thirties, who runs a business called Zed's Surfing Adventures. Boards were lined up on the lawn outside a beach house owned by Zed on the point, adjacent to which were a couple of flats that he leased out to visiting surfers. A few surfers were lounging around, watching the waves (which were not even half the size of those at the Soup Bowl) breaking to the left off the point, but they exuded the lassitude born of spending too many days in paradise. It was lunch time, hot and dry; the tide was starting to push back in, firming up the waves, and yet no one seemed to be able to find the energy to walk the fifty yards to the channel and paddle out, into the line-up, where yet another left swept off the point, pristine and unsurfed.

I found Zed and asked if I could hire a board. 'Sure, bro, no problem,' he said, in the same drawl as the surfer who had pointed me in his direction earlier. The Bajan accent is a curious mix of Geordie and West Country sounds, delivered unhurriedly as if there is all the time in the world. Which, in Barbados, there probably is.

None of the other surfers was tempted to join me, and so, once Zed had shown me the channel from which access to the point is gained, I had the line-up to myself. It was as near to paradise as I have found. While beachbreak surf breaks on a sandy seabed (whose bottom will vary according to swell conditions, thereby often creating variable surfing waves), point break surf carries a predictability because the waves break on to a rocky point, forcing the wave always to break to the left or right. Likewise, reef breaks, where waves emerge from deep water to hit a coral reef or rocky seabed, rising suddenly to break with precision to the left or right (and, sometimes, in both directions, as in the classic set-up at the

Banzai Pipeline in Hawaii). Whether a wave breaks to the left or the right is a question of the surfer's perspective: if he is paddling for a wave and it is breaking from right to left, as he is looking at the beach, the wave is a left. If it is breaking from left to right, it is a right. On that day in Barbados easy 2–3 ft lefts rose graciously from the point, in warm, clear water, and even the sun had come out. It was early December, and as I sat waiting for waves, I imagined what it would be like to be surfing in Britain, from which Barbados obtained independence in 1966. I knew the answer. It would, in all probability, be wet and miserable not because of immersion in the still relatively warm water, but because of the likelihood of howling gales and rainstorms. Moreover, it would be rare for one to be privy to the predictability with which these Bajan waves came off the point.

I had a few more days on the island, and whenever I got a chance I came back to Zed's place. There were always a few people either in the water or hanging around, pre or post surf, and Zed was always friendly, never once displaying the arrogance that some surfers seem to think is as much a *sine qua non* of their identity as blond hair and VW camper vans. On my last day, though, there was no sign of Zed, and, as it was when I first turned up, again the line-up was empty. Despite Zed's earlier efforts to persuade me to take up longboarding, I opted to borrow a mini-mal from Zed's stack of boards and soon found myself waiting in the turquoise water. A mini-mal is a hybrid between a longboard and shortboard, being easier to paddle into waves than a short, performance board but more manoeuvrable than a longboard. For a few minutes, sitting on my mini-mal, I had only a turtle, bobbing in and out of view, for company. Then I was joined by a young Bajan who helped out Zed. We shared a series of lefts in a sea that was constantly changing colour. To the south, the sky was a deep black, menacingly so, suggesting that we were as likely to be struck by lightning as to enjoy the surf. But to the north round to due east was cloudless and empty, save for the bright sun. The two deeply contrasting colours made for an extraordinary interplay of light on the ocean, as if to accentuate the sense of fluidity and rhythm that seems to exist simply in *being there*, in the sea, and made for one of the best day's surfing in my life.

Afterwards I talked to Zed, who had reappeared from a shopping trip to the island's capital, Bridgetown. Born in Barbados in 1970, he started surfing when he was seven. He grew up at South Point – round the corner from which is Freights, one of the best breaks on the island – and began competing at twelve. He always made it to the finals of international events held locally; indeed, his proudest moment was coming joint first with eight-time Association of Surfing Professionals (ASP) world champion Kelly Slater when he was nineteen, in a contest held at the Soup Bowl, the most famous wave in Barbados. Zed gestured to a board standing against a wall inside his beach house. The nose had been snapped off. 'You can't underestimate the power of the Soup Bowl,' he said, in his laconic Bajan way. 'My board was broken along with twenty-seven others at the last competition held there.' This turned out to have been just a couple of weeks earlier, in late November 2005. The swell had been up to 15 ft and the event – the Independence Pro Surfing Championships, the most prestigious surfing contest in the Caribbean – was won by a British surfer from Newcastle, Sam Lamiroy. At this, I raised my eyebrows. Brits have occasionally done well internationally and we have even had a world champion in Martin Potter (though he was not quite the real thing, having learnt his skills in South Africa, where he lived since early childhood), but ours is not a country that the world regards as synonymous with surfing. My incredulity was firmly rejected by Zed.

'A lot of Brits come over here and surf,' he said. 'And a lot of them are really, really good.'

I nodded, perhaps a little unconvincingly. 'I'm serious,' added Zed. 'Brits rip. Irish guys too. I see a lot of them here, tearing it up.'

To 'rip' is surf-speak for *to ride a wave with optimum skill*. It is not a verb that would often be deployed by the international surfing press – magazines like *Surfer* and *Surfing* – of British surfers. The surfing nations – the US (including Hawaii, though Hawaiian surfers have an identity that is not American), Australia and South Africa – would blanch at agreeing even that there are decent waves in the UK, let alone surfers who rip. But Zed was having none of it. 'The Brits are as good as anyone, here or anywhere else. Sam Lamiroy was on fire at the Soup Bowl. He was the best surfer in the water by far.'

Zed cracked open a beer and we talked some more. He told me that the best wave on Barbados wasn't the Soup Bowl but Duppies, on the north-west point of the island. I had visited it and had been struck by the way in which the layout of the reef created a whirlpool effect when just a small, two-foot swell caressed the shore. 'It's spooky,' said Zed, confirming the *Stormrider* heads-up. 'It holds fifteen to eighteen foot and I've had the best waves of my life there. Long walls of water, just incredible. But it's heavy, there's a rip and sharks. The name means "evil ghost" and that tells you a lot.' I asked if anything had ever compared to surfing Duppies. In reply, Zed did not mention surfing but told me a story.

'I was working at one of the hotels here, running watersports activities. For three days, this guy sat and stared at me, in the mornings when I'd arrive to pick up the guests and in the afternoons when I brought them back. I'd take them snorkelling or diving or waterskiing, sometimes even surfing, whatever they wanted to do. This guy, he just kept staring at me. He'd have the shakes as he did so and he started to give me the creeps.' Zed's tone and manner suggested already that this might be an unusual – and non-surfing – anecdote. 'Anyway, on the fourth day he walked over to me. I thought, Jesus, what does *he* want? He could hardly speak to me and stuttered and jittered and asked if I would take him snorkelling up at Sandy Lane, to see the turtles.' Sandy Lane is on the west coast of Barbados, has gentler seas and houses the island's posh hotels and huge villas. The super-rich stay there. Almost everyone who does goes snorkelling to look at the turtles. 'I tell this guy, "I can't take you unless you're in a group. It'll cost you too much." And I'm thinking what kind of drinker is this? Shaking like this early in the morning. What's he after, what's he want with me? But he says he wants to go alone, with just me, and he'll pay whatever. I think, OK, I'll go with it – and be careful. So I pick him up next day and we're driving to the beach. Halfway there he says stop the car. I did and he tells me there's something I should know. Says he's got Parkinson's disease and that's why he's shaking so badly, and asks me if I'll keep an eye on him in the water. I say "Sure" and we head on to the beach. We swim out and find the turtles. I look at his face as he's looking at them, and it's just amazing. He's beaming with delight. I've never seen anyone look so happy. Afterwards he asked how much he owed me. I told him nothing, the look on his face was payment enough. From that moment, I realized how lucky I am, and every day when I get up and look around and out to sea I say the same thing to myself.'

Zed wandered off to find his partner, Bettina. I fell to gazing out to sea, pondering Zed's words. I was struck by the charm of his tale but also by his sense of British and Irish surfing. This was a man of real surfing pedigree, and so far as he was concerned, *Brits ripped*. I knew that Britain and Ireland have great waves, and I knew that we have some great surfers. But what I had never encountered, overseas, was this perception of British and Irish surfing ability. Formerly a great seafaring nation, has our maritime soul metamorphosed so that we now have surfers on a par with the Californians, Hawaiians, Australians and South Africans who dominate the international surfing media? What is the state of surfing on our Atlantic, English Channel and North Sea shores? Do our surfers have Zed's sense of joy, good fortune and ease with the world by dint of episodes such as the one he related to me, or, simply, because of their involvement with the ocean?

Zed returned with Bettina and we continued talking. I told him about a break I'd read about a lot: Thurso East, in Scotland. 'It's one of the best right-hand reef breaks in Europe. It's as good a wave as the Soup Bowl.' This was a somewhat speculative assertion, given that I had only ever seen pictures of Thurso East in surf magazines and had surfed neither break, but I was feeling inspired by the scene at Surfer's Point, my own nice, easy lefts and Zed's uncommon *joie de vivre*. I was, in surf-speak, *stoked*.

'Cool,' said Zed. Bettina smiled and nodded enthusiastically.

I looked at Zed and said: 'How would you fancy surfing it?'

Zed pretended to shiver and made a self-deprecating comment about how he would fare in the cold. Then he broke into a grin.

'You're on,' he said. 'When are you going to be there?'

The idea for the book blossomed then. I would spend up to eighteen months exploring Britain and Ireland as a surfing nation. True, Britain and Ireland are separate countries. But British and Irish surfers seemed to me to share the same, perhaps predominantly Celtic, surfing psyche. They share the same language (albeit that Gaelic is spoken in many parts of Ireland, and, indeed, the Western Isles of Scotland), and while there are inevitably cultural, historical and sociological differences among all the surfers in this book – those of England, Wales, Scotland and Ireland, north and south – there is one indisputable point of commonality. Those surfers occupy the English-speaking fringe of western Europe, and, in so doing, they form a collective that, to the outside world, is largely perceived as homogenous.

So for this book, the nations would be as one. I would start in Cornwall at the UK's biggest surfing event, the Rip Curl Boardmasters, held annually in August, and then I would zig-zag around Britain and Ireland, generally always heading north, inching my way to Thurso in Scotland and beyond, to the Orkney and Shetland Isles. En route I would try to take in key surf-spots on British and Irish shores, with a detour to the Channel Islands somewhere along the line. It might be less *Endless Summer* and more *Infinite Chill*, but Zed liked the idea, especially as I ramped up the power and form of Thurso East. I confessed that I hadn't been there, but described the long, walling rights that I had ogled in British surfing magazines for the past twenty years.

'Call me just before you're going to be there,' said Zed, 'I'll come over and surf it.' I said I would, though I had my doubts about whether Zed would leave his island paradise for anywhere in Britain or Ireland, least of all the remote and freezing tip of mainland Scotland. But regardless: I'd find out if Brits really do rip, and assess the extent to which our maritime heritage now finds expression in what, for the Hawaiians, was, and still is, the Sport of Kings.

South African Antonio Bortoletto has that winning feeling at the Rip Curl Boardmasters, 2005, held at Newquay's Fistral Beach.

2

LOGO BEACH

Europe's 'biggest free lifestyle festival' was looking good. Crowds swarmed along Headland Road, Newquay, to Fistral beach, the home – between 1 and 7 August 2005 – of the Rip Curl Boardmasters, the UK's premier surfing event. The first day was blessed with perfect weather – a positively Mediterranean 22°C, an almost cloudless sky and the diffuse luminescence peculiar to Cornwall. Light in Cornwall is ever changing but as much a tangible presence in the county as its abandoned tin mines, holy wells and quoits. As holidaymakers and surfers made their way to Fistral on the tranquil Monday morning that marked the opening day of the event, there was something else in the air, too, something inchoate and yet evident especially among the crowd milling at the top of the sharp hill at the end of Headland Road. There, just before the road dips down to Fistral's new restaurant and shopping complex, the talk was of cutbacks, off-the-tops and aerials. This was surf talk, and its speakers oozed with the unique sense of anticipation that accompanies a large sporting event. Whether they could surf well was impossible to determine (nor did it matter); they were there to savour the Boardmasters, to live the life, to watch and learn and be part of the whole jamboree. With the weather as good as it was, and with some of the best surfers in the world due to compete at the Boardmasters, who could blame them? The scene was set for a cracking surf contest.

Except for one thing. The waves. Or, rather, the lack of waves. The weather gods had chosen to smile benignly on Cornwall in every sense but surfing. The sea was so flat that even a surf-hungry ant would have been unable to find a wave to ride. A few days earlier, tropical Storm Franklin had formed in the south Atlantic, promising swell, only to dissipate upon passing Bermuda. The organizers had no alternative but to postpone the start of the contest, but, said Anton Roberts, one of two commentators on the beach throughout the event, 'stick around, there's great swell forecast for Wednesday – it's gonna be pumping.'

Any sense of disappointment at the non-existent swell was not obviously apparent on the beach. Fistral was packed with all manner of people: men with paunches playing cricket with their sons; women with tattoos and pale skin in search of a tan; pre-pubescent children carrying inflatable dinghies to the water's edge; hippie chicks and dreadlocked deadbeats; teenagers cradling cans of lager; boys playing football and girls batting a ball back and forth under the midday sun. The British were getting on with their love affair with the seaside. It made little difference to the vast majority of people gathered on the beach whether the waves were ten inches or ten feet. Among them, a few professional surfers in the Boardmasters came and went. They were almost uniformly blond, often good-looking, and usually a little below average height. Well-developed upper bodies sat languidly on less impressive legs (surfers spend so much time paddling out through surf that they cannot but have strong and powerful shoulders, chests and arms; their legs are rarely worked hard enough to develop into the same athletic form). The surfers would wander to the water's edge and peer out to the horizon. There was nothing there – at least, nothing to give them any cause for cheer. Then they would turn and make their way back to Fistral's restaurant complex, only vaguely appraised by the crowd. To those in the know these people were heroes, but to most of Newquay's visitors they were simply rather better looking than the men with paunches, whose cricket game had been replaced by Frisbee.

The lack of consistent summer swell in Britain is a perennial problem for an event such as the Rip Curl Boardmasters. The 2005 event was a World Qualifying Series (WQS) competition, which meant that qualifying points for the ASP World Championship Tour (WCT) were up for grabs, but many professional surfers favour other WQS destinations over the Fistral showcase because the waves, in summer, are so unpredictable. They can – as in 1981, the year international surfing came to Newquay – be perfect, but more often they are disappointing or, as at the beginning of the 2005 Boardmasters, no more than a gentle nuzzle on the shore, not even suitable for beginners. Rip Curl, the sponsors and organizers, did not let knowledge of this seasonal unreliability deter them from insistent pre-competition publicity. 'This year's festival will be the biggest Boardmasters yet,' claimed a press release issued a week before the event, thanks as much to the 'absolute confirmation of the Nokia Unleashed Music Festival', to be held at nearby Watergate Bay, as the likelihood of good surf. Up to 130,000 people were expected for the week-long event, which would see ex-Harrow crooner James Blunt headlining at Watergate on Friday 5 August, supported by Donavon Frankenreiter, a man who, if it was down to surfing pedigree, should rightfully have been the star attraction. Born in 1972 in Downey, California, Frankenreiter grew up surfing and at thirteen secured a sponsorship deal with Billabong, one of the major global surfing brands. Billabong paid Frankenreiter as a 'free surfer', a role also carved out later in his career by three-time ASP World Champion Tom Curren, first with Rip Curl and later with southern California surfwear company The Realm. Both men were paid simply to surf, not in contests but in exotic locations; to be the embodiment of their sponsors' image. Many people, not least the men with paunches, tired from their cricket and Frisbee-throwing and seeking respite from their children, might well have found this impossible to fathom.

More readily comprehensible was the financial value of the

Boardmasters to its surfers. The prize pool was $125,000, split in less than politically correct fashion as follows: $100,000 to be shared among the leading men, with $25,000 for the women. The spoils and availability of qualifying points to secure their ongoing presence on the ASP men's WCT attracted four surfers already on the 2005 WCT: Tom Whittaker, Toby Martin, Victor Ribas and Rip Curl's own rider Darren O'Rafferty. As a Rip Curl press release had it: 'Make sure you check these guys out as the standard will not get any better in the UK this year.' The remaining male competitors were from the WQS tour, the under-series of events held in inconstant surfing locations such as Fistral to enable surfers to try to secure points for the WCT. Rather more WCT surfers turned up for the women's event – up to half including luminaries in female surfing such as Mel Redman-Carr, Rebecca Woods, Rip Curl rider Jacqueline Silva, Serena Brooke, Claire Bevilacqua, Laurina McGrath, Heather Clark, Melanie Bartels and Pauline Menczer. Quite why they should be competing for a prize pool so disproportionate to that available for the men was unclear, not least considering the droves of women now taking to surfing. Press reports throughout 2005 regularly estimated that women accounted for anything between 20 per cent and 40 per cent of newcomers to surfing in Britain. The standard of women's surfing was, as Rip Curl put it, 'pretty darn hot', or, as Kai Stearns, editor of *SG: Snow Surf Skate Girl* magazine said (rather more pertinently): 'There are aggressive, powerful surfers [on the women's World Championship Tour]. They're not just trying to surf as well the guys – they're getting their inspiration from other women now.'

At the Boardmasters, a rather more unreconstructed form of gender politics seemed in danger of prevailing, thanks largely to the 'Bikini Babes Competition', sponsored by *Nuts* magazine. 'No hounds, only foxes need apply,' said one of the commentators. 'If you think you're hot enough, go and see the guys in the Foster's beer tent and get yourself registered.' It seemed that fewer women than expected were rushing to enter, for the commentary team's requests grew in frequency as the festival wore on. 'We're still a supermodel or two short for the Bikini Babes contest,' said Anton, on the penultimate day, as the female surfers competed in 1–2 ft surf to reach the quarter-final stage. For good measure, he added that 'the winner gets a night with one of the judges – but that's unofficial'. Curiously, while it is difficult to imagine a commentary team talking in such terms at other British sporting events, Anton's comments were imbued with an unmistakable feeling of innocence – and no little irony. It was almost as if surfing was paying homage to its macho roots, without anyone believing a word of it.

Meanwhile, women were amply catered for in the trade village, set up in the car park on Fistral beach. That is, if you agree with the view of one male surfer in his forties, who did not want to give his name: 'The big corporates have realized that women love spending money on clothes, so there's been a major push to get them interested in surfing. Surf-wear is now trendy and fashionable on city high streets and worn by people who have never even touched a surfboard, let alone ridden a wave. So here we've got a stack of shacks selling gear mainly for the girlies.' I wasn't sure that the balance in the trade village was quite so pronounced in favour of women, but he was right about one thing. Surfing is big business, and no longer the preserve of a minority of die-hards. At the Boardmasters, a collage of logos and flags fluttered in the gentle breeze, from the big brands and major sponsors such as Rip Curl, Fosters, Vans and Nokia to the West Cornwall Pasty Company, the Chocolate Fondue Company, the Half-Price Surf Shack and Uncle Ho, the latter selling mainly Fairtrade shoes and hats and offering the chance to win a trip to Vietnam. Women's clothing was certainly on offer in the same quantity as men's, and those who had been blessed with the space to set up a stall were making a killing. People came and went all day in the trade village, spending a fortune on everything from skateboards, skim-boards and surf gear to fresh fruit juice and pasties, not to mention traditional seaside fare such as buckets, spades and fishing nets. Europe's largest free lifestyle festival was doubling up nicely as Europe's largest free-spending binge.

There was one group, however, that appeared in a world of its own – the skateboarders. A huge half-pipe had been erected at the end of the car park hosting the trade village, and next to it was its little sister, another half-pipe but of perhaps a quarter the size. On both pipes a collection of skaters and BMX riders strutted their stuff throughout the week, apparently oblivious to the possibility of serious injury, and captivating Fistral's visitors in a way that must have been the envy of the surfers. Against the skaters, what chance did the surfers have to inspire the crowds in waves that rose to a messy 2–3 ft in the middle of the week, only to disappear again by the weekend? In contrast, their close cousins had a $20,000 purse to contest, courtesy of the Vans 'vert' competition. 'Vert' riding takes place on the kind of mammoth half-pipe that stood overlooking the trade village, in contrast to 'street' skating, which takes place, unsurprisingly, on streets. Street skating can be more difficult (and just as dangerous), but the spectacle of a skater rising some 10 ft above the top of a skate ramp (which is itself already 12 ft above ground) cannot but enthral anyone lucky enough to witness such gravity-defying athleticism. Not that the skaters appeared athletic in the conventional Olympian sense of the word. Many of them smoked in between sessions, sported tattoos as much as lank hair and poor posture, and though some were billed as surfers as well as skaters, as a group they were possessed of an obvious counter-cultural animus, as if to acknowledge that the commercial world had caught up with them but that they had chosen to spurn its overtures.

At the beginning of the week, Christian Surfers International – 'we see ourselves as the bridge between the church and the beach' – had had a stall at the foot of the huge skate ramp. By Wednesday, they had moved, to be sandwiched between the Surf Shack, selling its mango, banana and coconut smoothies, and the Fruit Bowl, which dispensed similarly healthy produce. There was probably an entirely innocent explanation for the move, but I couldn't help but think that someone had spotted the inherent disharmony between the skaters and all they stood for and the

Christian Surfers. Skaters would wear the T-shirts of the Sex Pistols and Nirvana (for sale in the trade village, lest they had forgotten to bring their own) and generally appear to have embraced everything that the slogan 'Universal Suffrage is the Counter-Revolution' had to offer, while the Christian Surfers avowedly stood for brotherhood and selflessness. 'There is nothing inherently evil about surfing!' proclaims the Christian Surfers International website. 'God made the waves, the problem is the surfer!'

Railing against a perceived notion of superiority among surfers over fellow users of watercraft, the website says it loud, and says it proud: 'God doesn't care what you ride, it's his waves you ride for free, so we freely offer our activities to all regardless of ability, equipment or sex. Surfing naturally is predominantly male and youth orientated so our groups often reflect this, but don't be put off by that!' This blend of cosiness and evangelism, with a healthy dose of *esprit de corps*, sat uneasily beneath the scruffy, bruised and anarchic males flying through the air on the vert half-pipe. Call me a conspiracy theorist, but the two just didn't go together. No wonder Christian International Surfers found a different home.

But if Christian surfers and skateboarding do not make for easy congruence, surfing and skateboarding are flipsides of the same coin. Skateboarding began in America in the 1950s as 'sidewalk surfing', as Californian surfers adapted the wheels from roller skates to narrow, two-ply pieces of wood. The motion required to turn a skateboard is identical to that used on a surfboard, but what started as an outlet for surfers when there were no waves soon generated a momentum of its own. By the 1970s, skateboarding had become a televised sport, with riders such as Stacy Peralta, Jay Adams and Tony Alva becoming stars in their own right. Then, as suddenly as it had blossomed in relatively mainstream Western culture, skateboarding vanished, but an underground culture had been born and never went away. Skateboarding made a comeback into the mainstream in the 1980s, when wider boards were introduced and a trick that would influence hundreds of thousands of surfers and skateboarders was invented. The 'ollie' is the means by which a skater kicks the back of his board on to the ground, simultaneously jumping and arching his front foot along the deck. The board follows the trajectory of the skater into the air, and the trick explains how skaters can leap over seemingly insurmountable obstacles as if they were less problematic than a piece of gravel (a piece of gravel is, of course, still as perilous as ever to a skater). Now, skateboarding remains resolutely hardcore, practised seriously only by a dedicated few, perhaps because falling – which everyone does – hurts so much. My right shoulder first popped out when I fell spinning 360s in the car park at the University of East Anglia (a campus whose architect was surely a skateboarder), then another three times in ramps and bowls, and once more doing a 180 degree ollie on to a town centre bench before its final dislocation in Fuerteventura. I wouldn't dream of attempting an ollie now, as a dad in his forties (not least because my kids would never live down the inevitable injury), but countless surfers around the world have been influenced by the manoeuvre, using it and other tricks from skateboarding to push the limits of surfing into the realms of what, when surfing first reached mass consciousness in the 1960s, would have been regarded as impossible.

Unfortunately, though, the swell that Anton and co-commentator Nick Williams kept promising failed to materialize, leaving the majority of the crowd to wonder what all the fuss was about, or, perhaps, to ponder the irony of a reversal that now saw skateboarding, conceived as a second-rate option when there was no swell, a key component in the commercial success of a major surfing event. Alan, from Birmingham, was typical. Holidaying in Cornwall for the first time, he had brought his family along to Fistral from their nearby campsite to watch the Boardmasters. 'I didn't see any surfing for two days, and then I couldn't understand it when it did start,' he said, before glancing over to the half-pipe. 'But those lads skateboarding! Wow! Amazing,' he added, before heading off to the Foster's beer tent. It was easy to see that for Alan and many like him the temptation of a lager in the beer tent (complete with huge video screen) was too great to resist. Despite the efforts of Anton and Neil, who injected their commentary with urgency, jokes and information in equal measure, there was a palpable sense that, to most of the onlookers, the action in the water was incomprehensible.

A marginal but contestable swell arrived on Wednesday morning, accompanied by a modest onshore wind that made for messy conditions. Anton exhorted 'free surfers' to steer clear of the competition area, as the Boardmasters finally got underway with the women's heats. These 'free surfers' were not 'free' in the way of Tom Curren and Donavon Frankenreiter, but rather beginners – or 'kooks', to use the surf-speak term – who would accidentally drift into the area marked off by black flags for the Boardmasters. Anton rather kindly designated them as free surfers, but let slip his real sense of their status when telling the 'monkey man without the wetsuit' to move on, lest the lifeguard on a yellow jet ski be forced to come over. Later, his glee in the removal of 'two kooks' was undisguised. The lifeguard approached them on his jet ski and unceremoniously ushered them away after they had routinely ignored Anton's pleas. 'We know you can hear us, come on you two kooks, move away,' he would say, fruitlessly, altering this to a contented 'see ya later, boys' once the pair of miscreants were on their way.

Meanwhile, two of the best British female surfers were competing in the lacklustre waves. Porthleven surfer Robyn Davies – five times a British national champion, sponsored by global brand O'Neill and described by those in the know as 'a charger' (an accolade that is far from easily acquired) – fared badly, coming last in her heat of four, while Porthtowan's Sarah Bentley did a little better with a third. British interest continued as the first men's heat got underway, with Bude's Reubyn Ash prevailing over Welsh surfer Nathan Phillips, Spain's Luca Perdomo and Matt Capel, an Australian surfer based in south Devon. The blond, wavy-haired Ash, a goofy footer (which means that he surfs with his right foot forward, as opposed to 'natural stance' surfers who surf with their left foot forward), looked unfeasibly young, though not quite as young as his sponsors, Rip Curl, would have it: 'Still a young whippersnapper, Reubyn was only born in 1998,' said Rip Curl's web page for Ash. This would have made him seven for the Boardmasters, though the website did go on to add Ash's correct date of birth, 1 March 1988. The seventeen-, as opposed to seven-, year-old Ash surfed superbly, ignoring yet more free surfers who had strayed into the competition area, despite Anton's ever more exasperated imprecations: 'Free surfers, *please* pay attention to the lifeguards and move to the north. *PLEASE!*'

Also more than capable of shutting out the distractions was 2004 British champion Alan Stokes, described, occasionally with a hint of envy, as 'the David Beckham of British surfing'. Stokes is a Newquay local blessed with good looks and surfing talent in abundance. In fact, he does look a little like a younger, leaner David Beckham, but as I watched him walk up the beach having won his heat with some dazzling off-the-tops it struck me that when all was said and done the Rip Curl Boardmasters might not be the kind of event to which Posh would lend her yet leaner presence. There were cameras galore and video booths in the trade village, there was a large video screen on which the surfing was intercut with ads for Nokia, Rip Curl and Fosters, there was the prospect of Radio One DJ Jo Whiley hosting her show from the beach on Friday, and there was the Nokia Unleashed Festival to look forward to on the weekend, but somehow the event welded inveterate British seaside kitsch with the anarcho-cool of skateboarding and surfing in a way that didn't seem to possess quite the jetset chic to which Mrs Beckham has become accustomed.

Perhaps, though, I am wrong. David Beckham and a number of other world-famous footballers including Roberto Carlos, Ronaldinho and Thierry Henry appeared in a Pepsi ad dubbed 'Surf', which was not shown on mainstream television for fear of a backlash after the tsunami catastrophe of late 2004. The ad could, however, be seen on Pepsi's website, and opens with a group of football heroes refreshing themselves with ice-cold Pepsi on a tropical beach as they play 'keep-up' next to a beach volleyball net. In an allusion to the problems with localism that have beset certain surfing beaches worldwide, the footballers have strayed into an area designated by a sign as for 'surfers only'. A surfer arrives, gestures at the sign, and duly despatches the football out to sea. He did not, however, bank on the *uber*-athleticism of Beckham & co, who rise to the challenge of retrieving the ball by leaping on to surfboards stacked on the beach and paddling out to the kind of fearsome reef break that would kill anyone whose surfing ability was less than expert. The surf scenes were, indeed, shot at the Fijian island of Tavarua, a place as renowned in the surfing world as Hawaii. Professional surfers were made up to look like the footballers and, in the ad, they head and volley the ball among themselves in the sea, as their surfboards fly along the tubing waves or into the air. Eventually, Beckham himself volleys the ball back on to the beach, where it hits a coconut tree, causing a coconut to fall and slam shut the players' cool-box full of ice-cold Pepsi – just as a surfer was about to open it and seize the longed-for, and, of course, very healthy, drink.

Pepsi's 'Surf' ad is an enjoyable conceit and illustrates just how far surfing has come. Its alliance with the biggest sport in the world by way of an expensive ad has yet to enter popular consciousness, but it is only a matter of time before the act and imagery of surfing are harnessed for the benefit of football again or another commercially massive sport. Beckham himself reportedly took to surfing after filming the ad, taking lessons in Morocco. The *Daily Star*, however, suggested that his club, Real Madrid, had banned him from pursuing his new hobby: 'The Real Madrid star has been warned by club bosses that the risk of him being injured while having fun at the beach is too high,' wrote Daniel Kilkelly on 15 October 2005. Kilkelly continued in classic tabloid manner with pithy observations from a 'friend': 'A friend told the *Daily Star*, "David loves the thrill of surfing and would like to do it more often. He's naturally very sporty, has great balance and is supremely fit – so he was always going to be good on a surfboard. He might not be Keanu Reeves in *Point Break* just yet, but he's been pretty impressive riding a wave."' Quite how impressive Beckham as an outright beginner would be has to be open to doubt, but the friend neatly encapsulated surfing for the Beckhams: 'He had a couple of lessons in Morocco and picked it up really quickly. But he has to be careful because of the risk of injuries. David plans to surf a lot more when he retires from football. Victoria loves it, too, because Becks looks very cool on a surfboard. She's not as sporty, so she's happy just to watch.'

'Conditions are somewhat smaller than yesterday,' said Anton, 'but we're hoping to progress all the way through the women's finals.' It was Saturday, the penultimate day of the Boardmasters, and once again the surfers were forced to compete in poor, dribbly waves. Thursday and Friday had seen an improvement in the swell, with overhead waves and a diminution of the disruptive onshore wind. Ideal surfing conditions occur when waves are unaffected by any wind, but if there is to be wind, surfers will hope that it is blowing lightly offshore, directly out to sea. As Tony Butt and Paul Russell explain in *Surf Science*, 'The major effect of an offshore wind is to "clean up" the surf. It does this by attacking the short waves, eliminating them like weeds in a garden, and leaving the cleaner, more desirable, long waves.' Butt and Russell's book – written with the assistance of Hawaiian big-wave surfer and Professor of Oceanography Ricky Grigg – is a serious examination of the science of waves, as befits its authors' pedigree: Butt is a big-wave specialist, based in the Basque country, and a post-doctoral research fellow at Plymouth University, while Russell was twice the European Surfing Champion and is now a Reader in Coastal Dynamics in the School of Earth, Ocean and Environmental Sciences, also at the University of Plymouth. In less scientific language than that which Butt and Russell would deploy, even a light onshore wind can mess up what would otherwise be good surf.

The problem with 2005's Rip Curl Boardmasters was that when there was swell it suffered from an onshore wind. Thursday dawned with promising head-high waves but, once again, an onshore wind was doing its best to make life difficult. The waves refused to break cleanly and evenly, and white water would foam and roll down their faces rather than offer the curl – or 'lip' – that good surfers will exploit with moves such as off-the-lips, slashes, hacks, cut-backs and aerials. The crowd continued to appear drawn more to the giant video screen on the beach than to the water's edge, albeit that the size of the waves meant, at last, that the surfers could properly perform. Newquay local Mark Harris was unlucky to be outscored by Hawaiian Hank Gaskell, losing his heat by a mere 0.17. Surfers are allowed a maximum of fifteen waves per twenty-minute heat, in which their two highest-scoring waves are aggregated. Each wave is scored out of a maximum 10 points, divided into the following categories: 0–2.5 is a poor ride, 2.5–5.0 is a fair ride, 5.0–7.5 is a good ride and 7.5–10 is an excellent ride. Harris took an early lead in his heat with a 7.5, but it wasn't enough, and with Ash and Stokes having earlier been knocked out, British hopes were left with Micah Lester and Josh Lewan. Both are, as it happens, Australian nationals living in south-west England, so to pin British pride on their Antipodean shoulders was perhaps a little disingenuous. Ultimately, though, it didn't matter – the duo were eliminated by close margins in heats four and six respectively. On the same day, Brazilian Renato Galvão, the winner of the 2004 Boardmasters, was also knocked out, losing to Hawaiian Dustin Cuizon who bagged one of the highest heat totals of the contest with a 16.43.

By early evening on Thursday rain had swept in on Fistral's high tide, creating smoother waves and providing a platform for one of the best moves of the Boardmasters. Australian Yadin Nichol won his heat with a score of 17 out of the possible 20, with one wave rated a superb 9.17 thanks to a huge 'air' pulled off by Nichol. An 'air' or 'aerial' occurs when a surfer propels the board up and beyond the lip of the wave. It is a manouerve that owes much to both skateboarding and windsurfing, and one which accomplished surfers now routinely execute so that they turn self and board in mid-air, to come back down on to the wave where they continue surfing. At last, conditions allowed surfers to impress those of the crowd not deterred by the rain; it was unfortunate, however, that by then there were no British entrants – even of the Australian variety – left.

Plenty of uninitiated Brits were, however, taking to the water. The restaurant and shopping complex on Fistral beach is also the home of the British Surfing Association, designated by the Sports Council as the governing body for surfing in Britain. The BSA's head director at Fistral is forty-year old Barrie Hall, a man born in Wales who started surfing when he was six. Hall grew up in Plymouth, and had his first surfboard when he was ten. During the Boardmasters he was a very busy man, as, indeed, is the case from April to the end of October. 'We're solidly booked just about every day,' he said. 'Everyone wants to learn to surf.' The BSA employs four full-time staff but takes on between six and eight instructors during the summer. One, Nick 'The Disco Kid' Tiscoe, entered the Boardmasters only to be knocked out by Alan Stokes. Tiscoe and his colleagues appeared a relaxed crew, fit, healthy-looking and patient with the scores of people wandering up to the BSA office to book surfing lessons. But for all their evident surfing cool, the BSA's instructors have paid their dues to get where they are.

'We run a Surfing Coach Accreditation Scheme aimed at ensuring the public are properly looked after by instructors,' explains Hall, in the midst of taking seemingly innumerable bookings from beginners of all ages, shapes and sizes. 'There are four levels of BSA surf coach, and each one costs £225. A level one coach, for example, is a competent surfer who can teach beginners through to intermediate surfers. It's the bread and butter qualification for basic teaching, and is the minimum requirement of surf club coaches, teachers and anyone else who wants to teach surfing as a BSA-accredited coach. At the other end of the scale there is the level four award, which is for people into the advanced theory and practice of surf coaching – national team coaches, or coaches running advanced workshops.' At every level, aspirant BSA coaches must also hold an acceptable beach life-saving award, which, in practice, means taking one of the six-day courses (at a cost of a further £200) run by the Royal Life Saving Society or the Surf Life Saving Association. These courses require nothing less than excellent physical fitness. The whole kaboodle – from levels one to four (and beyond – the BSA also enables surf coaches to progress to trainer and assessor standard) is, according to Hall, one of the best surf coaching programmes around. 'The UK system rivals that of the Aussies,' says Hall, adding that the BSA's methodology is so well-respected that he was invited to South Africa to help develop a similar infrastructure there.

Hall moved to Newquay when he was 18, with the express intention of surfing as much as possible. He is a warm, mellow character, whose late-teen ambition has been amply fulfilled in a life that has seen surf trips to classic surfing locations such as Indonesia ('at least fifteen times'), California, Sri Lanka and South Africa, as well as destinations closer to home that are just as good, on their day, as their more famous cousins. 'I've done plenty of Euro road trips, to France, Spain and Portugal, and have surfed the Canaries and Morocco.' Hall's tanned face lights up as he recalls surfing in the Canaries. 'The place is awesome, just awesome,' he says, gazing as if at a tall, treasure-laden ship on the horizon that only he can see. Now he has settled down, marrying Mandy in Sri Lanka in 2003, with whom he has a young daughter. He still surfs almost every day, though, like many Newquay surfers, is often deterred by the endless crowds and so tends to surf other breaks than those of his home town. The BSA surf school closes at the end of October, leaving Hall with admin and paperwork until Christmas. 'It's good to ease off and take time out during the winter,' he says, adding that he will take off on a surf trip in the New Year. 'Somewhere warm,' he says.

Outside the BSA's office the Boardmasters hummed along. Surfers came and went, popping in to see Barrie and his colleagues at the BSA: National Director Karen Walton, Steve Berriman (membership and marketing) and Jo Hillman (coaching). Even those who had been knocked out retained an impressive equanimity, chatting amiably to the BSA staff and appearing considerably less competitive than many professional athletes, to the point where they even seemed pleased for their opponents' success. Certainly one of the most appealingly laid-back was Robyn Davies, a surfer I had heard a lot about but never met.

'Bad luck,' I said, having been introduced to her by Karen.

'One of those things,' she said breezily, smiling as if, in fact, she was through to the next round. I explained what my book was about and asked if we could meet up for a longer conversation. 'Sounds great!' said Robyn, again smiling with such openness that it was impossible to believe that she had ever said a bad word about anyone. 'Call me when you're down here again.' With that, Robyn was gone, but fortunately Karen gave me her email address. 'Good luck with her!' she said, with a wry smile the meaning of which was wholly lost on me.

On Saturday morning, once the cleaners had cleared the beach of the debris left overnight by the free-lifestyle enthusiasts, the women's heats got underway. Watching the women trying to find rideable waves – and doing so – it occurred to me that for all that the conditions offered nothing by way of a spectacle, it was a tribute to the ability of those in the water that they were actually up and riding at all. Many people who call themselves surfers would not have been able even to begin to find a wave to surf, let alone to pump and shimmy their boards along the minuscule faces, throwing in turns and manouevres that did not seem feasible.

Again, though, the contrast between the action in the sea and that in the trade village was marked. Scores of people continued to spend hundreds of pounds, and on the vert ramp professional skaters such as Renton Miller, Jocke Olsson, Vans winner Terence Bougdour and the UK's Pete King (not to mention eleven-year-old Newlyn ripper Sam Bosworth) were, as the saying in skateboarding goes, *tearing it up*. They put on a breathtaking display that saw passers-by stopping for much longer than a swift minute or two and skate fans whooping with delight. Or, as the Rip Curl website had it: 'To huge applause and cheers the riders produced death-defying tricks as they killed the ramp as they had never done before. Going ballistic and giving frightening combinations the crowds went mental as the riders showed no mercy.' No doubt many of the skaters' tricks – frontside tailslides, inverts, airs to fakie, half-cabs and fakie ollies – were even more mysterious than what the surfers were doing. But the difference lay in the immutable visibility of the vert ramp: it was simply there, at the end of the car park with all its free-lifestyle stalls, offering a stable, tangible arena for the art of skateboarding and drawing everyone in – so much so that I wondered if the organizers would be better off hosting a Rip Curl Skatemasters with surfing as the sideshow. But no, this will never happen. For all that the sight of Jocke Olsson winning the highest air award with extraordinary flights above the coping (the metal lip of the ramp) was mesmerizing, surfing is where the money is.

Sunday, finals day, dawned much as the Boardmasters had begun. A large crowd sat or stood shoulder to shoulder on the beach under a clear, sunny sky. A small blond boy of about seven ignored everything around him as he wandered the beach with a fishing net, wearing blue jeans and a green T-shirt sporting the words 'California Surfer 56'. Another, slightly older and tanned boy wore a bleached blond Mohican cut that suggested his parents were definitely not of middle England. The smell of marijuana wafted along the beach, blending oddly with the equally pungent aroma of Cornish pasties; girls of fourteen threw a tennis ball back and forth; small children and their parents built sandcastles; a dreadlocked dude waved *poi-poi* flags; a group of Manchester males played beach football, and Anton gave a plug to Surfers Against Sewage, or SAS, the environmental pressure group based in nearby St Agnes. Rip Curl, Nokia and Fosters banners fluttered everywhere along the beach, and beginners ventured forth either in BSA-led groups or on 'foamies' (10 ft sponge boards ideal for learning) hired for £8.00 a day from the surf-hire centre at the southern end of the restaurant and shopping complex. A text message popped up on the video screen, courtesy of 'Shaz and Allen from Exeter – the second sexiest city in the UK'. Presumably they rated Newquay, surf city itself, as the sexiest, but not, regrettably, because of its waves. Once again the Rip Curl Boardmasters was cursed by poor surf or, as British surfing magazine writer Tim Nunn put it in *Wavelength* magazine:

'Sunday, finals day, and I've had enough. It dribbled on in sunshine.'

Sadly, Nunn's exasperation – outlined in an entertaining account of the Boardmasters in the longest-running surfing magazine in the UK – was well-founded. As he said, opting not to pull his punches in describing Saturday's action but to deliver them as hard as he could: 'The surf is piss weak, the first few heats go down. It's dull. I'm over it. I realize that it doesn't matter how many sideshows and branded stands and beer tents you whack on the beach, if the surfing isn't in exciting conditions it is very boring to watch.' And he adds: 'It also doesn't help British surfing that all but four of Britain's entries got knocked out on the first day dribble fest, hardly giving them a chance to compete against the best in the world to improve.'

The best of the Rip Curl Boardmasters 2005 turned out to be, among the women, Silvana Lina of Brazil and, of the men, South African Antonio Bortoletto. The women's final, whose title sponsor was Nokia, was held on a low tide bank and proved to be a one-sided affair. Lina's adversary, Australian Serena Brooke, was unable to find much by way of decent surf and her poor score reflected this. In contrast, Lina surfed admirably though not quite so as to 'destroy everything in sight', as Rip Curl's website had it. There simply wasn't that much to destroy, but Lina was magnanimous in her victory: 'I am very happy to be in England,' she said. 'I want to congratulate Serena and thank everyone.' The organizers rattled through both the men's and the women's heats and before long the men's semi-finals were underway, the first pitting Australian Beau Mitchell – ranked 165th on the WQS before the Boardmasters – against Bortoletto. The waves remained lacklustre but the Durban-based surfer took the heat, leaving fellow South African David Weare to battle it out against highly regarded Brazilian surfer Yuri Sodre. Weare prevailed and, surfing in a white identifying vest as opposed to his compatriot's red, appeared to have wrapped up the final, too. He paddled into waves right in front of Bortoletto to score a creditable 7.0 and 7.27, which, with just ten minutes to go and given the parlous state of the surf, looked to have done the trick. However, even small surf can generate drama, and so it proved when Bortoletto found two waves good enough for him to score a remarkable 9.0 and 8.0. With seconds to go Bortoletto caught a small wave, heard the commentators counting down to the end of the final and knew he'd done enough. Jubilantly, just before his ride came to an end, he raised both arms to the air. Previously ranked 105th, his win saw Bortoletto shoot up to 50th on the WQS and gain invaluable points in his quest to secure a place on the ASP Tour. No wonder he looked happy, taking the applause of the thousands on the beach and a cheque for $12,000. Weare walked away with a cheque for $6,000, while the two leading women took home $4,000 and $2,000 respectively.

Back in the trade village, money continued to circulate, *sans* demarcation by gender. A teenager bought a T-shirt with the words 'Better a bad day in the water than a good day at school', and immediately donned it over his bare upper body. It was sunny and warm, so perhaps he was heeding Anton's oft-repeated advice to avoid the sun rays, either by covering up or by a bit of 'slip-slop-slap – especially if you're ginger, because you guys burn more'. Women bought flip-flops, necklaces and crop-tops, men eyed the surf gear and everywhere logos shone in the Sunday sunshine. Trade was brisk despite the hangovers being nursed from the refreshment consumed either at Judge Jules's live performance the previous evening in the Fosters' beer tent, or at Watergate Bay, where half-British, half-Swedish chart-toppers Razorlight – the majority of whose songs chronicle a romantically seedy, booze-fuelled London life – had done their thing, supported among others by Easy Kill, a local band who, save for their lead singer Kyle (who is learning), all surf. One stall was doing especially well – that for Footprint's *Surfing Britain*, a guide written by Chris Nelson and Demi Taylor. I'd always relied on the *Stormrider* guides, together with a supplement produced by *Carve* magazine at least a decade ago. I flicked through the Footprint book and, like hundreds of others at the Boardmasters who were curious about surfing or actively planning to surf our best breaks or just plain wannabes, bought a copy. Meanwhile, I heard that Caroline Steel from Leeds had bagged the *Nuts* Boardmasters Bikini Babe 2005 title.

In the distance, Newquay's Headland Hotel looked down on the seething mass of people. Its Victorian architects could never have imagined how Fistral beach would look in the early twenty-first century. As I made my way towards Headland Road, I caught sight of a stall I hadn't previously noticed. Perhaps it was its dark green canvas, a little understated compared with the other marketers and their temporary homes, or maybe it was because it was squashed to the side of an outlet for Yamaha jet skis, a form of watercraft with which the majority of surfers have, at best, an undecided relationship. Tucked just inside this modest stall stood a surfboard and on a fold-away chair next to a table sat a lean, weather-beaten man in his early forties. His name was Chris Hines, and he was at Newquay to promote the Eden Project's 'Eco Board', which, if Hines had his way, would become the world's first commercially produced wholly biodegradable surfboard. I knew of Hines through friends – he was a Porthtowan-based surfer, a founder member of Surfers Against Sewage and known for his radical environmentalism. We spoke briefly, and agreed to catch up again on my travels. Before I went, I asked him what he made of the Boardmasters.

'What do you mean?'

'Is it a true reflection of British surfing?'

Hines smiled. He looked at the jet skis, and the people milling everywhere, and gestured towards Fistral beach.

'This place is incredible. On its day Fistral is one of the best beachbreaks in Europe, and this event is massive. I mean, *look* at the people. Twenty years ago you'd have been certified if you'd said over a hundred thousand people would come along to a UK surfing event. It's amazing. But is it surfing? Is it British surfing?'

A fast-talking, intense man, Hines paused. He reached over to his cherished Eco Board and tapped one of its rails, then looked towards the sea, almost wholly obscured by the throng of people.

'Is this British surfing?' Hines shook his head. 'I don't know. I just don't know.'

It was as if he'd had the answer, only to see it slip away, like a wave that promises to rise into rideable form only to bulge harmlessly towards the shore.

The best reef break in England? Probably. Porthleven going off.

3

SIX FEET AND OVER

By the tail-end of 2005, the UK surfing scene was able to support no less than seven dedicated magazines. All were based in Cornwall, with the exception of *The Surfer's Path*, which as well as an office in Bude could list one in America, too. The longest-running is *Wavelength*, edited then by Steve Bough and based in Cornwall's county town, Truro. *Wavelength*, created in 1981, was for years the leading title but had seen stiff competition from Newquay's *Carve* magazine. The other, more niche or underground titles – *SurfGirl* and *ThreeSixty* (which share the same publisher as *Carve*), Joe Moran's often joyously unreconstructed *Pitpilot* and Helen Gilchrist's cult title *Stranger* – continue to grow in circulation, and by the end of 2006 had been joined by *Slide* and *Tonnau*. The former was set up by veteran surfing photographer Roger Sharp, while the latter, edited by Rachel Bell, was devoted to the Welsh surfing scene. Even then, there was room for one more magazine, with *Huck* – 'more than just a ride' – entering the fray to appeal to what its editor Vince Medeiros sees as a 'tribe' of surfing, snowboarding and skateboarding enthusiasts, people for whom these activities define their lives. In Ireland there are *Fins* and *Freeflow*, and even now the market shows no sign of topping out. For those already up and running, and, it seems, one or two newcomers, these are heady times.

The first issue of *Carve*, published in March 1994, featured Boardmasters' headline musician Donavon Frankenreiter on its cover. The long-haired, tanned Californian, with his toned body and blue boardshorts (and a mildly subversive tattooed upper left arm), provided an image of surfing perfection for the cover of what Chris Power, *Carve*'s editor, intended to be a magazine that would 'put the stoke back into surfing'. The shot of Frankenreiter throwing his body into a frontside off-the-lip at legendary Hawaiian break Off-The-Wall – spray flying everywhere as surfer and board are about to go into freefall down the face of the wave – was pretty much as good as it gets. It was taken by veteran British surfing photographer Alex Williams, a man whose photographs have featured so frequently in surfing magazines over the years that I have as often marvelled at his apparent ubiquity as his evident expertise. Williams did, however, share the honours for the debut issue of *Carve* with Mike Searle and Power, who himself is no mean snapper. Running to a modest sixty-eight pages, *Carve*'s first issue featured Hawaii, Portugal and Lanzarote. World-class spots, all, and replete with surfers tucking into exquisite tubes of turquoise waves, under suitably paradisiacal skies. At the back, though, was a feature that had as much, if not more appeal.

Power put together a 'Cold Snaps' collage of the best surf in Britain's winter of 1993–94. Surfing in Britain in winter is, as the accompanying editorial pointed out, 'a heavy experience. By December you're wearing a thick suit, boots and gloves that feel like dumbbells when you paddle. The water seems more dense, the lip comes down with a crack that'll hurt if you get it on the head. The beaches are deserted, except for a handful of surfers here and there when the wind's offshore.' The experience can, said the text, be 'pretty bleak'.

And yet the 'Cold Snaps' feature contained images to warm the coldest surfer's heart. Here were beautiful, barrelling rights in west Wales, empty reef breaks on the Gower coast, a surfer whose every body part save for his face was clad in neoprene executing a textbook bottom turn at the foot of a secret Cornish left, that day working at up to 10 ft, and a picture of a break near Land's End that Power chose not to name in 1994 but which looks uncannily like Gwenver, now a popular though deceptively tough (and, for its locals, fortunately all but inaccessible) wave. Above the image of Gwenver (if Gwenver it is) sat a small, quarter-page shot of a truly terrifying wave. It was about 8 ft and breaking to the left, the lip curling as the wave hit a reef to form a 'tube' or 'barrel'. A good surfer will drop down the face of a wave and race along inside the curl, stalling the board to do so if necessary, risking the might of tons of water smashing on to his head if the attempted tube-ride goes wrong. Surfing magazines the world over are full of images of expert surfers deep inside tubes, making the manoeuvre appear no more difficult than turning the ignition key in a car. Tube-riding is, though, less for the average among us and more for the Formula One drivers of the surfing world. To ride a tube or tuck inside a barrelling wave takes years of practice and an act of extreme commitment, but how much harder is it when faced with a wave like the one in *Carve*'s 'Cold Snaps' feature? For this was not a wave illuminated by immaculate light, the translucent blue of Hawaii, Portugal and Lanzarote; it was not a wave warm enough to require no more than a pair of boardshorts; it was not, in short, a wave that made it all look benign and easy. This was a wave of deep, dark murkiness, one that seemed to possess in its face a thousand lumps of concrete as well as the black strands of kelp that bubbled in the shorebreak. This was The Cove, in north-east England, and the caption summed it up well: 'The water may be brown, weird-tasting and freezing, but The Cove is fast becoming known as the best wave in the north-east. The late great Nigel Veitch reckoned he had the best tube of his life not in Indo or Hawaii, but here. When it's on, crews from Newcastle and Scarborough converge to race the speedy lefts.' Just visible at the pit of the wave, about to be buried beneath the exploding white water, was a surfer whose drop-in had clearly gone wrong. 'No doubt this guy was glad there's a bit of kelp covering the rocks,' concluded the caption.

On a damp September day I made my way through the streets of Newquay to find the author of the wry payoff in the caption about

The Cove. *Carve* is published by Orca Publications, whose home is on Berry Road, itself within paddling distance of the surfing beaches of Towan, Great Western, Tolcarne and Lusty Glaze. At low tide these four beaches combine to make a single mile-long stretch, collectively known as the Town Beaches, with Towan Head jutting out to the north ensuring that they offer sheltered, relatively unthreatening surf in all but the most massive of storms. The 1992 *Stormrider Guide Europe* – to which Power was a contributing photographer – notes the appeal of the Town Beaches to 'grommets' (children learning to surf) and holidaymakers and concludes, a little wearily, that 'locals head here only when there is no other choice'.

Power himself is not a Newquay local – not by birth, at any rate. Born in 1961 in the Home Counties, most of his upbringing was between Oxford and Reading, an area notable for rowing as its watersport of choice. Power took up skateboarding at an early age, thanks largely to the influence of his younger brother, with whom he would make skateboards and skate the local bowls. One day his brother returned from a local skate shop clutching an imported copy of US magazine *Surfer*. Power, a wiry, fit-looking man with black curly hair, was smitten. 'I took one look at the surfing shots and knew I had to give it a go,' he recalls, confessing that when he first turned up at a Cornish surfing beach he thought it would be easy. 'I arrived at Polzeath and the waves can't have been bigger than three feet. I assumed it would be a piece of cake. I was wrong. Like any beginner, I couldn't do it.' He chuckles at the memory, but practice makes perfect and soon Power was proficient enough to want to centre his life on surfing. He took a degree in geology at Southampton University, from which he made sorties to south-coast surf spots at Kimmeridge and Bournemouth in Dorset. After university he spent a few years 'doing odds and sods', such as selling windsurfers in Oxford and skiing and snowboarding in America.

By his mid-twenties, Power was freelancing regularly for the early British surfing magazines such as *The Edge*, *Surf Scene* and *Groundswell*, the BSA's own title. In 1981, he moved to Newquay having landed a job at *Wavelength* magazine. Power worked for

Wavelength under its now deceased editor John Conway for ten months, but I sensed that something of a clash may have occurred between the two men. Conway was a larger-than-life, brusque figure, one of the pioneers of the British surfing scene and, apparently, a man who didn't mind taking the occasional short cut. This is not Power's style. He is a quieter sort, reflective and thorough, the kind who prefers to play his cards close to his chest. It was no surprise that the relationship did not last long – nor that Power's intelligence and passion convinced him that he could do a better job than Conway.

'I looked at the UK surfing magazines and felt they lacked any spark,' he explains. 'The US magazines were amazing – full of inspirational pictures and stories that said "welcome to our world". By contrast, Brit surfers were getting a raw deal. The main titles back then [the late 1980s] were *Wavelength* and *Surf Scene*, and to be frank they were both looking jaded.' Power's ten-month stint as assistant editor of *Wavelenth* came to an end when he became uncomfortable about Conway's business practices. He spent a couple of years publishing the BSA's newsletter, *Groundswell*, then by chance ran into Mike Searle and Louise Webb – avid bodyboarders who had escaped sales jobs in London to live in Cornwall, where they set up *ThreeSixty* magazine. Power initially sold them some bodyboarding photographs and the trio soon started talking about setting up their own surfing magazine. Idea became reality in 1994, when, thanks to an investment of £5,000 each by Power, Searle and Webb, *Carve* hit the newsstands with a print-run of 15,000. 'We got a fantastic reaction,' recalls Power, who has remained editor since the magazine's inception, building up *Carve* to become the leading surfing magazine title in Britain. 'Our readership in the summer peaks at 30,000 per issue,' says Power, who credits the magazine's success to the enthusiasm of its staff and contributors. 'We're a small, independent publishing house and we all surf. That commitment comes across in the copy.' Or, as Power's editorial put it in the first issue: 'Our number one aim is to get you stoked, just itching to go surfing . . . being stoked is what it's all about.'

Power agrees that surfing in the UK is going through an extraordinary boom. 'It's been rising in popularity every year ever since people first started riding longboards at Fistral in the sixties,' he says, sitting at a desk awash with surfing magazines and photographs, 'but it's gone crazy lately. I don't know if it can continue at its current rate, but every time I think it's hit the ceiling something else happens – there's an ad on TV using surfing, or I turn up to surf a secret spot in winter to find it packed. It just seems to grow and grow.' Indicative of this, *Carve* is a much brighter, bigger beast than its 1994 ancestor, up to three times its original size, with copious advertising. Competition among the surfing titles is robust. As Power concedes, '*Wavelength* had its doldrums but it's catching up again. It's a tough business. To stay ahead you've got to slog your guts out.'

I asked him whether he thought that the changes were for the better. Diplomatically, Power batted the question away. 'I'm not old enough to tell you,' he said, 'but one thing is true – the breaks down here are twice as crowded these days.' I asked him which were his favourite breaks, but Power, who lives near St Agnes, preferred to maintain a discreet silence, so I turned the conversation to Cornwall's most revered wave: Porthleven, on the Lizard peninsula.

Is it as good as they say it is?

'On its day it's an amazing wave,' agreed Power, of the reef break off the rocks of Britain's most southerly working port. 'It's really photogenic. It's good at two to four feet but much more impressive when it's six to eight feet plus. You should try and check it out.'

I fully intended to, but before I left Power dropped a couple of the perennial nuggets with which he was to favour me during my odyssey.

'Make sure you talk to Robyn Davies – she lives there. She's by far and away the best female surfer in Britain. Better than most blokes. If you can find her, that is.' Power's smile reminded me of the look on Karen Walton's face when she gave me Robyn's email address at the Boardmasters. He paused, then recovered his thread. 'And talk to John Adams. He's in his sixties now and lives in Penzance. He can tell you about how surfing has changed. And he's the man who discovered Porthleven.'

Porthleven has legendary status in an English surfer's mind. I first heard of its right-hand reef break when at university in what one might believe to be the surf-free region of East Anglia. Not so. Norfolk and Suffolk have a number of mercurial breaks which were regularly surfed by what was then the East Coast Wave Riders club. Two surfers I met in this, the flattest part of the British Isles, linger in my mind precisely because of their obsession with Porthleven.

'It's the best wave in the country, no question, and it's on par with anything in the world,' would be the invariable pronouncement of Chris Martin, then studying Environmental Science at UEA, whenever the subject of great waves came up. I wasn't sure if Chris had surfed it, or whether this was a repetition of received wisdom, but another student, Greg from Venezuela, was even more of a devotee. I rarely spoke with Greg, who, in fact, was so taciturn that he rarely spoke with anybody, but I recall one term wondering where he'd got to. 'He's gone to live in Porthleven,' said Chris. 'He just wants to live there and surf.' Was that it? What about work, career, life? 'He has no plans other than to surf Porthleven,' said Chris.

As I drove into Penzance to meet John Adams, having left a voicemail for Robyn Davies telling her I was in the area, I wondered what had happened to Chris and Greg. I'd shared one or two flats in London with Chris for a few months after university, during which time I worked in a bookshop and he as a cycle courier. He stowed a custom-made 6′ 6″ thruster wherever we lived, and was always off on one trip or another. As much as Porthleven, he used to rave about Chicama in Peru, the longest left-breaking wave in the world. I can't recall whether Chris was a regular or goofy footer, but I'm fairly sure he made it to Chicama. We'd lost touch in our mid-twenties, but maybe, just maybe, he had settled in Porthleven. What odds, though, on a Venezuelan called Greg still being there, surfing the same wave that, as an overseas student on surfari, he'd fallen in love with some twenty years ago? Maybe I'd run into one or both of them on one of my trips; maybe, just maybe, John Adams had encountered them.

Certainly, John knew an awful lot of people. When we met he had just turned sixty-five, and had packed his life with experience, entrepreneurialism and enthusiasm for just about everything. He had run dance halls, exhibited surf movies, set up a video and DVD distribution company and, most recently, become a keen yachtsman. Throughout, he had surfed, and he was, indeed, one of the two men who discovered Porthleven.

'Back in the early 1960s the surfing scene was concentrated on the north coast of Cornwall, at Porthmeor beach in St Ives, Newquay and down the coast at Sennen Cove,' said John, a tall, well-built man with dark hair and the kind of permanent tan that comes from continual exposure to the elements. 'I used to surf a lot then with Mike Carr, the first secretary of the British Surfing Association, in the days before wetsuits were invented. We used to wrap plastic bags around our legs to keep warm, and no one surfed beyond November. And no one thought to surf the south coast. In fact, we used to get a bit of stick, living in Penzance, from the north-coast surfers. They'd tell us on the south coast that there was no surf where we were, but they were wrong. Mike and I used to drive around looking for surf, at beachbreaks like Praa Sands and Perranuthanoe, and we knew the south coast picked up swell. Then one day we clocked Porthleven. It must have been in 1965 or '66, I'm not sure. The wave was breaking at around four to five feet – a big, clean wave coming out of deep water and hitting a reef to the right of the harbour. Mike and I looked at each other and said: "Let's go!" So we paddled out and surfed it. The locals thought we were mad. Surfing then was regarded as either dangerous or full of drop-outs; people viewed us as aliens. So to see two blokes paddling out and catching perfect, clean barrels at an old, working port like Porthleven . . . well, I can see that it must have looked certifiable. But we loved it. That was the start, and we went back whenever the swell was good. It's my favourite wave, without a doubt.'

It was an overcast day, and I had met Adams at his house in Penzance. He uses the ground floor as the office for www.surfingvideos.co.uk, which, unsurprisingly, distributes surfing videos. There was little light downstairs, but one room is a sparkling Aladdin's cave of surf film classics, such as *Morning of the Earth*, *Big Wednesday*, *Children of the Sun* and *Free Ride* ('a spiritual experience that explores the very nature of stoke'), and, of course, Bruce Brown's *The Endless Summer*. Brown's film, made between 1962 and 1964, follows two surfers – Mike Hynson and Robert August – around the world in search of the perfect wave. Widely regarded as the definitive surfing film, *The Endless Summer* was first shown in the UK by Adams. The film is less a documentary and more a cinematic, and frequently turquoise, travelogue, but if its precise genre is elusive one quality is irrefutable. This is a film brimming with what can only be described as innocence. It was completed shortly after the assassination of John F. Kennedy in November 1963, predating Vietnam and hovering in a curious nether-zone of American history, immediately post-McCarthyism but on the cusp of the great American Dream starting to turn sour. It is a film made against a cultural and political background of the Cuban missile crisis, the Bay of Pigs invasion and the building of the Berlin Wall, a film unscarred by the American race riots of the sixties and, in surfing terms, one which is wholly unaware of the localism that would soon arrive on Californian and Hawaiian beaches. Brown's narration is ingenuously oblivious to anything beyond the film's premise – that two surfers would travel Africa, Australia, New Zealand, Tahiti, Hawaii and California in search of the perfect wave. I looked at Adams, as he told me how he had made a living distributing and exhibiting surfing films in the sixties and seventies, and wondered what it must have been like to be a surfer in the UK at that time. Was there the same kind of innocence, an undiluted enthusiasm for surfing, that is so evident in *The Endless Summer*?

'It was wonderful,' said Adams, whose eyes seemed to illumine the gloom as much as the beach-blues and -whites of the surfing memorabilia and merchandise in his house. 'There was a hippie, offbeat feel to it all, a feeling that it was all there, waiting to be discovered. Yes, we were freaks to some, but if people thought we were mad, they also looked up to us. It was a great time to be a surfer.'

Adams had never run into Chris or Greg, but twenty-five years after he had paddled out at Porthleven, some of his successors were coming in for a bad press. 'Are most residents [of Porthleven] in favour of surfing?' asked Les Edwards, the vice-president of the Porthleven 2000 group. He knew the answer – it was 'an emphatic NO'. The Porthleven 2000 group comprised local businessmen who wished to build a breakwater on top of the Porthleven reef, the aim of which was apparently to shelter the 300-year-old harbour and cliff-side houses from waves and prevent erosion. A related benefit would be that it would be easier for yachts to visit Porthleven, bringing much needed income to a close-knit and vibrant, but also poor, community. Chris Power mustered the armoury of his geology degree to scotch the plans of the Porthleven 2000 group in *Carve*'s first issue, in a piece entitled 'Goodbye Porthleven?'.

'The "reasons" [for the breakwater] appear to make little sense,' he wrote. 'First, the cliff in question is composed of very hard Devonian slate and is not being significantly eroded (and if it was, why would district planners have allowed two large stone houses to be built on the cliff-top in the last five years?) Incoming waves expend their energy as they break on the reef, not against the cliff. Second, during southerly gales large waves would probably be deflected by the proposed breakwater into the harbour mouth. So it looks as though the only difference the breakwater would make would be to wreck the wave for surfing. Could this be the real reason behind the plan? For years Porthleven residents have complained about a minority of badly behaved surfers. Perhaps now they've decided enough is enough?'

A quote from Les Edwards seemed to confirm Power's fears. '[Surfers] bring little or no income to Porthleven. They defecate in people's gardens, do strip shows, block the road and park illegally.' And he warned: 'You surfers have a lot to do in building a better image in this area.'

Nothing seems to have come either of Edwards' scaremongering or the Porthleven 2000 group's plans. There is no breakwater, and Porthleven continues to be acclaimed in every guidebook on British surfing as either the best or very nearly the best wave in England. As I drove into Porthleven, after meeting Adams, I hoped to see the wave in all its glory. It was, though, a windless, grey September day, and Porthleven needs a large south-westerly swell, held up by a north-easterly wind, for its right-hand reef break to work. I parked the car on the harbour side, opposite a Christian bookshop, and made my way to the cob, not expecting all that much. If Seneca is right – that to be happy we should expect disappointment, so that when it inevitably comes we are unruffled (and perhaps even pleased to have been vindicated) – my lack of optimism was a good call. There was not a wave – of the surfable variety – in sight.

A few days later, on 1 October 2005, California-born surfwear company The Realm announced that its European arm, based in Wales, had joined forces with the Porthleven Surf Club and co-sponsors Etnies and Electric to host a big-wave contest at Porthleven. Thirty-two of Britain's best surfers would contest the 'Six Feet and Over Porthleven Challenge', so long, that is, that the ocean cooperated and produced the requisite swell. Local hero and British student champion Dan 'Mole' Joel was one invitee among an illustrious list that included fellow Porthleven surfers Jake and Sam Boex, Britain's top pro surfer Russell Winter and Geordie champion Gabe Davies. In order to provide the best showcase possible for the surfers and Porthleven as a surf spot, the 'Six Feet and Over' contest would have a waiting period of six months. Only if the conditions were perfect within that period would the contest be held.

If a six-foot wave sounds large but not especially fearsome, still less much to wait for, due regard should be had for the way in which surfers measure waves. It may seem illogical, but most surfers, once they have achieved a standard beyond average, measure waves from the back, rather than the front. This means that what to an observer on the shore looks like a six-foot wave will generally be described as two or possibly three foot. This system is derived from Hawaii, and has always struck me as having a little too much testosterone in its foundations. But to those in the know, a six-foot wave has a face of anywhere between twelve and fifteen feet. And for the chosen few, the Porthleven challenge was the real deal: a contest featuring the country's best surfers to be held at a dangerous reef break – and only in the kind of surf that would, in all likelihood, seriously injure, or perhaps drown, anyone not used to it.

But would the right conditions prevail? There was a close call on Saturday 14 January 2006, but after an early morning assessment the judges decided that the waves were not 'of the size and standard required to run the challenge'. In other words, they were big, but not big enough.

On another visit to Porthleven, this was put into perspective by Dan 'Mole' Joel. 'The Hawaiians would call this flat,' he said, gesturing across the harbour to a surfer taking off on a forbidding grey lump of a wave. It was late January 2006, and the surfer shot down the face of the wave before crouching low and executing a bottom turn to his right. He then rode the fast, near-barrelling wave back up its face and down again until the wave was no more. As he arched his body back towards the lip of the wave, it was clear that he was standing a foot or two beneath a wall of head-high water.

'Surely that's a four-foot wave?' I said.

'Well, yes, the face is maybe four foot or thereabouts,' said Joel, sounding unconvinced. I could tell that he thought it was two foot, if that. 'But the Hawaiian measuring system means that, really, it's flat today.'

A statement like this from a certain kind of surfer can sound ludicrous. Some will be relatively new to the sport, and eager to impress; hence to downsize a challenging, sizeable wave as a mere two foot is to say 'I am beyond you, my fellow surfers, also out there riding those four-foot waves today. To me, those waves are of little consequence.' These people often tend to sport the latest equipment and yet stare meaningfully, not to say contemptuously, at larger waves (as if deciding whether they are worth the effort) rather than paddle out into them. One also needs to factor in the natural human tendency to hyperbole. Every surfer, at some stage in their development, will have recounted a tale of derring-do which might, after an extra pint or glass of wine, sound a little better by adding a foot or two to the wave face or a more jagged sheen to the reef which was, of course, a mere six inches beneath their board. But then again, there are those drawn to surfing for whom the phrase 'size matters' was invented. For these surfers – big-wave riders – only large waves can give them what they are looking for from the ocean. These surfers do not describe the surf as 'flat' or 'too small' for any other reason than that, to them, the Hawaiian measuring system is spot on. Dan Joel is one of them.

Joel was born in Helston, an old market town a mile or so inland from Porthleven. Helston was also the birthplace of the first Britain to become a world heavyweight boxing champion, Bob Fitzsimmons, and to this day the town bears a hardy demeanour, which grows yet tougher in Porthleven. Once a major boat-building centre, Porthleven remains a busy working port, with fish caught daily and sold either locally at the Quayside Fish Centre or in nearby Newlyn's outdoor market. The main catch is cod or haddock but includes crab and lobster. Facing due south-west, Porthleven is exposed to everything that the prevailing south-westerly Atlantic gales can throw at it. The sea wall built along the main beach is some thirty feet high, and yet winter storms regularly generate waves that crash over its top on to Loe Bar Road. Perched at the end of the harbour road, almost on the granite cob, is a seventy-foot clock tower built in 1883 as a literary institute by William Bickford-Smith of Trevarno. The tower achieved fame in 1989 when the nationals carried photographs of it engulfed by waves, but on a day when the Porthleven reef is working it provides a perfect vantage point from which to watch the surfers dropping into clean, tubing waves. Indeed, part of the joy of visiting Porthleven – which sees a large influx of tourists every summer – is the sense that everything here has an elemental and yet theatrical aspect: boats are still built, fishermen set off every morning and bring home their catch, surfers catch powerful, serious waves, all within easy view. Moreover, there are no amusement arcades, no tacky gift shops, and, despite what may be presumed to have been the wishes of the Porthleven 2000 group, there is no marina. Life in Porthleven is unambiguously concentrated on what goes on in and near the water, so that it seems to have avoided sacrificing its age-old Cornish charm, and yet remains as far from kitsch as could be imagined. The port – with its narrow streets and steep hillsides, reef break and fishermen – seems impervious to the march of what passes for progress; so much so that it is difficult not to conjecture that because of where it is Porthleven has itself become so intricately welded to the full force of the Atlantic that it can be no more, and no less, than it is now.

The port's inhabitants are hewn from the surrounding environment as much as boxers like Fitzsimmons are often moulded by hard manual labour and endless hours in the gym. And yet for all that Dan Joel – born in Helston and raised from the age of eleven in Porthleven – is not only one of the best surfers to ride the Porthleven wave but also one of the country's best big-wave riders, he is also a grounded, likeable man.

'Porthleven is the jewel in England's crown,' Joel told me over coffee in a café, set back a little from the harbour. 'When it's on, it's the best. You just can't beat it at four to six foot, with the sun out. It's a hollow wave, super-fast, a dry-hair paddle out, very ferocious and dangerous because it breaks on to shallow rocks. But if you know what you're doing, you can tuck into barrel after barrel. The only problem is the Internet.'

I must have looked bemused, because Joel quickly clarified what he meant. 'Porthleven has always suffered from crowds but the Internet has made things a lot worse. Now everyone checks message boards online, so it's not just a handful of people who know it'll be on, it's a busload.' This, indeed, is a lament of many long-time surfers in the better known surfing areas of Cornwall and Devon. The 2004 British champion Alan Stokes has described the advent of webcams at many well-known breaks as 'lame', bemoaning (at the age of twenty-four) the good old days of having to pour over newspaper weather pages and drive around from beach to beach to find a decent wave. He has a point. Webcams mean that anyone, anywhere, can click on a shot of a given break and simply decide to turn up, but at the possible expense of the knowledge and essential wave-craft only learnt by studying maps and weather charts and seeing if one's reading of them has proved correct (there is, though, a counter-argument to this: while popular beaches, complete with webcams, will become yet more crowded, those still prepared to work at finding a wave may actually encounter fewer crowds when they do so).

But despite the crowds, Joel is dedicated to Porthleven: 'The place is part of me. I started surfing at beachbreaks like Praa Sands and Gwithian when I was ten or eleven, and I've surfed in a lot of places, but I'd rather surf Porthleven than anywhere. I began surfing the left off the pier and then when I was fifteen progressed to the reef. I know all the good surfers here, locals like the Boex brothers and Robyn, and I think they'd say the same. I'd even say that I'd rather surf *onshore* Porthleven than offshore Gwithian. I've centred my whole life on it. I'll be stoked if the Realm contest is on in good surf.'

Porthleven has a surf club, established in 2002, consisting of some thirty or so local surfers. Joel had not heard of Greg or Chris, but named Budgie, Bernie Robinson, Pete Edkins and Dave Burr as 'the old-school crew here – they're always out when it's good'. I asked him how Robyn Davies, as a woman, compared to what I imagined was a predominantly male surfing scene. 'She's a charger,' said Joel. 'She surfs better than most blokes out there.' I asked him if he knew whether she was in town on the day we met. 'I'm not sure,' said Joel. 'She can be difficult to get hold of. Have you got her number?'

I did, and after leaving Joel I tried it again. There was no reply. Half wondering if she might emerge, a bubbly, vivacious presence amid the greying winter afternoon light, I took another stroll around Porthleven. I found myself standing in front of William Bickford-Smith's literary institute, looking across to my right at Porthleven's right-hand reef break. In front of me, to the left of the cob, some bodyboarders in their early teens were playing in the waves. The sea wall, to my left, loomed large along the length of the beach. It is a near vertical mass of granite and concrete, perhaps of the same height as Bickford-Smith's tribute to literary endeavour, scarred by the tumultuous seas of the region and adorned, as if with supplicants doomed to frustration in perpetuity, by scattered lumps of granite rocks at its base. The beach here is, as a sign placed by Kerrier District Council puts it, 'prone to dangerous shore dumps and undertows'. It is patrolled by lifeguards between 24 July and 5 September, but if the massive sea wall is not enough to make any swimmer – or surfer – think twice, Kerrier D.C. not only recommends a trip to the gentler environs of Praa Sands, a little way along the coast, but has placed another sign, this one nearer the cob.

'WARNING,' it says, in red lettering, continuing to advise that 'Persons using this pier do so at their own risk.' The reason? 'EXTREME DANGER IN BREAKING SEAS. Pier closed when red ball is raised.'

Next to this sign is another, advertising the Atlantic Inn and its warm welcome. It struck me that Porthleven's surfers – who, like its fishermen, would be just about the only people genuinely capable of ignoring the warning signs – would deserve the pub's homemade specials, grills, steaks and local fish dishes on the day the Six Feet and Over contest finally took place. But as for Robyn Davies, my efforts to will her into existence were in vain.

Definitely not unjazzed: Fuz, Susan, Sam and Sandy Bleakley.

4

THE LEGIONS OF THE UNJAZZED

Sam Peckinpah is the highest profile film director to have been drawn to the landscape of west Penwith, a peninsula jutting out into the Atlantic whose most famous landmark is, ironically, that which celebrates the point at which it vanishes, Land's End. In *Straw Dogs* (1971), a young couple arrive in a remote west Penwith village so that the man, played by Dustin Hoffman, can concentrate on his work as a mathematician. His wife, a self-consciously luscious Susan George, appears to be sexually frustrated, and to know some of the locals, though this does not yield an even superficial welcome for Hoffman. The incomer's efforts to be treated with dignity and friendliness – to behave, albeit as a man of science, with Christian principles – are met with derision, with relations between Hoffman and George souring by way of an ever more uncomfortable parallel. The outright violence that descends upon the isolated cottage in which the pair are staying is almost a relief, such an air of foreboding has Peckinpah given to life among the rugged moorland hills of west Penwith, and yet even when tensions have finally imploded Peckinpah gives no quarter. George is abused by two of the locals in a harrowing scene, and soon the cottage is besieged. Dreadful violence ensues, and for all that Hoffman somehow manages a peculiar, ambivalent smile at the end, his visit to Penwith has not been a pleasant one.

Peckinpah took a staple of modern cinema – the journey to unknown parts by sophisticated metropolitan types and their consequent fate at the hands of hostile, indeed downright malevolent, locals – as a red herring. *Straw Dogs* is less *Deliverance* and more analysis of the dysfunction and unspoken violence underlying the relationship between the Hoffman and George characters. When considering the venue for the film, whose tagline – 'In the eyes of every coward burns a straw dog' – is one of the more memorable of the genre, Peckinpah chose west Penwith. *Straw Dogs* was filmed at St Buryan, a village near Penzance, as well as Tor Noon Farm, Morvah, and Lamorna Cove.

Even today, more than thirty-five years after the making of *Straw Dogs*, west Penwith remains a wild and, on occasions, disorientating place. Known locally as 'the seat of the storm', the peninsula is so exposed and remote that it is easy to feel that you are on the edge of the known world. In fine summer weather, this feeling of detachment makes for a perfect 'getting away from it all' experience, but in severe winter storms the ghosts of *Straw Dogs* seem to snap at one's sodden ankles. Penwith was always merely a cipher for the imagined horrors of Peckinpah's vision, but this is, irrefutably, an area where solitude is never far away, where the sense of the elemental infuses one's soul like sea salt on a seal's whiskers. There are secluded coves, high moors dotted with holy wells and stone circles, windswept cliff walks, abandoned tin mines (west Penwith is arguably Britain's first post-industrial landscape) and, everywhere, the sea. Here its texture, its moods, its subtleties and secrets, its rages and radiance are never less than immediate.

In summer, the area's principal towns – St Ives, St Just and Penzance – will be full to bursting with tourists, many drawn to the strong artistic tradition in west Penwith or to its literary history. Artists and sculptors such as Terry and Anthony Frost, Patrick Heron, Barbara Hepworth and Peter Lanyon are but a few of a long list who have lived and worked in west Penwith, captivated by its exquisite light and stirring landscape. D.H. Lawrence lived for a short time in the village of Zennor, now a beacon for tourists but less congenial for the writer and his German wife Frieda von Richthofen during the First World War. Convinced that Lawrence and von Richthofen were using clothes hanging on their washing line to send coded messages to German U-boats, the locals reported the couple to the police, who forced them to leave.

As befits its artistic and literary heritage – Virginia Woolf spent summer holidays at Tallend House in St Ives, which provided settings for both *Jacob's Room* and *The Waves* – west Penwith is a little different from other surfing areas. The area's main surfing beach is Sennen Cove, 290 miles from London, one and a half miles from Land's End and nine miles from Penzance. This is mainland Britain's most westerly beach (only the Isles of Scilly and their reputedly non-surfing beaches lie beyond) and its glistening white sands are pummelled by swell virtually every day. The beach faces north-west and stretches in an arc from the village dwellings near the breakwater on the left round to the northern end, a less accessible area known as Gwenver. To follow this trajectory is to go from beginners' waves to serious surf of excellent quality, but each part of Sennen Cove shares one thing in common. The sea here, a comfortable 19°C in the summer, is crystal clear. Better still, it is almost always surfable. Of Gwenver, my *Stormrider* guide has this to say: 'One of Cornwall's most consistent beaches. Faces west and is exposed to all swell – if there's no swell here there's no swell anywhere.' Some time earlier, just a year after Peckinpah and his film crew were back and forth among the country lanes of west Penwith, Carl Thomson, in *Surfing in Great Britain*, wrote of Sennen Cove: 'There is surf on this beach for about five out of every seven days, and out of those five days, three will have well-shaped waves at about six feet, with a good curl, giving excellent rides.'

When Thomson's *Surfing in Great Britain* was published in 1972 – the first guidebook to waves on these shores, with a glossary including a definition for the term 'brown outs' ('dancing around in the nude – usually at beach parties') – Sennen was the scene of Britain's first (and only) 'surfing village'. Chris Tyler, an ex-architect, ex-trawlerman and surfer, set up the Skewjack Surf Village in 1971 as a surf camp and focal point for surfers in the south-west. Skewjack's heyday was in the mid-seventies, with the BBC turning up to film an episode of *Holiday '76* there, and despite its location – which, to be precise, was about a mile and a half inland from Sennen Cove – the distance from the surf proved no deterrent to visitors wishing to avail themselves of a week's accommodation for, in the early seventies, £8.50 per week. *The Times* sent Penny Radford to have a look at Skewjack, and her piece, published on 9 August 1971 with the headline 'Skewjack, Cornwall: Surf City of UK', provides a glimpse of UK surfing's early, innocent days. Surfing terminology may have remained consistent, wrote Radford, but its *raison d'être* was changing: 'The surfer saw himself as a species of super-aggressive Canute, who wrestled with the waves – instead of telling them what to do – in a futile but satisfying struggle, sometimes to death, with the forces of nature. But all that has changed to a back-to-nature search for harmony with the sea, harnessing its powers for one's own pleasure.' For this reason, wrote Radford, surfing was 'a very deep sport'.

Skewjack closed in 1986 and was demolished in 2000, but evidence of its place in surfing folklore can be found at www.skewjack.co.uk. One picture posted on the site, of a man drinking from what looks like a bottle of wine against the sun setting on Sennen Cove, is captioned 'Godfrey, Pipe and Plonk = Tranquillity at Gwenver', and this image probably encapsulates the Skewjack soul as well anything. Perhaps, in part, because many of Skewjack's staff still live in the area, the village's counter-cultural spirit continues to animate the sense of surfing in west Penwith. *The Times* may have dubbed Skewjack 'surf city' in 1971 (though it was also known locally as 'Screwjack' thanks to an advertising campaign promising 'two girls for every boy'), but that honour rightfully goes to Newquay, whose hustle, intensity and commercialism are barely known in west Penwith. Even the six-year-old Chapel Idne surf shop overlooking Sennen Beach has been fashioned of natural wood to resemble a chapel, and its owner, Pat Dowling, is a down-to-earth man who believes not in image and profit but in helping people to get the best out of their surfing. Sennen today remains a free-surfing stronghold, whose essence is perhaps best illustrated by long-time residents the Bleakley family.

Alan 'Fuz' Bleakley, fifty-eight, has lived in a cottage over-looking Sennen Cove with his artist wife Susan since 1996, having been in the area since 1978. Fuz grew up in Newquay and was among the town's first wave of surfers, having first taken a board to sea in 1964, when he was fifteen. With Paul Holmes and the late Simmone Renvoize, Fuz published the magazine *Surf Insight* in the mid-1970s and is the father of one of Britain's best surfers, former two-time European longboard champion Sam Bleakley, twenty-eight. While Fuz's home breaks as a teenager were those of Newquay, Sam has been brought up surfing the pristine waters of Sennen Cove and Gwenver. A Cambridge University graduate, Bleakley junior is a writer and professional surfer, sponsored principally by Surftech, Oxbow and Vans, and by his mid-twenties had visited more than thirty countries. And yet no matter how many immaculate overseas waves he gets to surf, for Sam, Sennen Cove is the best place on earth.

'There's nothing like it,' he says, sitting in the kitchen of Fuz and Susan's cottage, looking out to the Atlantic and down on to the beach below. 'This is still my favourite place to surf. I think it always will be.'

There is something magical about Sennen Cove. Tucked into the south-east corner of Whitesand Bay, Sennen is a wild and rugged place with sundry weather-beaten houses etched into the hills surrounding its unblemished waters. This is a place where basking sharks, seals and dolphins are regular visitors to the line-up, and where – so far – the Skewjack legacy of chilled-out bonhomie remains the norm. The standard of surfing varies considerably from the outright beginners, who will hire boards from the surfing centre tucked just underneath the superb restaurant ('The Beach' owned by Phil Shannon, who is also the UK's longest-serving lifeguard), to the likes of Sam, who will usually be found playing amidst the peaks of Gwenver. Sam is easily distinct from the crowd, given an elegant longboarding style that sees him walk the board to hang five or ten or carve sweeping roundhouse cutbacks with equal fluidity. Sennen has also been the scene of tow-in surfing by Dan Joel, who, with another top UK pro surfer, Sam Lamiroy, has surfed Cowloes reef, a serious break that lurks further out in Whitesand Bay. The Bleakleys are huge admirers of Joel and Lamiroy and the boundaries they are crossing in performance shortboard surfing, but for them the philosophy of surfing lies elsewhere.

'I call it "joined-up surfing",' says Fuz, an academic, writer and poet who as well as working for the Peninsula Medical School still surfs regularly. 'Surfing is about flow, not about zapping. Surfing well is akin to the way a jazz musician plays just behind the beat. A good surfer understands how to tolerate this feeling, how to embrace an ambiguous state of giving oneself over to the wave. Surfing, then, becomes "joined-up" – it's what I see from the moment Sam takes off to the moment he kicks out. The wave becomes one whole piece. Rhythm is key.'

Fuz's aesthetic approach to surfing meets its physical representation in Sam. 'Sam Bleakley? He's a cat,' were the words of Steve Winter, one of Newquay's best surfers and brother of the UK's most successful professional surfer, Russell. The Winter brothers – including big-wave specialist Dean – could not be more different from the Bleakley clan. They are intense, tough and powerfully aggressive men, in and out of the water, more likely to enjoy watching a bare-knuckle boxing video than settle down to read poetry. And yet Steve could not compliment Sam enough. 'There's no one who surfs as gracefully as him,' he told me, as the Rip Curl Boardmasters in 2006 got underway, this year in decent surf. 'You watch Sam surf and just don't know how he does it.'

This is high praise indeed from someone of Steve Winter's

pedigree, but to talk to the Bleakleys is to come away yet more impressed. Sam is a handsome man, with the surfer's stereotypical long blond hair, and keeps himself in prime condition thanks to a careful diet and near-constant immersion in the ocean. In a lesser individual, his gifts could translate themselves into arrogance, but there is not a trace of this in him. Instead, there is a humility and curiosity about the world, not least when he and Fuz are discussing surfing.

I sat in the Bleakleys' kitchen, overlooking the Atlantic, on various occasions to chew the fat about surfing, contemporary and past. Often the conversations would entail my asking questions of Sam and Fuz, and sometimes we would be joined by Susan and Sam's wife, Sandy. I confess to feelings of envy during some of those conversations, for Sennen Cove is my favourite surfing spot, a place I wish I had grown up, and the setting for one of those moments that stay with you all your life. It was a mild October day, and I paddled out into beautiful clean three-foot surf just in front of the beach café. The water was still warm, it was sunny, there was the lightest of offshore breezes, and the line-up, though busy, was not insurmountably packed. Moreover, friendliness among everyone was the order of the day. There were one or two rights but the surf was predominantly left-breaking, meaning that I, as a regular footer, was surfing on my backhand (with my back to the wave). This stance is, for most people, not as congenial as riding waves frontside (with one's body facing the wave), and I am no exception. However, for some reason, on that gentle mid-autumn day, I surfed well to my left, catching wave after wave and enjoying myself so much that I was unable to resist saying 'just one more wave' and paddling back out each time I had earlier resolved to head back to shore. Eventually, sitting on my board waiting for another wave, I fell to simply gazing at the water, alternately watching the bulge of waves and the way in which they broke just a few yards ahead of me, and then turning to look to the horizon to wonder at the waves gleaming as far as the eye could see, like blue silk rippled by an invisible force. Was this Melville's 'image of the ungraspable phantom of life', the key to it all, as Ishmael reflects at the outset of *Moby-Dick*? And then, as stillness seemed to descend despite the sea's constant restlessness, a silver-grey seal popped up next to me. He (or she – I am no expert on these things) was no more than ten feet away, and chose to stare at me for perhaps ten seconds. I stared back, marvelling at such a beautiful creature, and then turned to shout excitedly to the surfer nearest to me. 'Look!' I said. 'A seal! Check it out!'

This may have sounded overtly communicative, perhaps rather non-adult, and is not my style on dry land, where being English perpetually stymies such ingenuousness. Certainly, the surfer looked at me with bemusement, and when I looked back to my new friend's position, he – or she – had vanished. But I loved that moment, and, along with many other good days' surfing at Sennen Cove, it is why I love surfing there more than anywhere else.

In the course of many digressive conversations in the Bleakleys' kitchen, the language of surfing was a recurring theme. Given that he is the author of acclaimed poetry such as *Hermes in the Kitchen Drawer*, Fuz was unsurprisingly intrigued by what surfing's argot – incomprehensible to outsiders – might betray. 'There's a very male kind of surfing,' he says, 'and it's often reflected in the language used to describe what, to me, is less about "slash and burn" shortboarding and much more to do with flow. Metaphors are important, but terms like "hacking", "slashing" and "gouging" are emblematic of a male world view, a desire to dominate and control the environment.'

These terms describe manoeuvres on the face of a wave, but if their precise meaning may elude the non-surfer, their innate aggressiveness is obvious. This, Sam felt, was not a problem: 'You need to be pumped up to make certain moves, to surf well, to get deep inside a barrel at a place like Pipeline or Teahupoo or make an air over a sectioning wave. It's still the case that ninety per cent of surfers are men and so this kind of aggression is normal. In fact, it's inherent in surfing's progression.' Fuz, though, was not so sure. The poet in him meant that such language could not be taken for granted. 'Metaphors determine how we see the world, they influence our kids and life in general. There's a danger that you can become oblivious to your environment if you uncritically accept a language system that is overtly male. You become dull to the world, what I call "an-aestheticized". The point is to become aestheticised, to use your senses, to notice things.'

Surfing – whether 'slash and burn' shortboarding or styling on a longboard – is, for both father and son, a fundamentally life-affirming act, a means by which dullness to the world is avoided. Fuz has finely considered views on this, given, especially, that he is currently heading up an inter-disciplinary research project by Exeter and Plymouth universities, the premise of which is that a culture of prescription-for-profit has become institutionalized in the medical profession, thanks to the major pharmaceutical companies. As he puts it: 'We live in a world where Prozac is now prescribed for kids. We continually seek to desensitize ourselves to our environment. People pop a pill for virtually any reason, and doctors are encouraged to let them do this, because there's money in it for the pharmaceutical companies. But reality should be experienced, not prettified or avoided, and we're losing the ability to do so. But for those who still want a dose of real life, what better than to go surfing?'

From Fuz's formative years of surfing Newquay's beaches in the mid-sixties – a time 'when you had to find someone to go surfing with' – to the present, surfing has, for him, always been 'a transcendental act. The experience of total immersion in the ocean is, for me, what it's all about. I was never a brilliant surfer, but I was good enough to enjoy it from 1964 onwards and surfed in Australia [where he worked on *Tracks* magazine], the east coast of the USA and California, where Sue and I were married and where, at San Onofre, Sam caught his first "real" stand-up wave.' Fuz gestures to Gwenver, lying resplendent beneath the Bleakleys' cottage, and explains how he can tell, from the white water on a particular rock, how good the swell is. 'Mind you, the size of the waves isn't my interest,' he adds. 'You can be stoked to be out on a small, messy windblown day.'

For Fuz, surfing offers a spiritual experience that is simply impossible *without* surfing. As he puts it: 'There are two things that define the uniqueness of surfing and its spiritual core. The first happens when you're out the back, sitting in the line-up on a strong offshore day, and you can see rainbows on the backs of breaking waves. You take off, drop down the face, the spray is blowing back at you and again, if you look round, there's a brief, flickering rainbow. People on the shore just can't see this, they can't experience this feeling. Then there's surfing with dolphins. Just brilliant.'

I wondered if Fuz was about to embark upon something of a New Age soliloquy, but this wasn't the point. 'Surfing with dolphins is spiritual, but it's not relaxing – in fact, it's about as far from New Age cosiness as you can get. These are wild, powerful animals, and you haven't a clue what they're going to do next.'

The same goes for surfing with seals, the 'selchie' so much a part of the stories and folklore of the west coast of Ireland, Scotland and the Western Isles, hauntingly captured in David Thomson's *The People of the Sea*. As Thomson writes of the grey Atlantic seals that have, since time immemorial, occupied the strange hinterland where the land ends and the sea begins:

As to the seals themselves, no scientific study can dissolve their mystery. Land animals may play their roles in legend, but none, not even the hare, has such a dream-like effect on the human mind; and so, even though many creatures share with them a place in our unconscious mind, a part in ancient narrative, the seal legend is unique. Walk on their lonely beaches, climb onto their rocks with the knowledge that the sea stretches unbroken to America, that for thousands of years people believed what you now feel – that you are at the uttermost edge of the earth – and when all is quiet except for waves and sea birds, you hear an old man gasp. It is a seal that has broken the surface of the water to take a breath, and, very often, seeing you it will raise its whole torso and stare back at you to assess the danger, or from curiosity – then disappear silently.

Or, as Fuz put it, 'Surfing gives you a feeling of what it is like to live as a seal, of being a water animal. What else gives you this? Sailing doesn't. People in boats spend all their time trying not to fall into the water. For a surfer, the fluidity of the ocean – of being in it – is what matters.'

If the sense of the spiritual looms large among west Penwith's surfers, so too do concerns about the ever increasing commercialism of surfing. Whether surfing has 'sold out' is a question that recurs throughout the world with the predictability of certain waves. To look at waves peeling off the point at Malibu, CA, or Jeffrey's Bay, South Africa, is to look out on machine-like precision, something – barring a natural catastrophe – that simply *will* occur sometime between March and November (Malibu) or April and September (J-Bay). And just as those and many other waves have been arriving for centuries with mysterious certainty, so has the question of surfing's soul – or, more accurately, its whereabouts – become a perennial point of debate.

The *Guardian* posed the question in an article appearing during summer 2006. Its *G2* cover for 17 July was illustrated with a goofy-foot surfer riding frontside inside what could well be a Pipeline barrel (the shot is from an agency; neither surfer nor wave are identified), with the apocalyptic words: 'How surfing went mainstream – and lost its soul'. Inside, Patrick Barkham's otherwise neutral text is heralded by the headline: 'A bigger splash, a lot more cash', with the following strapline: 'Time was when surfing in Britain was reserved for the hardy few. But now a wave of seamless wetsuits and rampant consumerism is robbing the sport of its rebel image, while the flood of BMW-driving stockbroker surfers is causing tension among the locals.' The feature is centred around Watergate Bay, a couple of miles north of Newquay, where brothers Will and Henry Ashworth own a hotel and beachside complex that attracts hordes of surfing converts on a year-round basis. Those converts are pictured in the principal photograph for the piece. Some twenty to thirty people who have hired 'foamies' or who are being given surfing lessons are all crammed into a thirty-yard space, competing for half a foot of incoming white water.

Barkham wrote of how surfing in Britain was 'once the exclusive domain of gilded young men', only for its democratization to sweep away elitism in favour of brands, brands and more brands, so that now the wannabes vastly outnumber the diehards. At first blush, this is a view with which it is easy to have sympathy. Even in the cold waters of Britain and Ireland, surfing is no longer the preserve of distinguished few. Bristol-based law firm Burges Salmon chose, in January 2005, to advertise for recruits in trade magazine *The Lawyer* by using a photograph of one of its associates, Mark Shepherd, clad in a Rip Curl wetsuit and manhandling one of two surfboards on to the roof-rack of a rather shiny VW estate, with what Shepherd and his brethren might classify as the 'invitation to treat' being 'the elite firm outside London'. The message is unambiguous: Burges Salmon offers smart young professionals a better, healthier life than the metropolis, one whose trappings include gleaming black cars and surfboards in equal measure. Shepherd may well be a fine surfer, but surfing's rebel image – one deftly summed up in Californian beachside graffiti with the imprecation 'Surf Now – Apocalypse Later' – has only latterly embraced lawyers. Now that it has, the axiom that where there are lawyers there is money, holds true for modern surfing. A number of surfing companies have long since eclipsed their humble garage-and-back-room origins either to become listed on various stock markets (for example, Quicksilver, Billabong, and, with supermodel Elle Macpherson on its board, Hot Tuna) or to emerge as private conglomerates whose tentacles appear to reach into every continent (Rip Curl, O'Neill, Reef, Roxy). In the biggest desert town of them all, Las Vegas, photographs of surfers tucking into turquoise barrels jostle for attention with gambling's traditional aspirational imagery – fast cars, beautiful diamond-bedecked women – on the walls of the labyrinthine casinos. Even a delusional poker hustler, it seems, might look up and dream of a life at play in the ocean. And perhaps most extraordinarily of all (in a peculiarly British way), at around the same time as the Rip Curl Boardmasters 2005 a Newquay surf school owned by Anthony Rowlett was put up for sale with a price tag of £2 million. It is not so much that Rowlett's business, begun from the back of a camper van a decade ago, should command such a figure that is surprising (particularly given that it included the Reef Surf Lodge, an eighteen-bedroom establishment capable of housing up to 109 guests, as well as the Reef Surf Centre and a beach café), but more the identity of the estate agent acting on the sale. Step forward Knight Frank, estate agents more commonly associated with the landed gentry than a layback tail slide.

Such developments seem as alien to the landscape of west Penwith as a windless day in winter. Fuz Bleakley, for one, has reservations about surfing's unhindered embrace of the free market, castigating 'the sweat-shop labour in third world countries' used to produce the ubiquitous logo-covered merchandise, as well as the danger that commercialism creates a breed of surfer for whom 'the simulacrum precedes the real. So many people come to surfing now thinking that they, too, will be deep inside a Pipeline barrel within just a couple of weeks. They've no idea how difficult surfing is, and don't understand that the surf media's idealized images don't represent most people's real surfing experience.' And albeit that he is paid to be a surfer, Sam echoes his anxieties – if, also, to take them in a slightly different direction.

'There is a feeling of fracture between the fat cats making all the money and the practitioners,' says Sam. 'Surfing has been cursed by its airhead heritage, and you have to work your socks off to make a living out of it. I feel that the big companies could do more for grass-roots surfing. There's also a problem with so many people taking up the sport – they simply don't appreciate and understand the values and etiquette of surfing, also its dangers. There are rips, currents, waves can hold you down – it's not classed as an "extreme" sport for nothing.'

Throughout our conversations, Sam was ever the diplomat, aware of the upsides to surfing's ongoing boom as much as he was empathetic with the disillusionment felt by older surfers. His intelligence and ability to think laterally would give the lie to anyone's *idée fixe* of surfers' bleached-brain vacuity. Another topic on which he was notably eloquent was that of the original form of surfing – riding a longboard. Polynesian culture knows of two kinds of board – the *olo*, used by island chiefs, and the *alaia*, used by commoners. The former was hewn from the *wiliwili* tree, the latter from the *koa*. Both were huge, but for many years represented the paradigm for surfboard design, at least so far as length and looks were concerned. Not until the so-called 'shortboard revolution' of the late 1960s did boards shrink to what would have been unimaginable to the Hawaiians of the nineteenth century, whether of royal extraction or not. Shorter boards allowed for faster rides and greater manoeuvrability, but as the new millennium dawned the longboard made a triumphant return. And, for many, riding a longboard – strictly speaking, anything over 9 ft in length – is the purest form of surfing, at once a respectful nod to surfing's heritage and an embrace of style for style's sake that the shortboarders, their vision occluded by adrenalin, might be in danger of missing.

As Dave Parmenter put it in an edition of *The Surfer's Journal*: 'The biggest trend in surfing today is a worldwide shift to the longboard . . . demographically, longboarding is modern surfing. Or, more exactly, post-modern surfing.'

Twice a European champion, Sam is one of our best long-boarders, a man who has emerged following the trailblazing of the likes of Welshman Chris 'Guts' Griffiths and stylists such as Lee Ryan to form a link between a new breed of younger riders, not least Elliot Dudley and Ben Skinner (who scored a remarkable second in the 2006 World Surfing Games, surfing's Olympics). For Sam, the public need to know that longboarding and short-boarding are different things: 'People lump us all together, and this kind of homogenization misses the point. There's a beauty and grace to longboarding – hanging ten, walking the board, drop-knee turns – that gets overlooked. And our waves are often better suited to longboarding, anyway.'

For Sam, riding a longboard – 'like a cat', as Steve Winter has it – is 'all about flow. The ocean is constantly changing and you have to able to flow with it, like Billy Hamilton playing Matt Johnson in *Big Wednesday*. The joy of surfing is in its aesthetic, in the pleasure of either riding a wave in the pocket, playing just behind the beat as Dad says, or in watching someone with real style.' One man who inspired Sam with his ultra-stylish longboarding is Californian Joel Tudor, about whom he wrote an article for *Carve* magazine's summer 2005 'retro and longboard special' entitled – in an allusion to Miles Davis – 'The Birth of Cool'. It transpires that Tudor is a jazz-lover, too. Sam quotes him thus: 'I went to visit a friend in New York who'd been nagging me to go to some jazz clubs for years. I went, and that was it. I went from listening to Slayer and seeing tons of crazy punk concerts to jazz. I'd never seen anything like it, or heard the way it sounded – the pauses, the tones, the beats. It went with footsteps, like cross-stepping a log. Lots of people were trying to ride longboards like shortboards, but that's not the thing. Longboarding is meant to be stylish. All of a sudden that music – jazz – and a certain style of surfing made sense to me. It made me really slow down everything.'

Davis fans will understand the idea of endless reinvention, of silence being as important as sound, of less being more. So, too, the Bleakleys' – father's and son's – approach to surfing.

But the Davis acolyte might find one strain of dissonance, perhaps in the way of the John Coltrane tenor sax solo on 'Kind of Blue'. On the one hand, Sam could argue passionately for greater public understanding of his craft as a longboarder, while, on the other, he readily comprehended the downsides to commercialism. And therein lay a conundrum. Greater understanding meant a more pronounced alliance with the mainstream media, which, in turn, risked introducing yet more people to the beaches and, ultimately, inducing yet more sales of branded merchandise and environmentally unsound boards (there are few better examples of toxicity in practice than modern surfboard manufacture). This, surely, epitomized one of the paradoxes of surfing. Sam nodded, and his father had this to say.

'Yes, it does. It's a sport that has always worked against itself.'

No such ambiguity was evident in the tanned, healthy and strong frame of west Penwith local surfer and furniture maker Jonty Henshall, forty. I met Henshall in the midst of the Rip Curl Boardmasters for 2006, and to say that he was struggling with surfing's commercial side would be an understatement. Though evenly spoken and temperate in nature, Henshall, a surfer for twenty-five years, is finding the going tough in the early twenty-first century.

'It's very frustrating to be a surfer nowadays,' he told me, as we admired artwork in the Yew Tree Gallery near St Just. 'People's attitudes have been moulded by a perceived sense of what they think a surfer should be, which is driven by the corporate marketers. But many so-called surfers have no idea about basic etiquette in the water. They cover themselves in logos, paddle out at unfamiliar breaks and behave ignorantly, making the whole experience of surfing unpleasant. Worse, they're in danger of doing themselves and others harm.' Henshall was far from enamoured of the Rip Curl Boardmasters: 'I don't think it's representative of British surfing. Its ethos of commercialism and exclusively shortboard competition is worlds away from most people's experience of surfing.' Henshall was alluding to the unpredictable surf that abounds on our shores, meaning that knowledge of the right equipment is essential if surfing is to be enjoyed: 'You see people going out with tiny shortboards because that's what they think looks cool, when they can barely stand up on a mini-mal. Or parents taking their children out in swells that most surfers can't handle, because they assume surfing is as easy as it looks in the adverts. It's not.'

Henshall grew up in Cheshire, and used to holiday in

Anglesey, where he discovered surfing by means of a wooden bellyboard in 1970. Having learnt to stand up he switched to wind-surfing, again around Anglesey, though returned to surfing when he attended Exeter University. Given that we are the same age, Henshall would very likely have been paddling out at North Devon breaks or windsurfing off Exmouth in south-east Devon in the late 1980s, at the same time as me, but our paths did not cross then. Instead, we were discoursing on the state of surfing in an art gallery in west Penwith, a little over a stone's throw from the cottage setting of the young couple's trauma in *Straw Dogs*. Beyond, some mile and a half away, lay a mild blue Atlantic whose swell lines could not, from that distance, be detected.

Isn't it a good thing to have so many people getting into surfing, I asked?

Henshall seemed to agree – saying that it was good that such a diverse surfing community existed in Britain and Ireland – but his furrowed brow soon found verbal expression. 'The trouble is that so few people have a clue what they're doing,' he said. 'Yes, it's great that people get stoked through surfing, but it's time to do what Nat Young did on Australian beaches – put up signs explaining the basic rules of surfing etiquette. People need to be educated about surfing's unwritten rules – and its dangers – before they paddle out. I'm not in favour of localism, but I am in favour of education. There are too many surf tourists and wannabes who think they have a right to abuse local beaches. They take surfing for granted.' For that reason, Henshall is a devotee of what surfers call the 'dawn patrol'. 'I prefer surfing on my own. So I'll get up at four-thirty in the summer if it means I can find a wave to myself.'

Henshall was a likeable man, capable of expressing his dismay at surfing's commercialism without rancour or bitterness. After talking to him I drove to Sennen Cove to check the surf. It was a summer evening, and while good surf had prevailed for most of the week it had now dropped off at Sennen. An unfeasibly large number of surfers were competing for the one or two peaks that were working, but I paddled out nevertheless. I had a good enough session – as the branded T-shirts say, a bad day in the water is better than most things. As I loaded my board on to the car, I thought of the Bleakleys, jazz, Jonty and surfing, and I recalled a line from the great Pipeline pioneer Phil Edwards. For Edwards, non-surfers were 'the legions of the unjazzed'. Was it a good thing if the unjazzed remained the majority?

Beauty in the Badlands.

5

BADLANDS

H*e was 25 years old. He combed his hair like James Dean. She was 15. She took music lessons and could twirl a baton. For a while they lived together in a tree house. In 1959, she watched while he killed a lot of people.*

So runs the tagline of Terrence Malick's 1973 classic, *Badlands*. Martin Sheen and Sissy Spacek play an outcast couple whose killing spree is based on that of Charles Starkweather and Caril Ann Fugate in 1950s South Dakota. Sheen is a loner who falls in love with naive schoolgirl Spacek, only for her father to disapprove of their relationship. Sheen's character opts to shoot the father by way of what proves to be his inimitably blunt dispute-resolution methodology. The pair escape to the wilderness to enjoy a bucolic existence until the police arrive. Then the killing starts, and there is a lot of it. Malick's badlands is a place made all the more disturbing for the detachment displayed by his lead characters, whose love story is a haunting accompaniment to the senseless slaughter of anyone who gets in their way. The badlands, for Malick, is a place of psychological disorientation, of the usurping of conventional mores and morality by primeval self-interest, as much as it is a physically intimidating landscape, one where life only ever hangs by a thread.

Cornwall has its very own Badlands. Few people seem to know how or when the term was coined, but it describes the coastal area stretching to the north-east from St Ives to Crantock, the last break before Newquay. For some, the Badlands goes yet further, south-west all the way to Sennen Cove, but if its borders are hazy there is no doubting its epicentre. St Agnes may appear as the quintessential picture-postcard Cornish village, but it is the heart of surfing's Badlands.

The *Stormrider* guide heralds the area thus: 'This area is often referred to as the Badlands for a number of reasons, not least the insularity and intensity of local spirit here, which can be challenging to outsiders. Not surprisingly, SAS was born in the Badlands and now they knock heads in Europe as well as at home.'

The SAS in question is not, thankfully, the elite military regiment. Badlands locals may be tough, but they're not – at least, to my knowledge – trained to deal with terrorists or engage in warfare. The SAS to which *Stormrider* refers is St Agnes-based pressure group Surfers Against Sewage, set up in May 1990 to campaign for cleaner seas following a public meeting in St Agnes village hall. This particular SAS has, arguably, been just as effective as its military namesake, thanks in no small measure to the dedication, commitment and energy of its founder members. I caught up with one of them, Chris Hines, in the Blue Bar in the neighbouring village of Porthtowan on a grey September day in 2005.

I'd previously met Hines at the Rip Curl Boardmasters in the summer, where he had been publicizing the Eden Project's Eco Board. My memories of our meetings have him in surf-wear the first time, and wearing a suit the second. I am not sure if this latter is accurate. There is little about Hines that suggests conformity, and suits don't seem to be his thing. But, suited or not, Hines was eloquent about SAS and its work.

'The plastics industry did a lot for environmental awareness,' says the man who grew up on the edge of Dartmoor and surfed his first waves at Widemouth Bay when he was twelve. 'The advent of panty-liners meant that you could really *see* sewage slicks. Condoms, panty-liners and other plastic refuse made for a visceral, and visual, reminder of pollution.' Hines was living in the St Agnes area by his late-twenties, but along with the rest of the Badlands' surfing population grew sick and tired of paddling out into water whose glistening barrels would often be sullied by untreated sewage. Ear, throat and gastric infections were the price to be paid for going surfing. 'It just wasn't right,' he recalls, saying that one of the abiding images from that era was seeing seal pups 'living amongst human excrement'. A meeting took place in local surfer Martin 'Minzie' Minns' house, to be followed by the one in the St Agnes village hall. 'The whole village turned up. There were mothers and businessmen as much as lifeguards and surfers,' says Hines. SAS was born, with an initial focus on South-West Water. Soon, though, its desire for clean seas – whether to swim, surf or canoe in, for use by humans and the protection of its marine denizens – was being emulated up and down the country. 'It was amazing,' says Hines, a founder member along with Gareth Kent, Jason Ledger, Andrew Kingsley-Tubbs and 'Butties'. 'I only intended to work on an initial project to target South-West Water, but ended up staying for ten years. The campaign just snowballed.'

The SAS campaign went from a small gathering prepared to take on South-West Water to an organized environmental pressure group capable of lobbying parliament 'for an end to the discharge of raw and partially treated sewage and toxic waste into the sea and inland waters'. Surfers around the country were mobilized in a movement whose common denominator was a love of the sea. 'We had surfers from Brighton, Wales and the north-east, from Cornwall and Devon, from everywhere, really, all ready to get anywhere within twenty-four hours to publicize an environmental issue,' says Hines. 'There was a lad called Robbie from Hartlepool who'd bunk off school to come and help us. I've no idea where he is now but he was typical of the spirit we had.'

Help meant donning wetsuits and gas masks and waving a six-foot inflatable turd underneath politicians', councillors' and local water authority apparatchiks' faces whenever possible. SAS secured acres of newsprint through media-friendly publicity stunts, and marched outside the House of Commons in 1991. The group also lobbied the European Parliament in Brussels, and prior to Labour's 1997 election victory Hines was asked to advise shadow environment minister Michael Meacher, with SAS ultimately giving evidence to the House of Commons Select Committee Inquiry into Sewage Treatment and Disposal in the UK. At its peak, in 1994, SAS had 18,000 members, and now, even if, as Hines says, 'many of our original goals have been achieved', there are still 8,000 members looked after by a voluntary committee of directors and executive staff, four of whom are full time.

One of them is Richard Hardy, SAS's campaigns director. Originally a surfer from Brighton, Hardy joined the group in 1991 and became more and more involved in its activities until he was appointed campaigns director in 2003. By then he had worked for various NGOs, and is happy to describe himself as 'a campaigner who surfs, rather than a surfer who campaigns'. Hardy has lived near SAS's base among the old tin mine workings of Wheal Kitty, outside St Agnes, since 2002, and is perhaps indicative of the mature, heterogeneous surfing constituency to which SAS now appeals as much as its early radical environmentalists. 'We've become quite sophisticated campaigners now, and while the old imagery – things like the surfer with a gas mask, or the inflatable turd – is still there, we're not just surfers and we're not just about sewage. There are many other issues that we face and we're able to tackle them both as the most dynamic group in the watersports user spectrum, and as a group with a proven record that gives people a voice. We give everyone involved in coastal living an opportunity to make a difference, to be heard, and you'll see many of our members' children on campaigns now, as surfers have grown up and had nippers.'

SAS's early focus was, Hardy agrees, concentrated on the problems of raw sewage. On one occasion when we met, he had just returned from a trip to Guernsey, whose sewage treatment programme is woeful by comparison with that of its near neighbour in the Channel Islands, Jersey. Hardy's brief was to help lobby for a full sewage treatment programme, but bad weather had resulted in delays and barely any sleep for thirty-six hours. Despite this, the 35-year-old eloquently summed up the early work undertaken by SAS: 'We commissioned medical studies to prove that the health risks were real, and created a database of all illnesses reported by SAS members. The industry began to listen as surfers proposed cost-effective, viable solutions to pollution problems. The existing mechanism of "treatment" – pumping out sewage through a long sea outfall – barely deserved the name, but we showed that full treatment using ultra-violet disinfection or micro filtration could remove bacteria and viruses from sewage, rendering it harmless. Jersey was a working example of the success of UV processes, which meant that water users even next to a fully treated outfall wouldn't fall ill. It's a great shame that Guernsey is still lagging so far behind.'

Hardy's predecessor, Chris Hines, looks back on a decade of active involvement with SAS and feels proud that, 'We won the argument that all sewage discharge should be treated to secondary level as a minimum requirement,' so too that UV must be provided for an additional eight million people. It was SAS that opened the country's first full-treatment UV works at Welsh Water in 1994, and the first micro-filtration plant for Wessex Water in 1997. Hines' and his colleagues' work was a factor in Labour's victory, with many marginal seats in coastal constituencies swinging to the left thanks to promises that the SAS message would be fulfilled. That the campaign has worked is undeniable, with the work of the founder members and their teams summed up on www.sas.org.uk: 'The SAS campaign has had considerable impact on the whole sewage debate and the UK is now on its way to having some of the cleanest beaches and bathing waters in Europe.' There is, though, still work to be done, says Hines: 'Toxins today are less visible than when the SAS voice was first heard. There are other issues such as the oestrogen effect and marine energy that need our input. It's vital to continue to monitor the situation and carry on working with local authorities and politicians so that the need for safe and clean recreational waters isn't forgotten.' His views are echoed by Hardy. 'There is still a lot of work to do,' he says. 'In recent years, we've extended our remit to include the inland recreational waters of lakes, rivers and estuaries. A nation-wide clean-up will not only benefit all recreational water users and beach users, but will also boost the economy, both locally and nationally. The coastal and inland water environment must be recognized for the valuable resource it is. To preserve and maintain the UK's natural heritage provides not only financial reward, but also assists in slowing down the degradation of the planet.'

This last is, indeed, as much a focus for SAS in its contemporary incarnation as local issues. 'We're facing global climate change at such a rate that if we're not careful, we won't even have any waves to surf, let alone waves that require better sewage treatment,' says Hardy. Global warming and its attendant problems mean that SAS has come down in favour of a controversial proposal to create a renewable energy source off the north coast of Cornwall. The 'Wave Hub' scheme caused outrage on various online surf forums when it was first announced, but Hardy believes that there is no alternative. 'We have to look at alternative energy resources, and the vast power of the sea is an obvious place to start. We've analysed the Wave Hub proposal very carefully and we don't believe that it will cause any meaningful disruption to the quality of the surf. In fact, any change is likely to be undetectable.'

The Wave Hub concept entails the building of an electrical grid connection point twelve miles offshore into which wave energy devices would be connected. Advocates of the Wave Hub, which itself lies on the sea bed, argue that it will provide a well-defined and monitored site with electrical connection to the onshore electricity grid. Power is absorbed by underwater connection units from a number of wave energy devices on or just beneath the surface. So far, so environmentally friendly, but some surfers along the stretch of north Cornwall from Gwithian to Newquay – designated as the first site of the Wave Hub, should the scheme go ahead – fear that it will impose obstacles on incoming swell where previously there were none. By way of exemplifying that the NIMBY mindset is as alive and well in surfing as its more usual habitat of middle England, one or two anguished and apocalyptically minded locals have demanded that the Wave Hub be relocated to Scotland or Ireland – anywhere, indeed, but the north Cornwall coastline, whose waves and surfing industry they believe will be destroyed by the plans.

This view meets with little sympathy from one of SAS's neighbours at Wheal Kitty, surfwear manufacturer Finisterre. Founder Tom Kay, who set up and ran Finisterre from a bedroom rented from St Agnes surf shop owner Chops Lascelles in 2002 before moving to Wheal Kitty in September 2005, is unyielding in his commitment to the environment despite the fact that if the Wave Hub was approved for north Cornwall, his own surf spots might be affected. 'There's a picky attitude among some surfers who would claim that they're environmentalists,' he told me one bleak winter afternoon, as I shuttled between meetings with Finisterre and SAS. 'These people are often perceived as being at one with nature, but then the moment a sensible – crucial, even – development like the Wave Hub comes along they start moaning and saying that it'll mess up their waves. They don't seem to mind if it's relocated – and might mess up someone else's waves – but what they don't see is that if we don't start finding renewable energy sources and using them instead of solid fuels, we won't be able to live our lives as we do, let alone go surfing. Global warming is a fact and it's going to change surfing radically by the next century if we don't start doing something about it.'

Kay is a man who practises what he preaches. Originally from the coast of East Anglia, he studied Marine Biology at university only to drift into a career as a surveyor in London's West End. 'I hated it, being in London, away from the sea,' he told me, and the way in which Kay speaks – compact body moving ever so slightly to accentuate his words – it was as if he was recalling the oppression of city life afresh. Shaking his head, he went on. 'I had to get out and knew I had to do something that'd be fulfilling. I'd always surfed and suddenly got the idea – I'd make technical apparel for surfers, the kind of clothing they need in this country.' Kay launched www.finisterreuk.co.uk after eight months of research, by the end of which he had hit upon creating fleeces, jackets and base layers that were 100 per cent recyclable and expressly designed for the feeling of post-surf extreme cold that the UK's and Ireland's winter surfers know all too well. Finisterre gives a percentage of its turnover to SAS and the Marine Conservation Society, and insists on making the people who buy its products think about consumerism – what Kay calls the 'how, where and why' of materials – by campaigns such as 'Offset the PLC'. The title might, at first blush, be seen as an offsetting of the big surfwear corporations, some of which (for example, Billabong and Quicksilver) are listed on public stock exchanges, but the 'PLC' in question is actually the 'product life cycle'. Kay wants his customers to think about their purchases and their own environmental footprint, and dreams of a world in which everything that we produce is recyclable and recycled. That dream is shared by Brazilian Carlos Burle, one of the greatest big-wave riders in modern surfing, whom Kay and Finisterre's marketing director, Ernie Capbert, persuaded to act as the company's ambassador. Acquiring a name such as Burle, for a small company in St Agnes, was no mean feat: the 39-year-old held the record for the largest wave ever surfed (Todos Santos, in Mexico, at 68 ft) for some time, and is renowned as the kind of man who makes his own choices, at his own pace, rather than those driven by the marketers. Burle has since given popular talks on surfing at Plymouth and Falmouth Universities and has undertaken trips with Finisterre to pioneer cold-water big-wave riding in Ireland.

Finisterre took its name from the old shipping forecast district now known as Fitzroy. Kay had always loved listening to the shipping forecast, and Finisterre – meaning 'Land's End' – was engraved in his consciousness from an early age. So, too, as I left Kay and said my farewells to Richard Hardy, did I note that the word 'Badlands' had been etched in thick black lettering on a gate adjacent to the SAS building. Beyond were green fields and, then, the sea.

When he finished working full time for SAS, Hines took some time out. 'I went surfing, relaxed, made a documentary on waste for West Country TV, just bits and pieces, really.' Soon, though, his involvement with environmental politics took him to the Eden Project, which opened near St Austell in south-east Cornwall on 17 March 2001. The brainchild of Dutchman Tim Smit, who previously oversaw the restoration of the nearby Lost Gardens of Heligan, the Eden Project is arguably the most successful of Britain's millennium projects. Two giant biomes house plants of rainforest, semi-desert, sub-tropical and Mediterranean origin. Set up at a cost of £90 million, the well-designed biomes – set in an easily navigable environmental theme park – have helped accrue income, employment and visitors to an area of Cornwall whose china clay mountains appear, unlike its tin mines, to be in rude health. In marked contrast to the disastrous Millennium Dome in London's Greenwich, Eden's biomes have provided nothing but upside, garnering critical acclaim and public acceptance in equal measure.

Hines now works within the Eden Zeitgeist developing his cherished Eco Board. For half a century, surfboards have been made out of polystyrene foam and fibreglass resin, but such manufacture entails toxicity on a large scale. Urethane foam is made using toluene diisocyanate (a poisonous and irritating liquid) and polyether compounds, while fibreglass cloth is often treated with toxic chemicals such as chromium. Breathing fibreglass dust is not only unpleasant but dangerous, while polyester resins, comprised of dicarboxylic acids and dihydroxy alcohols, release volatile organic compounds (VOCs) to the atmosphere when they cure. Epoxy resin has been developed by some manufacturers in place of polyester resin, and has lessened some of the above problems. However, the fact is that the creation of a surfboard – which, in its modern form, is one of the most resolutely non-biodegradable products on earth – is, paradoxically given surfing's image, an act of hostility to the environment. A newer UK pressure group, the EcoSurf Project, sums up the problem thus: 'As surfers we get through around three quarters of a million boards a year. Currently only a tiny percentage of these are made from sustainable, biodegradable or even recyclable materials.' Hines, along with three Cornish companies, aims to change all that.

The Eco Board began life with a bang. A huge balsa wood tree fell to earth in Eden's Humid Tropics biome, and Hines, with colleague Pat Hudson, saw the potential for a surfboard blank, or core, made from wood. The first prototypes were too heavy, but Hines was not deterred. An alliance was formed with three other Cornish companies, Homeblown Surf Blanks and Foam Systems from Redruth, Sustainable Composites Ltd and Hillzee Surfboards. The result – on display at the Rip Curl Boardmasters 2005 – is a board made of a 40 per cent plant-based blank, laminated in hemp cloth and a bio-resin. Tris Cokes, Homeblown's managing director, is convinced that the Eco Board is the future: 'This is one in a series of prototypes but we are moving rapidly and hope to progress the foam and get to market in the near future. We will continue working in pursuit of the ultimate goal – a one hundred per cent natural surfboard that can be used by everyone.'

That goal seemed to have moved a step closer following the closure of surfboard manufacturing giant Clark Foam in December 2005. Clark Foam, set up in Laguna Niguel, California in 1961 by Gordon Clark, had cornered as much as 90 per cent of the global surfboard manufacture market for polyester blanks thanks to undercutting the competition and an extraordinary output that saw as many as 1,000 surfboards produced a day. The demise of the company sent shockwaves around the global surfing community, but it was no surprise, to environmentalists at least. In a letter to customers explaining the closure, Clark produced a curious blend of *mea culpa* and self-justification that may have lawyers – probably his own – scratching their heads for many years to come. He explained that he had been increasingly at odds with state and local government owing to his unique, and rather mysterious, production techniques, not to mention the admitted use of toxic and polluting chemicals. But still, in the good old days 'it was a far different California. Businesses like Clark Foam were very welcome and considered the leading edge of innovation and technology. Somewhere along the way things have changed.' Clark commended contemporary efforts by the State of California and Orange County California 'to make a clean, safe, and just home for their residents', but bemoaned his previous battles with the authorities over safety issues, one of which had cost some $400,000 in legal fees for a compensatory payment of $17,000. 'Our safety record is not good,' he admitted, adding that, 'We have three ex-employees on full Workman's Compensation disability – evidently for life. There is another claim being made by the widow of an employee who died from cancer. According to the claim, the chemicals or resins at Clark Foam caused the cancer.' The net result of such travails and the translation of increased environmental awareness into a regulatory framework was that Clark Foam was no longer able to do business viably; indeed, as Clark illustrated in his letter, a parallel with communism was apposite:

> Some years ago I read that the old communist Russian tractors had a negative economic value. They were so poorly built that the raw material used to build them was worth more than the tractor that would rarely work.
>
> I find that due to this 'standards' thing my equipment and process has a negative economic value. Why sell something for a dollar when you are risking a lawsuit that could cost you anywhere from the dollar to everything you own? Since I am the 'standard' I am liable for everything that was built to my 'standard'. Therefore, I am not going to sell any of this equipment or the process. The liability is far too great. Furthermore, most of the equipment can be dangerous if it is not operated properly.

Clark was not merely jumping ship, he was scuppering it in the act of abandonment. Production would cease immediately, nothing from the business would be sold, and the dream had soured once and for all. 'I should have seen this coming many years sooner,' wrote Clark, 'and closed years ago in a slower, more predictable manner. I waited far too long, being optimistic rather than realistic. I also failed to do my homework.' He concluded by saying that he anticipated spending a lot of time in court over the next few years, and thanked everyone for their 'wonderful support over the years'. After all, it had been 'a great ride with great people'.

Clark's honesty and willingness to write such a letter on the brink of a full-scale federal investigation was laudable, and there is no doubt that for all the problems with his business he was held in high esteem by many in surfing. But even in surfing, the sport of kings and hippies, beats and airheads, wannabes and druggies (depending on which media stereotype you're reading) the market looks after itself. Where once was Clark Foam, there may soon be the Eco Board.

As Tris Cokes put it, announcing that Homeblown would be opening a new factory in San Diego in early 2006: 'I've been making boards for forty years and in that time surfing has become a huge global industry with global environmental and social impacts. When Clark Foam announced their shut down in December last year, we immediately saw the opportunity, and this opening is a great landmark. We are pleased that the chemistry and processes used in Homeblown production comply with the US Environmental Protection Agency's tough regulations. Our unique delivery system also means highly efficient use of materials and energy and reduced waste streams.'

Chris Hines joined Cokes at the opening of the new factory, where he presented the Eco Board. Prior to their departure, Hines had this to say: 'Showing a prototype surfboard to the Californians may seem like taking coals to Newcastle but we believe that the new version of the Eco Board represents a hugely exciting leap forward for the industry and sport. For manufacturers and surfers to be won over by them, Eco Boards must be as good if not better in terms of performance [than existing designs], and cost competitive. Ultimately we believe all surfboards will be made from sustainable materials sourced from the indigenous plant base.' And by way of reducing surfers' carbon footprint, Homeblown was also determined to reduce 'surfboard miles'. The small Cornish enterprise also opened in South Africa's Jeffrey's Bay, with Cokes opining that, 'It's a form of madness to transport surfboard blanks halfway round the world. Big volume and low weight being transported long distances equals a big negative environmental footprint. By following this policy we reduce the carbon footprint and global warming impact of the sport.'

Cokes and Hines are two Badlands locals whose imagination extends far beyond St Agnes. To believe the surfing myth of the area, though, other inhabitants of St Agnes and its environs are rather more insular. If localism is not as pronounced as on the North Shore of Oahu or at certain Californian and Australian breaks, the grandeur of the Badlands coastline – full of dramatic coves whose leeward slopes are dotted with scores of limpet-like cottages, as well as the remnants of the once-thriving tin and copper mining industries – is not accompanied by an analogous elevation of the human spirit on the beaches. To paddle out at, say, Chapel Porth, Trevaunance Cove or Porthtowan is, if you believe the hype, not far short of an act of hubris. Chris Nelson sums up the feelings of foreboding in *Surfing Britain*:

> The world has many Badlands. To me, as a young grommet surfing Yorkshire in the late 1980s, there was only one true Badlands – the 'locals only' breaks around St Agnes. The name alone was enough to keep us away when we made the occasional foray to the south-west. A magazine article here, an urban myth there. Tales of spontaneous acts of violence, regular drop-ins and a very warm welcome – but not of the pleasant variety. We didn't think our scruffy blue Datsun would really benefit from flat tyres and a 'locals only' wax job on the windscreen. Hey, there were other beaches, other waves. We never even ventured down to check the place out.

I know where Nelson is coming from. Despite many sessions at Perranporth, a huge expanse of sand smack in the middle of the

Badlands, and a few at Chapel Porth, a low-tide break a couple of miles to the south, I have never surfed St Agnes. It is not, though, that I fear for my safety (or for that of my car), but because the standard of surfing at St Agnes is so high that anyone less than expert cannot but feel intimidated. My place is not in the line-up at a small, intense and competitive break like Trevaunance Cove. Fortunately, I know this, and so wouldn't make the mistake of taking on the hollow waves that surge into St Agnes in big swells. What, though, of an unfamiliar face who does give it a go? Is the Badlands vibe a product of myth or reality?

Steve Bough, *Wavelength*'s editor until summer 2006, agrees that there is a 'very localized' spirit at St Agnes. 'You need to be careful how you conduct yourself in the water at Aggie,' he says. 'Don't drop in, don't hassle, be respectful and you should be OK.' 'Dropping in' is, indeed, the cardinal sin in surfing, given that surfing's primary rule is that *the surfer who is already on the wave has right of way.* If you paddle for a wave, catch it and drop down its face in front of a surfer who is already up and riding, you have 'dropped in' and made it all but impossible for that surfer to maximize or even enjoy the remainder of the ride. As Bough says: 'If there's one piece of advice for newcomers to surfing more important than stressing just how dangerous the sea is, it's to make sure that they never, ever drop in.'

The point is made with some humour by 19-year-old St Agnes local Josh Ward. As with many Badlands' surfers, Ward comes from a family that has surfed in the area for generations. His uncles, Drustan and Dave, surf, as do his father and mother. As the bleach-blond-haired Ward says: 'My whole family surfs, from my nan to my little brother.' But then comes the Badlands punchline: 'But watch out, my nan shreds low-tide Aggie and she'll wax your windscreen if you drop in on her . . .'

It is difficult to gauge the extent to which the undeniably close-knit community of St Agnes can be accused of being overly protective of its waves. Localism in the form of outright violence or vandalism to anyone unfamiliar is to be abhorred, but a part of the surfer's rite of passage is earning a place in the line-up. If this means behaving respectfully towards those who live in a given area – whether it's the Cornish Badlands or Tierra del Fuego – then a community that is prepared to enforce its codes of conduct is not doing any more than looking after its own interests. It is all, no doubt, a question of degree. Two local surfers provided some illumination as to how far the pendulum had swung in St Agnes in *Surfing Britain*. One, surfer, shaper and owner of Best Ever Surfboards, Steve Bunt, put it thus:

> I think it [the origin of the Badlands legend] was between 1981 and 1985. We didn't like the outsiders coming in and taking over our break, really. We decided to make it 'the Badlands' – put people off. It was bad karma to come down and surf here. It really did work and it still does. There are a lot of people who won't come down and surf around Aggie because it's 'the Badlands'.

The other, Josh Ward's father and Chapel Porth lifeguard supervisor Martyn, explained what might happen in the water:

> I think the original idea came from a sticker, but it does keep people away. They do let people come and have a surf, but if there's something they don't like about somebody, they'll close up. They can get a bit angsty sometimes, yeah.

Peter 'Chops' Lascelles is one of St Agnes' most prominent members of the surfing industry. An Australian émigré who fell in love with Cornwall as a young man, Lascelles' surf shop is full to bursting throughout summer, and his boards, made under the Beachbeat brand, are sold throughout Britain and Europe. Lascelles is unique in being able to count Damien Hirst as a client. The most prominent member of the Young British Artists is married to Maia, herself described by the *Guardian* as 'a Californian surfing nut', and it was his wife's passion for clean seas that led to Hirst agreeing to paint two boards designed by Lascelles that would be auctioned to raise funds for SAS. The boards (Spin 41 and Spin 42) sold for £21,000 and £38,000 respectively, and Hirst came back to ask Lascelles to make a couple more boards that he would like to give as presents. Despite the fact that two of Hirst's homes are in surfing locations – Zihuatanejo, Mexico, and somewhere in north Devon near Saunton Sands – the artist himself does not surf, for, as he once told the *Guardian*: 'You're battling the elements. The odds are stacked up against you. I only do things I know I can win.' Maia's world was one that 'I didn't know exists . . . She's like an alien to me.'

As with everyone involved in the surfing industry, it is not in Lascelles' interests for prospective customers to feel alienated, still less that they are too scared to go surfing for fear of the locals. And yet, as I was beginning to find at every turn in this surfing odyssey, as usual there was a conundrum that seemed impenetrable.

'I don't agree with localism,' said Lascelles, a tanned, jovial and heavy-set man in his early fifties whose formative surfing years were spent on Australia's Gold Coast. 'But it does exist, especially round here. If you paddle out and try to dominate, the local guys will have words with you.' That, though, appeared to be the limit. 'We don't really beat people up round here. It's a bit of a myth. Besides, a lot of the blokes aren't tough enough to back up what they say. It's a myth. But it's a myth that's worked. Chapel Porth and Trevaunance Cove are two of the hardest places to get a wave in Britain.'

Why?

'Because the guys will just close ranks. If they don't like you they'll bunch up and close the peak off. You can paddle as hard as you like but you won't get a wave.'

There was an unmistakable twinkle in Lascelles' eyes as he told me this. Despite what would be his imagined vested interest – to encourage people into the water everywhere, but especially at his home break – not to mention his declaration that he didn't agree with localism, an understanding and tolerance of why localism might arise underlay our conversation. Lascelles was a realist, a man who had surfed all his life but who had chosen St Agnes as his home because of its natural beauty, sense of community and innate 'spiritual feel'. Indeed, so enthusiastic was he about this part of Cornwall that he was almost evangelical about its merits. He was also as unflinching as the hardest Hawaiian local when looking at the issues confronting surfing today.

'It's much more crowded than when I got here thirty-five years ago,' he said, as employees came and went, rearranging the boards and merchandise in his shop. 'The wetsuit has changed the face of British culture. In the 1970s, the beach was a bit of a novelty, now it's a way of life even here because the cold doesn't matter any more. All sorts of people turn up at the beach now. When I first surfed here you were lucky if there were fifteen guys in the water, on even the best days. Now there are fifty people out there. And only fifteen of them can surf.' Lascelles agreed that St Agnes was more than usually close-knit, but pointed to Newquay and Croyde as two other well-known surf spots where localism is prevalent. Increased crowds meant not only a diminution in locals' wave-counts but also brought safety issues. 'There's a rip at Trevaunance Cove that takes you straight out the back. Trouble is, getting back in isn't so easy. Everyone surfing needs to know their limits, and, in a way, that St Agnes has a local vibe – even if it's largely a joke thing – helps stop people who shouldn't be out there getting themselves in trouble.' The primary task, for Lascelles, of those at the top of the tree in surfing is to educate those new to the sport. 'People need to learn the fundamentals like not dropping in and not throwing your board away when a wave's about to land on your head. So many people try to paddle out, get caught by an incoming set and just throw their boards behind them without looking to see who's next to them. A board smacked into someone's head by an incoming surge of white water can do a lot of damage. I'd say that water safety is the main issue in surfing today.'

Lascelles had strong opinions on surfing's commercialism and what an obsession with image is doing to domestic prospects of competition success. He was proud to be a year-round employer in St Agnes – 'I'm one of the biggest employers in the village, and have been for some time, even though it wasn't until five years ago that the Chamber of Commerce asked me to join them' – and estimates that he has shaped over 20,000 boards in his career. He may sell up to 1,000 boards a year but seemed a little lackadaisical about the Rip Curl Boardmasters, describing it as 'a bit of a media circus'. He was much more animated about young surfers' prospects in a landscape still, in his view, not given its due respect by the principal surfing nations. 'To a degree, Britain is regulated by the international surfing community, but they still don't believe we have good surf and surfers. The fact is that we're the first country in Europe to produce a WCT top forty-four surfer, in Russell Winter. We *have* got great surf and a lot of good surfers, but there are two problems: one, our amateur structure isn't very good, and two, the image of surfing fostered by the magazines and the corporations is all about the Kelly Slaters of the world and beautiful turquoise tubes from paradise.' Lascelles felt strongly that having four countries compete against one another – England, Scotland, Wales and Ireland – was inimical to competition success, and that the corporations needed to do more for grass-roots surfing in Britain and Ireland. 'It's not just about image,' he said, 'it's about training and encouraging our surfers.'

I was struck again by the fervour with which Lascelles, speaking in a distinct Australian accent, referred to 'our' surf and surfers. His three sons, Sean, twenty-four, Brennan, twenty, and Marcus, fifteen, all surf, so perhaps his passion was motivated by paternal pride. Certainly, Lascelles was also eager to tell me about Sean's band Easykill, who had supported Donavon Frankenreiter and James Blunt at the Nokia Unleashed gig during the Boardmasters. As our conversation came to an end, he pressed 'play' on the shop's CD player and Easykill came blaring out of the speakers. The music was raw and fresh, intense and together – just the kind of music you'd expect from the Badlands.

On another visit to the area I met Dominique Munro-Kent, a British longboard champion and one of the best female surfers in the country. To categorize her in this way is, in fact, to do Munro-Kent a disservice, as it is when talking of any number of prominent women surfers. The likes of Munro-Kent, Robyn Davies, Irish champion Nicole Morgan, Badlands local Sarah Bentley and Welsh surfer Beth Mason surf as well as, if not more capably than, many men. Munro-Kent is also a superb teacher of surfing, as I learnt one summer's day when I booked a morning's tuition for my two sons, then aged ten and eight.

The boys were apprehensive, being of an age when the female of the species is more than usually perilous. Within minutes, though, Dominique – who looked every inch the surfer girl with her blond hair and taut physique – had put them at ease. She had an easy manner and communicated information fluently. Beginning with a talk on the beach about safety, Dominique carefully explained rip currents, drawing a diagram in the sand to illustrate the way in which they work. For those not familiar with surfing or the sea generally rips are mysterious, unfathomable beasts. Put simply, a rip is a strong current flowing out to sea, formed when a channel is created between the shore and a sandbar. Once they have broken, waves find the channel as the line of least resistance back to the sea – the surge of water then becomes a rip current. Rips are features of UK beachbreaks in medium to large swells and, when identified by an experienced surfer, can be utilized to make the task of paddling out slightly less wearisome. The unwary, though, often find themselves caught in rips. Panic is usually the first reaction, meaning that the person caught expends vast amounts of energy trying in vain to swim *against* the rip. The secret, if you are reasonably fit, is to swim at a 45° angle across the rip to the breaking waves, and, once there, to swim another twenty or thirty yards parallel to the beach. Then you swim (or bodysurf) back in with the surf. If you are not fit, the only option is to float with the rip. Lifeguards are present on virtually all UK beaches in the summer, and on many popular Irish beaches, and they will spot a swimmer or surfer in difficulty. It is best to stay calm, conserve your energy and await rescue, but still better to identify a rip in the first place. Dominique's diagram in the sand and accompanying explanation had the boys engrossed. After explaining what a rip was, she told them how to spot one.

'Rips will usually have a darker colour, thanks to sand stirred up from the bottom, than the surrounding water, showing that deep water is flowing along a channel. Waves will break further out to sea alongside the rip, and the surface will be smoother. You need to be able to stand on the beach and spot a rip before you go surfing.'

The boys were itching to get into the water, but after the safety talk there were stretching exercises and tips on how to get their feet. The act of standing up on a board should be achieved in one motion, when the surfer has paddled into a wave. A common mistake is to paddle and *think* that you have caught the wave, only to stand up and find that it has continued its journey without you. So, with the board facing directly to the beach, or at an angle once you have become proficient, you paddle as a wave approaches and always take an added stroke or two to be sure that the momentum of the wave is carrying you. Then comes the hard bit. Placing your hands on the deck of the board, near the rails, you perform a press-up movement and, in one movement, jump to your feet. If you are right-handed you will almost certainly be a 'regular foot' surfer, and so you leap up with your left foot forward in 'natural stance'. The curious cultural stigma attached to the left-handed among us continues in surfing, if not to the degree evident in Roman Catholic thinking prior to the twentieth century, when being left-handed was seen as an indicator of Satanic influence. In surfing, a left-handed person will usually be inclined to be a goofy-footer, standing with his right foot forward. Leaving aside other imponderables such as the fact that the English word 'sinister' meant originally in Latin 'left' but by the time of the Classical Latin era had come to denote 'evil' or 'unlucky', what is beyond doubt is just how difficult – whichever foot you choose to put forward – the act of standing up on a surfboard is. Unlike its close cousins, skateboarding and snowboarding, surfing requires athleticism in conjunction with a moving surface, a wall of water that is never the same, always subject to quirks and changes. Even when the mechanics of getting to your feet have been mastered, beginners will find that they fail to distribute their weight evenly, so that the board 'pearls' – noses into the water at the foot of the wave – or they go 'over the falls', a nasty experience that means you have been summarily dumped from the top to the bottom of the wave in white water.

Dominique comes from a well-known St Agnes surfing family – her father, lifeguard Robin Kent, and her brother Jamie are well-known chargers – and knows as well as anyone the mistakes beginners will make. But her tuition and her enthusiasm yielded dividends for my sons. She had them jumping to their feet within just a few waves; even better, they were soon turning to the right and left, surfing along the thin wisps of white water. A mother herself, Dominique knows all too well that children soon grow bored of the repetition of one activity, and so she had the boys riding in on their backs, crossing their legs, and, in Elliot's case, surfing in backwards (though I think this may have been accidental).

Back on the beach, I asked Dominique what she made of the Badlands tag. 'It's very intense here, for sure,' she said. 'It's a really competitive line-up and the surf at Aggie is as good as it gets. It's a fast, hollow and powerful wave, and there are a lot of really hot surfers out there. Chops and his boys, the Ward family, Minzie, the Bunt family, the Hendy brothers, even my own brother James, all of them rip.' James had just arrived, and looked a little askance at his sister's tongue-in-cheek recognition of his prowess. But it was easy to see in James Kent the quintessential Aggie surfer. Of medium height, powerfully built and intense, with a hint of attitude about him, he wasn't the kind of surfer you would want to drop in on. 'Everyone's aggressive and assertive in the water,' continued Dominique, 'there's constant paddling for position, jockeying and shouting. Aggie is not an intermediate surfer's wave.'

But while Dominique clearly had no problems with aggression, some surfers in the area did – especially women. Dominique, who runs surf schools at north Cornwall spots including Porthtowan, St Agnes, Gwithian and Portreath, counselled a much greater level of assertiveness among her female charges. 'There are more and more women taking up surfing now,' she told me, but 'too many girls get to intermediate level and can't make the jump beyond. They sit on the shoulder and don't take enough waves. They need to be assertive, sit on the peak and paddle into waves as aggressively as the guys. I spend a lot of time coaching girls to do this, telling them to be more committed, more confident, angry even. They're not out there to be nice and smiley. They're out there to catch waves.'

As I shepherded Harry and Elliot into the car, I looked back to the surf at Porthtowan. A father and daughter were walking briskly to the beach, surfboards under their arms. It was sunny, with a gentle onshore wind. The waves were far from classic, but they were surfable. Some twelve or so surfers and bodyboarders were in the line-up, and closer to shore, taking white water rides, were perhaps fifteen beginners. Dominique was rapidly loading up her car, about to sprint off to another lesson at a nearby Badlands beach. She seemed as full of energy as the waves themselves, and I recalled the words of Chris Hines when I asked him what was so special about surfing.

'It's a reason for being alive that most people don't ever experience,' he said.

For some people, riding big waves – and photographing them from the water – is fun. Likely suspects Llewellyn Whittaker and Duncan Scott take on The Cribbar, while in the water, behind the lens and soon to suffer for his art, is Tony Plant.

6

CRIBBAR GREEN ROOMS

Love it or hate it, all roads, in surfing, lead to Newquay. The town first offered surfboards for sale in 1963, a year before the publication of John Severson's book *Modern Surfing around the World*. Severson was a surfer, photographer and writer who began surfing in the late 1940s, and, although proving himself in the big waves of Hawaii and winning the 1961 Peru Internationals, is perhaps best known for his work as the editor of *Surfer* magazine. By the time Doubleday & Co. published *Modern Surfing* in 1964, Severson had travelled the world in pursuit of his passion, but the only European nation to be mentioned in the book's section of 'Surfing Capitals' was France. The other surfing nations, according to Severson, were Hawaii, the US, Mexico, New Zealand and Peru, with two chapters devoted to 'Australia's Great Potential' and 'South Africa Unlimited'. The idea of there being quality surf in the UK had evidently not filtered through to Severson, and even now there are plenty around the globe who are yet to be convinced. Well-known Australian cricketer Shane Warne encapsulated an oft-heard view when asked by the *Observer* in October 2006 whether he went surfing: 'I haven't got the time. I play cricket six days a week. I haven't surfed since I was seventeen. I used to surf as a kid, but was never that good.'

Besides, he said: 'There's not too much surfing over here, is there?' *Surfer* ran an article in 2006 on 'Merry Olde England' in which England was only half-jokingly described as 'too often the court jester of European surfing', a tag belied by images of superb surf from Porthleven and a secret spot in the far west of Cornwall. But if Severson was unaware of the quality of surf on the northern Atlantic seaboard when he wrote *Modern Surfing* (or, perhaps, if he decided that such surf was simply too cold to merit inclusion), two Newquay lifeguards were, in the early 1960s, blazing a trail that has now become etched in the consciousness of the surfing *cognoscenti*.

In 1963 the men, Doug Wilson and Bill Bailey, met a genuine 'Malibu surfer' in American Doug McDonald, on his way home to the US and happy to sell Bailey a 10′ 6″ foam and fibreglass Bragg surfboard. At the same time four Australian lifeguards – Bob Head, Ian Tiley, John Campbell and Warren Mitchell – arrived at Tolcarne beach with boards fresh from Sydney shaper Barry Bennet. The exemplary surfing of the Australians, especially Bob Head, inspired Bailey and Wilson, and before long Bailey was selling home-produced boards from a garage in Newquay. The nascent surfing community surfed Newquay's town beaches as well as nearby Watergate Bay, with Bob Head also producing his own boards and Wilson running a rudimentary surf shop. Soon Bailey, Head and Wilson had joined forces with Plymouth businessman Freddy Blight, setting up Bilbo, now one of the best-known European surf brands and one which is an amalgam of Bailey and Head's Christian names. Bilbo started producing surfboards from a factory in Pargolla Road in Newquay in 1965 and opened its first shop at 6 Station Forecourt, Cliff Road, just above Great Western beach, in spring 1967. A year later another Bilbo shop in the Mumbles, near Swansea, had been opened.

Forty years later, Bilbo is still at 6 Station Forecourt, though now it is one of countless retailers in Newquay selling surfing merchandise. It is impossible to move more than five yards without encountering a surf shop, or one which at the very least plays on the surfing image. Within a stone's throw of one another on Fore Street, for example, are Smile, Revolver, North Shore, the Quicksilver shop, Fat Face, Fat Willy's, Enigma, Oasis, Double Six and North Shore Girls. The Newquay Surf Centre is in their midst, as is the Red Fort pub, a place that does not, from the outside, look to have embraced the culinary principles advocated by Jamie Oliver, Britain's superstar chef and ad hoc advisor to the government, whose fare is, however, available not more than two miles from Newquay. Amusement arcades sit side by side with the surf shops, above Newquay's ancient harbour, all of them jostling for custom in the epicentre of British surfing, a town heralded by a sign welcoming visitors to the 'Coast of Dreams'. Dreaming might take on a rather down-at-heel feel if one were to confine oneself to Newquay's main shopping thoroughfares, where glitz, gaudiness and greasy food seem in danger of countervailing the healthy surfing vibes, and the faintly seedy feel threatens to continue on Headland Road, where a succession of surf lodges oversee both the waves of Fistral beach and the town's golf course. Most offer 'quality budget accommodation', though this is difficult to believe of the battered and crumbling Western Ocean Holiday Flats, whose better days, given its current state of disrepair, are not hard to imagine. But all year round, Headland Road sees surfers of every age and ability walk its smooth, skateboard-friendly surface to reach Fistral and its low-tide neighbour, Little Fistral. Local teenagers – the 'grommets' of surf-speak – head for the beach after school, often already in their wetsuits, riding bikes with surfboards under their arms. Even on wintry afternoons when the surf is no better than a messy, windblown two foot, there will be people surfing in Newquay, with a fair proportion being transient surfers: Australians, New Zealanders, South Africans, the French and other Europeans, all on extended 'surfaris', making time for a stop in surf city. If they stay long enough, those visitors – perhaps staying at the Cribbar Green Rooms Surf Lodge on Headland Road – will realize that Newquay has more than the barrels and walls of Fistral to offer, more, even, than the varied attractions of its numerous bars and nightclubs. For Newquay has its very own big wave, a surf spot that has become the stuff of legends: the Cribbar, a rocky point beyond the Headland Hotel.

The Cribbar has been blessed with mystical qualities by the national media. It is treated almost as a bizarre, much larger version of the Severn Bore (the tidal surge that regularly sweeps up the River Severn), something sacred that appears 'perhaps once a decade', and entirely of its own volition. In fact, the Cribbar breaks as a surfable wave a good deal more often than once a decade, and with the advent of tow-in surfing is set to be surfed more than ever. Surfers first attempted to ride its giant walls in the mid-1960s, as beautifully captured in *You Should Have Been Here Yesterday*, a book subtitled *The Roots of British Surfing* by two surfers of the era, Rod Holmes and Doug Wilson. The mildly hazy sheen of Wilson's photographs of the Cribbar breaking at size, being surfed by the pioneers of British surfing, including Roger Mansfield, Trevor Roberts and Chris Jones – as well as the American big-wave specialist Jack 'Mahogany' Lydgate – perfectly distils the delicate velocity of its pristine, cold, blue and terrifying walls of water. And as the caption to one image of the Cribbar breaking on a clean, offshore day puts it: 'What would it take to make you paddle out? Money? Fame? Or a priceless personal memory to last you a lifetime?'

One man who knows the answer to that question is South African surfer Chris Bertish. On two occasions in late 2005, Bertish rode the Cribbar in surf estimated to be 20–25 ft. The second session, on Thursday 9 December, was widely reported, not least by the *Sun* newspaper, with headlines varying from 'Huge Cornwall of Water – surfer Chris Bertish has a swell time riding a monster' and 'Chris on crest of wave – super surfer Chris Bertish told yesterday how he conquered the Cribbar – the biggest wave in Britain'. Both stories were illustrated by photographs of Bertish racing down the line of an immaculate right-breaking Cribbar wall, a wave that whether measured by its face or using the Hawaiian system was certainly in the 20–25 ft range. The *Sun* fell prey to the classic surfer's hyperbole, explaining how 'daredevil Chris spent three hours riding the 35 ft-high monster' having scrutinized weather charts for weeks in the hope that the right combination of swell, wind and tide would prevail. When it did, Bertish had the wave to himself, said the *Sun*, because 'The wall of water thunders towards the beach at forty miles an hour and is too dangerous for most Brit surfers.' Bertish apparently told the paper that he had 'a whale of time', for surfing the Cribbar was 'really exhilarating, a real adrenalin rush and great fun'.

Bertish, a Gul wetsuit representative, is a big-wave specialist who, in *Sun*-speak, can legitimately claim to have 'conquered' a number of other legendary surf spots. 'I've got a lot of experience of surfing big waves at places like Teahupoo, Todos Santos, Jaws and Mavericks,' he told me. But the 30-year-old émigré finds the Cribbar as congenial, if not more so, than any of its more photographed brethren. 'I love surfing the Cribbar. There's something really special about the wave. Maybe it's the cold, maybe it's the unique history surrounding it. This isn't an over-exposed break – it's a wave that only a handful of people have ever paddled out into, let alone ridden.'

But the Cribbar's status as an almost mythological wave seems set to disappear. Local surfers have for years entered the inclement Atlantic at all times of the year (even in snow), and wetsuit technology is now so advanced that often a surfer will be warmer in a winter sea than on the beach, but another development in surfing is driving yet more people to take on waves such as the Cribbar. Tow-in surfing was pioneered in Hawaii by legendary waterman Laird Hamilton and occurs when one surfer tows another behind a jet ski. The surfer being towed holds on to a ski rope, as would a water-skier behind a speedboat. When the surfer has caught the wave – when he knows he has been successfully 'towed in' to it – he lets go of the rope, and surfs the wave. The technique has revolutionized surfing, for it enables surfers to catch and ride waves that are travelling too fast for a human to catch by paddle power alone. Remarkably, Bertish's 2005 Cribbar sessions were the result of his own paddling ability, but he and an elite group of UK and Irish surfers are in the vanguard of what is rapidly being perceived as the last frontier: cold water, big-wave, tow-in surfing. Surfing's ongoing search has taken on a new dimension; as Bertish put it: 'We've found breaks that are completely inaccessible to normal surfers. Feeling that you're pioneering surfing in new locations is definitely part of tow-surfing's appeal.'

New waves are being discovered all around Ireland and the British Isles, and the surfing of known big-wave spots has become a media event. Just two months after Bertish's 9 December exploits, the Cribbar was again in the news. Two tow teams selected a freezing mid-February day as perfect for a practice session when the results of a storm born a few days earlier on the US eastern seaboard finally came crashing on to the coast of Cornwall. Sam Lamiroy and Dan Joel were joined by Newquay-based South Africans Llewellyn Whittaker and Duncan Scott, on the kind of grey and bitter English day that, in many people, induces nothing but the desire to stay inside next to a warm fire and drink soup. Not so for those anywhere near the Cribbar. A large crowd gathered just yards from the scene of summer 2005's ill-served (by the surf gods) Rip Curl Boardmasters, and the action, this time, was infinitely more enthralling. It may only have been a practice session, but there was no denying the drama of watching the four men flying down the faces of the Atlantic bombs, nor the sheer terror when Lamiroy dropped down the face of a massive wave, only to find that it closed out. This means that rather than, in this case, continuing to break to Lamiroy's right (as he is looking at the shore), the wave collapsed in one fell swoop. Lamiroy had nowhere to go, and what happened next was entertainingly described by Roger Sharp in *Slide* magazine:

> You hold on in survival stance as long as you can before the maelstrom knocks you off; hit a big breath before the inevitable drubbing and go down. Deep. So deep you begin to wonder if you're going to come back up. Climbing up the leash the only clue as to which way fresh air lies. Stars start swimming in front

of your eyes before you break the surface, take a lungful of sweet air and turn around to see the next mountain of whitewater three feet from your head. No time to swim, or dive, it takes you. Down. Beating you down and then deeper, over what seems like an underwater waterfall, into dark calmness. So dark it's eerie. The fight for life starts again. The next Cribbar smackdown is waiting for you.

Lamiroy found himself in the impact zone of five Cribbar waves, and was just two feet from the rocks at the foot of the headland when Dan Joel was eventually able to manoeuvre the jet ski in position to rescue him. A gully lurks beyond those rocks, making for caverns into which the raging sea cannot but surge. Had Lamiroy not been rescued, he would almost certainly have been swept into the gully. And once there, it is very likely that even the super-fit, solidly built Newcastle man – who eschewed gloves or a hood for the February Cribbar session – would have drowned.

A similar fate could have been shared by a photographer out in the water during another February Cribbar session. Newquay's Tony Plant is a tall, intense man in his forties who, as well as representing south-west England in swimming and water polo, has surfed since he was six years old. He has a degree in fine art from the Chelsea School of Fine Art, and makes a living combining his passion for surfing with that for art and photography. Plant can be found in the water whenever breaks such as the Cribbar are working, camera (complete with water-housing) in hand, to capture images of surfing that, once published, bear an unmistakably painterly feel, but which on the way to their creation entail Plant dicing with death. Presently involved in making a 'no sponsors and no bullshit' DVD of big-wave surfing in Cornwall, Plant's website – www.surftwisted.com – hosts a gallery of images from a February Cribbar session whose terror is enhanced by the stark words he has chosen in accompaniment: 'It ripped my fins and board off, lost, gone forever.'

I have met Plant on various occasions, and each time our conversation veers towards the Cribbar his deep brown eyes burn with yet greater intensity, his brow furrows and he seems, in short, lost in awe. As he says: 'I've been watching the Cribbar since I was a kid. I've seen it barreling like you wouldn't believe, and I knew it was going to be good that day. I got there to find Ben Skinner [a top British surfer based in Newquay] coming back in. He'd paddled out – can you believe that? It was a monster swell but Ben had paddled in to it while the other guys were going to tow-surf it. Ben told me not to go out, but I'm comfortable swimming in big seas and I know there's a great water shot to be had of the Cribbar. I want to be the one who gets that shot, so off I went.'

Plant's experience of the ocean as a surfer and all-round waterman is a *sine qua non* of surfing photography. Only a fool would endeavour to swim into a heaving line-up with a camera and take pictures without having first attained a decent level as a surfer or boogie-boarder. In Plant's case, he has also sailed extensively in the Southern Ocean. 'I've sailed a ketch from Perth to Sydney in eighteen-metre surf,' he says. 'It was like a liquid version of the Lake District. The angles were simply impossible.' In common with many surf photographers, Plant often uses a bodyboard to get out into big waves. Body-, or boogie-, boards are, in effect, shortened surfboards whose front is squared off rather than angular. They are made up of a foam core comprised, variously, of polyethylene, arcel and polypropylene, leading to practitioners being dubbed by stand-up surfers as 'spongers'. There is, indeed, a degree of usually light-hearted banter between conventional surfers and bodyboarders, best summed up in the words of a friend when I mentioned that I was thinking of getting into bodyboarding: 'Don't bother,' he said emphatically. 'You've a long way to go yet before you're dead.' My friend was referring to the fact that bodyboards are almost always ridden in the prone position, though they can also be ridden in a drop-knee stance or even (just) standing up. To me, looking at the bodyboarders taking the vertical drops on the waves of my local break, there is much to admire in their art, and for the likes of Plant, the bodyboard is a vital part of his profession. By lying on the board and using flippers, Plant makes the journey to the line-up that much swifter, easier and, in most cases, safer. The Cribbar, though, is the kind of wave that can take the notion of safety and chew it to smithereens in one cataclysmic surge of primordial power. And so it was when Plant made it outside that day.

'I'll never forget being out there. It was scary as hell. The noise was deafening, the wind was ripping up the faces of the waves and all around was a huge, seething mass of white water. The handles of the ski rope were being whipped around on the wave faces, it was just carnage. The boys [Sam Lamiroy and Dan Joel in one tow team, Duncan Scott and Llewellyn Whitaker in the other] were yelling and whooping and whistling, and I was just firing away, trying to get as many shots as I could. After I'd shot one ride I turned to the horizon to see a humungous wave bearing down on me. It tore my boogie-board off me and destroyed it, and when I came up from that wave another set was about to land on my head. The next wave ripped my fins off, leaving me holding a camera in one hand and the other to swim with. I took an absolute hammering and knew it was time to get out. I stuck my arm up and Duncan and Lew came and got me.' The pre-surf risk analysis paid dividends: all those in the sea at the Cribbar then had carefully considered how they would cope in the event of any problems. As Plant says, 'The safety issues are paramount – it's not about show-boating when you're in that kind of surf. You have to remember that the jet ski is there to get the surfer on to the wave but also to get him out if it goes wrong.'

Plant took a beating, but was 'raging on adrenalin' for days afterwards. 'I couldn't sleep. All I could think of was what it was like being out there in all that immense power.' But Plant would not be tempted to try surfing the Cribbar himself. 'Nothing on God's green earth would get me doing that,' he said. 'I mindsurf the place all the time, but those guys surfing it get to a far scarier place than me. They take extraordinary risks. I've got every respect for them.'

To accept the dangers of big-wave tow-in surfing may strike many as grossly irresponsible, but it is useful to recall that individuals such as Lamiroy have not decided to attempt surfing the Cribbar, or, say, Waimea Bay on Oahu's North Shore (the spiritual home of big-wave surfing, a place that Lamiroy has surfed in the 25–30 ft range) without building up the requisite levels of experience and expertise. Just as most mountaineers contemplating an attempt on Everest are only able to do so because they have put their time in on lesser peaks, so too do the surfers riding the Cribbar only put themselves in such jeopardy because their training means that they can evaluate the dangers sufficiently to turn what would otherwise be suicide into a fair risk. Indeed, one might go further and hypothesize that, unlike ascents of Everest where commercial organizations now routinely haul barely competent Alpinists as close to the summit as they can get them, such practices will simply never occur at a place like the Cribbar. Big-wave surfing occurs in far too fluid an environment to take even the slimmest of chances, and anyone less than expert would find it all but impossible to cope with the extraordinary amounts of water avalanching around them. Such a person would be a liability in a form of surfing that inverts its norm of pure individualism, for in tow-in surfing the sport moves from the selfish to the team mentality. The two surfers must be able to have absolute faith in each other; they must believe to the core that both are premier watermen. As Bertish says: 'Tow-surfing is about two surfers working together. Training, teamwork and solidarity are vital.' There is also, at this outer extreme of the sport, so much more to consider than the act of surfing. The jet ski needs to be in perfect working order. It needs the right amount of fuel. Safety equipment such as flares and life-vests are essential. The tow rope must not be frayed, carabiners must function correctly, the radio must work. The analogy with mountain climbing remains apposite: tow-surfing anywhere, but perhaps especially in winter and autumn in Britain and Ireland, is nothing short of a mission that has to be planned and conducted with all the rigour of the Everest ascent.

That safety is paramount is well understood by the likes of Bertish, Lamiroy and Joel. Their attitude to so hazardous a pursuit is, indeed, epitomized by the formation of the British Tow-Surf Association (B-TSA) in July 2006. The B-TSA's chairman is Bertish, with its vice-chairman the ever exuberant Duncan Scott. Its mission is to promote awareness of tow-surfing to the public at large but also to ensure that it is carried out in as safe a manner as possible.

'There are now between ten and twenty teams of tow-surfers in the UK,' says Bertish, who, in 2001, became the first person to paddle into Maui's notorious monster wave, Jaws. 'Tow-surfing is undoubtedly getting more and more popular but people have to realize that it is potentially very dangerous. Our aim is to promote awareness of the need for proper safety precautions and educate surfers about the risks involved. It is important that a responsible voice for the tow-in fraternity emerges at the same time as the sport develops.'

The B-TSA has set up a website, www.b-tsa.co.uk, and, of the plethora of surfing sites online, it has to be one of the most minimalist. At the time of writing there were no images, merely a series of statements outlining the association's aims, objectives, agreed safety requirements and membership criteria. Its geographical area is designated as 'permitted launch and surfing sites in and around Great Britain', and its safety advisors for 2006–2008, the RNLI.

That the B-TSA should be understated rather than otherwise struck me as a good thing. Not so long ago – and maybe even to this day – the Newquay harbour master did not take kindly to young athletes with jet skis and surfboards launching from within his domain to do battle with the Cribbar. Indeed, one of the added complexities of tow-surfing the wave was hoping that it would break on the harbour master's day off, so that access would be unhindered, by him at least. Anything that would highlight the seriousness with which Bertish & Co. went about their business had to be a good thing. Perhaps, one day, it might even change the harbour master's mind.

The Cribbar is Britain's most high-profile big wave, but Newquay is about much more than slotting into its elusive green rooms. Not only is the town the home of the BSA, it also houses the English Surfing Federation and the new kid on the block, the British Professional Surfing Association. The ESF is situated along Headland Road, having taken up residence in the Cribbar Green Rooms, while the BPSA's office is on the opposite side of town, overlooking the left-handers of South Fistral. Sandwiched in between both of them, on Fistral beach, is the BSA, with whom Dave Reed, the man who set up the BPSA, used to work. Paul Jeffrey, an amateur boxer as well as surfer, runs the ESF, and if anyone is concerned that there are too many acronyms in domestic surfing, this is a worry that gains momentum when one considers that there is also the Welsh Surfing Federation (WSF), the SSF (Scottish Surfing Federation) and ISA (Irish Surfing Association). Disentangling who does what is not, to ingénues, an easy task and, as I learnt in talking to Reed and Jeffrey, politics is alive and well even in the world of sex wax and super tubes.

I met Jeffrey for a coffee at the Headland Hotel, a short walk for the dark-haired Englishman in his mid-thirties whose workplace is to be found amid the hostels and lodges of Headland Road. At its rear Jeffrey has set up boxing paraphernalia, which he uses to coach various Newquay surfers. 'I've always loved boxing,' said the man who hails originally from Swindon, at whose amateur club, Walcot, I trained for a few years. 'Surfers and boxers have similar physiques, and the fitness acquired through boxing training is perfect for surfers.'

Jeffrey is right about this, and he is not alone in pursuing the two disciplines. Europe's most successful ever surfer, Russell Winter, comes from a family of three brothers all of whom practise various martial arts. Jeffrey coaches Winter and another of Newquay's well-known local surfers, Spencer Hargreaves.

Jersey's Ian Battrick has boxed as an amateur, as has Newquay's Jamie Owen; so too yet another Nequay surfer, Nathaniel Hooton. But by far the most remarkable of the surfer-boxers is a 26-year-old goofy-footer from Sennen Cove, Sam Smart.

Smart's prowess at both surfing and boxing means that he might, one day, have to decide between the two. Smart runs www.bluelagoonsurf.com, a surf school in Sennen Cove, and is a professional surfer sponsored by Relentless, Surftech and C-Skins Wetsuits. He is also a hard-hitting and skilful southpaw who, boxing as a middleweight, has won all thirteen of his amateur bouts, seven by knockout. Smart is highly rated by the two clubs at which he learnt his ring-craft, the St Just Amateur Boxing Club and the Camborne and Redruth ABC, whose coaches believe he has excellent prospects in the national Amateur Boxing Championships. Smart himself takes a pragmatic view of his options: 'I don't think it's realistic for me, as a British surfer, to think of winning an event at Pipeline. Maybe it'll happen one day for an up-and-coming Brit, but it's tough surfing here – we don't have machine-like reefs and points that fire up all the time, we have mostly beachbreaks that shift and change. Conditions here mean that you can't refine your surfing in the way that many overseas surfers can. But boxing – boxing's different. We've had plenty of world champions and there's no reason why we won't have some more. I'm happy to combine the boxing and surfing for now, but it's true, I love boxing and I want to take it as far as I can. If I could turn pro, I would. I can always come back to surfing.'

Jeffrey's passion for boxing is as ingrained as Smart's; so, too, his convictions about domestic surfing. Or, more precisely, his belief about what is wrong with surfing in the UK.

'Surfing is no longer a minority sport,' he told me. 'Look at France or Spain – surfing is now their national sport. Here in Britain most beaches cater for surfing, even in places where the swell is fickle. We're ranked in the world top ten and every year more and more people get into the sport. And yet there are problems at almost every turn.'

Such as?

'Well, look around you.'

I peered beyond the terrace of the Headland Hotel, down to Fistral beach. The surf was reasonable enough and a few people were up and riding. I wasn't sure what Jeffrey was getting at and looked at him quizzically. He was quick to elaborate.

'The restaurant complex was built what, last year? It was supposed to be the grand new creation but it's not geared to surfing.'

'But there are plenty of surf shops and you can hire boards, get a meal, have a drink. What's the problem?'

'This is one of the busiest beaches in Britain, and you have to *pay* to have a shower. It attracts thousands of people every year to go surfing, and the lifeguards are put in a Portakabin. In the plans, there was detail about how there'd be a showcase centre for surfing, something providing a permanent record of the history of British surfing, but that hasn't happened. The car park prices are way too high. The whole thing is a classic example of something created on the back of surfing that gives nothing back to surfing. There's been no improvement on the old wooden café and I think that some of the unity has been eroded. There's no focal point anymore.'

Jeffrey was unsparing in his criticism of other aspects of modern surfing. 'In Newquay, the surf schools are well regulated and proportionate, but go to a place like Polzeath. Have you been there? Have you seen what it's like these days?'

I confessed that I had indeed been to Polzeath, both recently and many years ago. I have some very fond memories of surfing in Polzeath in my mid-twenties, and, on making a return visit in summer 2005, found it difficult not to agree with Jeffrey's bone of contention: there were simply too many surf schools on the beach. I wasn't sure that I'd go as far as Jeffrey – 'There are too many people on the take, milking the surfing boom' – but that Polzeath is replete with kindly souls only too eager to dispense their surfing knowledge is indisputable. So, too, that, during the summer, their surfing lessons are booked to the hilt. The BSA has a liaison officer whose job it is to check each surf school and try and ensure that they are BSA approved, but Jeffrey felt that there were unscrupulous operators (if not in Polzeath then elsewhere) who might not be inclined to listen to a word he said anyway.

Jeffrey himself moved to Newquay when he was five, though he did not start surfing until he was fourteen. 'That was it, then,' he said, shaking his head as if to recapture a bitter-sweet memory, 'goodbye school, surfing was everything. The lifestyle – being on the beach, the girls, partying – was irresistible.' He grew up surfing with long-time, well-respected Newquay pro Lee Bartlett and the Winter brothers, but knew that he was not at their level and so started to carve out a career on the other side of the fence, both as a judge and in surfing administration. 'I've been all around the world judging, which is a great way to asses how surfing has moved on. It's constantly progressing, and while there are those who think contests are uncool I have no problem with them. They drive surfing to the next level.' As an administrator, Jeffrey now runs the ESF, a voluntary position in a non-profit-making organization which, as he says, is 'on a mission. We want to inject a level of professionalism into English surfing that will guarantee future champions. The likes of Russell Winter, Lee Bartlett, Robyn Davies and Alan Stokes have all benefited from ESF support and gone on to represent England at the highest level, but we need to bring on and harness the talents of the likes of Reubyn Ash, Tom Butler, Holly Butler and Jayce Robinson. The problem is that we're not funded. England is the top-performing nation country of the home nations, but in contrast to Wales and Ireland we don't get any funding. How are we ever going to compete against, say, the French surfing team, which gets major financial backing from the French government?'

Jeffrey was realistic about surfing's image problem. 'Too many people think it's all about being chilled and laid-back, but I want to show them another side to surfing – especially modern professional surfing. The top pros are athletes who train and work as hard as athletes in other sports. There is still a recreational side to surfing, and it'll always have its hippie soul-surfers, but their world is very different from that of the likes of Russell Winter. He's on a plane every five minutes, dealing with jet lag and logistical problems, competing against the best, but he could only do this and achieve the success he's had if he kept himself in top shape, like an Olympic athlete.'

The reference to the Olympics begged a question. What price surfing as an exhibition sport for the 2012 London Olympics?

'I'm working on it,' said Jeffrey.

On the other side of Fistral beach, perhaps half an hour's walk from the Cribbar, is the office of the British Professional Surfing Association. Set up by Reed and business partner John Owen in 1998 under the corporate auspices of UK Surf Promotions Ltd, the BPSA runs a series of contests between April and November each year. Past champions since the first BPSA Tour event – held, appropriately enough, at Fistral beach in August 1998 – include Geordies Sam Lamiroy and Gabriel Davies, and Newquay locals Mark Harris, Alan Stokes and Lee Bartlett. More recently overseas-born surfers have scooped the BPSA title: South African Reubin Pearce in 2005, and Australian Micah Lester in 2006. The thinking behind the creation of the BPSA was, says Reed, 'to bring greater professionalism to UK events. We also wanted to highlight the quality of British waves. On their day our surf spots are as good as anywhere in the world.'

Reed, now in his early forties, started surfing aged ten, and is well-placed to run contests such as the BPSA Tour given his experience of the sport. 'I started surfing at Bantham in south Devon,' he explains, 'and then got involved with surf-lifesaving. Being in the water as much as possible became my life.' In the late '70s and early '80s, Reed was a good enough surfer to be asked to represent England, but always had a clear sense of his own abilities. 'There were other people who were better than me. Especially, at the time I was asked to surf for England, Nigel Semmens.' Semmens is another Newquay legend who won the BSA's British Nationals in 1979 and who now runs Ocean Magic, a surf shop on Cliff Road. Reed knew that he would never beat surfers of Semmens' calibre, 'and so in around 1981 I decided my role would be to help promote the competitive side of surfing as much as possible. Competition isn't everything – surfing will always, for most people, be about paddling out and just having fun – but it has grown massively from the early days.' Reed undertook a BSA judging course with Mike Cunningham, another well-known figure in British surfing, and by 1983 found himself working as a judge on certain events on the ASP Tour. He won 'best judge' on a couple of occasions, and became a full-time ASP judge for four years, finishing in 1989. As he says, with more than a hint of nostalgia, 'It was a great life. I travelled to all the best beaches in the world and surfed the best waves. I was hardly ever home and lived out of a suitcase, but it was brilliant. For a young man, you couldn't pick a better life.'

Reed was unique in being the only British judge on the ASP Tour. I asked him how surfers from Hawaii, Australia and California greeted his presence on the judge's stand. 'To begin with, they did wonder if I knew what I was doing,' he says. The consistency of his marking was a factor in gaining their respect – that, and dealing with the politics of professional surfing. 'I was good at it initially,' says Reed, 'but towards the end it began to wear me down.' In 1988 it couldn't have been much more wearing, as Reed was one of three judges to make a crucial decision in the Pipeline Masters, an event held in December on Oahu's North Shore which doubles as professional surfing's most iconic contest and the climax of the professional surfing season. Throughout the 1988 season, Australian Tom Carroll had been the front-runner, but the title swung to Barton Lynch when a paddling interference was given against Carroll. Reed takes up the story: 'Carroll was an amazing surfer, probably the best ever to surf Pipeline, but he was careless that day. Pipeline was pumping at ten to twelve feet, Carroll was wearing a helmet and didn't have peripheral vision. He was up against East Coast US surfer Todd Holland, who was out to prove himself. Carroll was acknowledged as the greatest Pipe surfer, and all he had to do to win the world title was keep his head. But I think he just didn't see Holland. It had to be a paddle interference, and I called it with two others from the five judges. Making this decision – which Carroll never complained about – meant that he effectively surrendered his title hopes to Barton Lynch.' Carroll may never have complained about the decision, but there was no doubting its controversy at the time – and its effect on the powerhouse Australian, a man who still, in his forties, competes as a wildcard in the giant surf of Tavarua, Fiji. 'I really wish I had achieved that third world title at Pipe in eighty-eight,' Carroll has said. 'It affected me physically and mentally for a couple of years after. In retrospect, maybe I should have had a break after that. Instead, I tried to push through. I didn't want to let it beat me, but it was a big loss.' Carroll went on to win two more Pipeline Masters titles, but Reed decided that it was time to return to the UK. He gave up working full time as a judge for the ASP, though kept his hand in judging world championship contests held in Europe as well as homegrown ones such as student events. He worked in marketing, and there was also a stint as a national director for the BSA, though Reed admits that 'all isn't completely harmonious between me and them these days'. I wasn't sure of the reasons for what seemed to have been a falling out, but one thing was clear: for a long time, the idea of running his own domestic surfing tour had been bubbling away in Reed's mind.

When the idea eventually became reality in 1998, it soon proved popular with domestic surfers. 'A growing number of surfers compete on the Tour,' Reed told me, as we looked out at good-sized, relatively uncrowded surf breaking at South Fistral. Prize money is far from enough alone to motivate competition, but sponsorship and exposure through magazine coverage of BPSA events – as well as kudos – lures around 200 professional surfers to contests in such places as Croyde, North Devon, Newquay, Freshwater West in Wales and all the way north to Thurso at the tip of Scotland. As well as running contests, Reed and Owen have other plans. 'We're developing the BPSA further so as to introduce a twelve-month rolling membership scheme, not just for pro surfers but for everyone, and will offer travel and personal accident and liability insurance. There's no doubt that people need it – it's estimated that at least a hundred thousand people go through the surf-school system each year. By taking out the cover you can surf with peace of mind.'

I wondered if Reed feared the dread spectre of litigation arising from incidents at UK beaches. In *Point Break*, an entertaining if largely nonsensical Hollywood romp in which an FBI agent goes undercover to catch a gang of bank robbers who have turned to crime to fund their surfing (as the tagline says: '27 banks in three years – anything to catch the perfect wave!'), Lori Petty half snarls, half pouts to Keanu Reeves' lawyer-turned-FBI-agent, quarterback-turned-surfer that 'Lawyers don't surf,' only for Reeves, not unexpectedly, to confound this stereotype. Stereotype it may be, but law and surfing have rarely walked hand in hand, either owing to the fact that so few lawyers (until recently, that is) do, indeed, surf, or because surfing, unlike, say, mountaineering and other so-called 'extreme sports', has largely escaped claims for personal injury compensation. Did Reed worry that surfing's unstoppable increase in popularity would result in litigation? And, if so, could this have a knock-on effect on the public's access to beaches?

Reed, a taller than average man whose black hair is either curly or wavy (I could never work out which) but always wild, was not too concerned at this potential Doomsday scenario. 'I don't think it'll ever get that bad,' he said, as a group of surfers continued to ride South Fistral's left-handers despite the gathering darkness. 'It's a worry but I think people who are attracted to surfing would rather sort things out amicably than go through the courts.'

Others are not so sure. Here are two lawyers' thoughts:

As surfing continues to grow the danger must be that it will resemble skiing, where a number of claims are made each season owing to collisions on the slopes. The role of local councils is also likely to come under scrutiny. There are health and safety issues given that they will often control access to beaches, and in the absence of appropriate warnings they may unwittingly create exposure to litigation. – Jeff Zindani, managing director of Forum Law.

If an accident or injury is caused by the negligence of another person, and was foreseeable and therefore preventable, then it may be possible to pursue a claim. If it can be shown that those running a surfing school negligently allowed someone to surf when they were aware that conditions were dangerous, that the person was not properly equipped or had the right level of experience for the conditions, then it may be possible to pursue a claim. – Jennie Walsh, a personal injury lawyer with Thompsons Solicitors.

There is something about lawyer-speak that cannot but make one feel that Lori Petty was right. This is not the fault of lawyers themselves but the system to which they adhere, a system that they also promote, whether consciously or not, in their use of language. The law is everything that is grey about human life: it seeks to impose order on ambivalence, and, in the attempt, cannot but analyse and over-analyse until even the minutiae are crying out for respite. Surfing has to be its antithesis. Surfing is about flow: flowing with the wave, with the ocean, with one's immediate environment, in an unselfconscious manner; it entails a literal, physical immersion in the water and a temporal one in the here and now. And once a wave has been surfed, there are no traces of the surfer – his or her artistry has proved as evanescent as the wave itself, as meaningful as the sound of a wave breaking, no more, no less. There is nothing in this of the law, nothing of lawyers and their modes of thought, and albeit that Karen Walton at the BSA echoes concerns that legal action may well flow in surfing's wake – 'Although there have been only a few minor claims so far, with more people taking up the sport the risk of injury will increase,' she told me – it is to be hoped that surfing remains an inspiration for frustrated office-bound lawyers rather than a source of income. To envisage a High Court judge being asked to comprehend how a frontside off-the-lip went wrong and resulted in injury to someone on the way to the line-up is to invite a barrage of legal quips of the 'Who is Gazza?' variety. Amusing, but expensive and of no benefit save to lawyers' wallets.

It is a relief, on this point, to note that even in America it does not appear as if surfing and litigation have formed an alliance. There is an Association of Surfing Lawyers, formed in Santa Monica, California, in 2002, but its aims seem uncontroversial and, indeed, laudable. Its website – www.surfinglawyers.com – sets a nicely informal tone, one that if adopted by the majority of domestic lawyers might make them rather more appealing individuals: 'The ASL is a non-profit organization of attorneys who promote and preserve the lifestyle, causes and concerns of surfers around the world. [We] aim to foster goodwill, balance, camaraderie and networking among surfing lawyers.' The home page then sets out 'A Surfer's Code' by 1977 World Champion Shaun Thomson, one of surfing's most intelligent and articulate sons:

I will never turn my back on the ocean
I will always paddle back out
I will take the drop with commitment
I will know that there will always be another wave
I will realize that all surfers are joined by one ocean
I will paddle around the impact zone
I will never fight a rip tide
I will watch out for other surfers after a big set
I will pass on my stoke to a non-surfer
I will ride, and not paddle in to shore
I will a catch a wave every day, even in my mind
I will honor the sport of kings

Reed and I talked for well over an hour, interrupted just once by a phone call from a surfer in Jersey ('You must go to Jersey,' said Reed afterwards, 'it's played a massive role in the development of European and British surfing'). Throughout, his gaze kept drifting to the waves breaking just a stone's throw from his office. Had he already been surfing that day?

'Oh yes,' he said, as we watched a Newquay local drop down the face of a five foot wave and turn to his left, 'I go out every day. I'm just wondering if there's time for one more quick session.'

Dusk was not far off, but I could tell that Reed had itchy feet. I left him to wax his board, and headed north.

Newquay's Lee Bartlett takes a short hop along the coast to
the crisp walls of Watergate Bay.

7

EXTREMELY WATERGATE

Two miles north-east of Newquay lies Watergate Bay, a two-mile stretch of sand offering excellent beachbreak waves on all tides that has attracted surfers for half a century. An undated but ancient-looking Tor Mark Press guide entitled *Cornwall's Best Beaches and Coves* talks thus of Watergate's charms:

> Watergate Bay (otherwise known as Tregurrian Beach) is a fine open expanse of sandy beach extending more or less north and south from Trevelgue Head for something like two miles. It is backed up by cliffs up which there are one or two paths. The easiest access is by the hotel midway along the length of the beach where the road comes down to sea level. Here there are toilets, car parks and a café. If you are interested in surfing or in invigorating bathing in the surf, Watergate Bay is a 'must' and it is recognized as one of the best beaches in the country for this.

Of the new fad of 'Malibu surfing' the Tor Mark guide had this to say:

> Malibu Surfing is true 'wave-riding'. The large Malibu boards are specially constructed, usually of rigid plastic foam covered

121

with fibreglass, and fitted with a skeg at the back to give directional stability. They are beautifully streamlined and, although as long as a small sailing dinghy, weigh only about thirty pounds – for greater maneuverability. The name is taken from that of the Californian beach where they were first introduced.

To go to Watergate Bay today is to see a vastly different world from that described by Tor Mark's unidentified writer. Where once the village abutting the beach seemed to be imbued with an air of decay almost as tangible as the scent of the sea, now it is the epitome of modern surfing in the UK, a place whose waves are rarely ever empty any more and which is emerging on the map for overseas holidaymakers as much as a homegrown market. Watergate Bay's metamorphosis from an artless if unambitious village to a thrumming centre of surf-related enterprise is largely down to the vision of the Ashworth Brothers, Will and Henry, owners of the Hotel and Extreme Academy, Watergate Bay. It is a vision that has attracted no less a figure than celebrity chef Jamie Oliver, one of whose Fifteen restaurants opened from a base overlooking the beach in 2005, and it is a vision at which the Ashworth brothers' parents – from whom they took over the running of what was originally the Watergate Bay Hotel in 2000 – must surely marvel, not least when each summer's day brings yet another invasion of surf-hungry tourists. The new, all-bells-and-whistles Watergate Bay is, however, inconceivable without surfing, as Will Ashworth is the first to admit.

'The increase in the popularity of surfing is staggering,' says the Hotel and Extreme Academy's managing director, a slim, smartly dressed and articulate man in his early thirties. 'Our surf school teaches five times as many students as it did ten years ago and the proportion of female surfers has risen from ten per cent to forty per cent. In the summer there can be as many as two hundred and fifty surfers in the water at one time – both locals and visitors alike. Surfing has radically changed Cornwall's leisure industry.' In 2001, indeed – when surfing was, comparatively speaking, still seen as an underground or even marginalized activity – the BSA published research suggesting a staggering £200 million annual turnover for an industry whose employers are generally no larger than Chops Lascelles' Beachbeat. A report around the same time by Cornish Enterprise found that nearly a quarter of that sum was confined to Cornwall alone – a county reportedly blessed with over 150 surfing-based businesses – and then, in 2004, another report put Cornish surfing turnover at £64 million. The BSA says that its membership is up 400 per cent to 10,000 since the turn of the century, and reckons that there are 500,000 regular surfers in the UK. As Ashworth says: 'Five years ago, surfing was important. Now it's fundamental to what we're doing.' The major global surfing brands – O'Neill, Rip Curl, Quicksilver and Billabong – have all targeted the UK (and, increasingly, Ireland) as key to the growth of their European markets (along with, tellingly so the cynic might add, Russia), and hotels such as this one have emerged in pole position to capitalize on the ocean-bound Zeitgeist.

Not everyone wants to move with the times. There remain plenty of hotels and B&B establishments in Cornwall and other surfing locales of the UK and Ireland whose embrace of surfing has been lukewarm. This is far from the case at Watergate Bay, where packages are tailored to surfers, aspiring or otherwise, and two surf schools exist: one is an O'Neill academy, while the other is run from the hotel. The hotel itself exudes California beach chic, with one refurbishment seeming to follow another so that few rooms are *sans* sea view and all are possessed of a slick ocean-blue décor, often with shutters and solid oak flooring. A brasserie overlooks the privately owned beach, children and dogs are not merely welcome but actively encouraged, and the overall feeling is akin to The House, which I visited in Barbados, and yet better even than this rather exclusive of luxury destinations: cool and chilled, relaxed and easy-going, and yet with a seemingly endless choice of activities on offer. All centre on the sea, in keeping with Henry Ashworth's original dream: to create a ski resort on the beach. With that in mind, the brothers merged what had been two separate businesses – the Hotel and, a stone's throw away, the Extreme Academy – in March 2005, so that now visitors can enjoy any number of adrenalin sports, from surfing, kitesurfing and waveski riding to mountain boarding and traction kiting.

With Jamie Oliver having chosen the first floor of the Extreme Academy as the location for Fifteen Cornwall, guests can avail themselves of après-surf relaxation courtesy of a top-class chef's seal of approval. At mid to high tide, diners in Fifteen Cornwall – a part of the chain inspired by the Channel 4 TV show *Jamie's Kitchen* – have a vantage point from which to observe surfing that is perhaps unrivalled in the UK. But despite its swish, not to say romantic, location, Fifteen's roots are in the metropolis: the original TV show followed Oliver's attempts to create a restaurant run by young people from disadvantaged backgrounds, and spawned the popular London eaterie Fifteen, near Old Street. Amsterdam acquired its own Fifteen in 2004, and now Oliver's vision is bang in the middle of Watergate Bay. Fifteen Cornwall retains its founder's ideals, according to Will Ashworth: 'It's been set up to provide a means of access for young people in Cornwall to the one part of the Cornish economy that is going from strength to strength – leisure and tourism. We've gone through a huge transformation from traditional British three-star hotel to a vibrant year-round destination in keeping with the modern Cornish environment, and Fifteen is a part of that process.' The new restaurant will also help two Cornish industries that have suffered in recent years – fishing and farming – for Ashworth says that Fifteen will use 'over ninety per cent of local Cornish produce'. He is confident, moreover, that it will become 'one of the iconic sights in Cornwall'.

Those sights include the Tate St Ives, the Eden Project near St Austell, Rick Stein's Padstow restaurant and any number of natural wonders, such as Bedruthan Steps, near Watergate Bay, Gunnard's Head on the Penwith Peninsula and Kynance Cove on the Lizard. Ashworth's belief that Fifteen Cornwall will one day join such illustrious company is far from fanciful, chiming as it does with the surfing boom – one which often seems to draw as much custom from the city in which Fifteen first came into being as the rest of the UK put together. Aside from the push by the leading surfwear companies – whose shops can be found in Leeds, Leicester and

London as well as more obvious communities such as Newquay and Plymouth – the influx of city-bound surfers to the Watergate area is helped by www.bigfriday.com, a Newquay-based company whose name is a play on one of surfing's paradigmatic films – John Milius' 1978 *Big Wednesday*. Milius, a southern California surfer in his youth, had a large hand in the surfing scenes in Francis Ford Coppola's *Apocalypse Now*, and in *Big Wednesday* (one of whose taglines – 'A day will come that is like no other . . . and nothing that happens after will ever be the same' – manages to resonate despite its linguistic flaws) he used surfing as a metaphor with which to confront the ebb and flow of an American society moving from the innocence of *Endless Summer* to the Vietnam War and beyond. In *Big Wednesday* surfing's relationship with the commercial world is seen as, at best, ambivalent. The chief character, Matt Johnson, slides into alcoholism as his childhood mentor, Bear, sets up a surf shop, but despite Johnson's irreversible decline he contrives to remain heroic, a toned yet bewildered cipher of soul surfing as literally represented by Pipeline legend Gerry Lopez, whose cameo appearance in the film is perhaps one of cinema's most immaculate, because virtually all that we see of Lopez is his exquisite wave-riding. But while *Big Wednesday* is tinged with melancholy, as if Milius cannot quite decide whether surfing would have been best served by being frozen in the Malibu of his youth, there is only optimism among the staff and clientele of Big Friday.

Big Friday, set up in 2002, is targeted – according to co-owner and surfer Rhona Gardiner – at 'mid-twenties to late-thirties people with attitude – young professional Londoners who are sociable, active and looking for something different to do with their weekends'. Big Friday's effervescent website ably conveys the zest behind its enterprise, one centred around what, in a different era, might have been analogous to Ken Kesey's Magic Bus. Today, the Merry Pranksters of the metropolis have left behind the LSD in favour of good vibes at the beach. From mid-May to the end of October, at 5.45 pm on a Friday, the Big Friday bus departs Shortlands Street in Hammersmith, West London, where it has collected a diverse array of people whose sense of adventure leads them to Cornwall's Atlantic rollers. Gardiner says that many will be new to surfing, though 'there are often one or two Australians and New Zealanders who've heard that England has waves, and want a no-hassle way of getting to the coast'. Big Friday takes away the strain, ferrying clients to Cornwall and sourcing accommodation and surfing lessons for them once there. During summer 2005, devotees could also sign up for yoga classes at the Hotel and Extreme Academy, Watergate Bay, thanks to a partnership between the hotel and Cornwall-bred surfer and yoga instructor Mara Luke. In 1991 Luke was ranked second in British women's surfing, and now teaches yoga twice a week in Newquay. For her, yoga is a perfect complement to surfing: 'I've been surfing for fifteen years and teaching yoga for eight, and found that yoga really helped my surfing,' she told me. 'A lot of surfers come to my classes, whether beginners, intermediates or experts. Surfers often have extremely well-developed upper bodies but neglect their lower back and leg strength. Yoga is a counter to this – it's relaxing and restores balance to the body. Yoga helps a surfer's flexibility and suppleness, and that means more fun in the water.'

Luke is in good company. Eight-time ASP world champion Kelly Slater is similarly enamoured of yoga, as are Gerry Lopez and Tom Curren. All have faultless physiques and appear, like Peter Pan, to defy conventional signs of ageing. Perhaps this, indeed, explains another of surfing's appeals, particularly to anyone stuck in an office, confronted each day not by blue skies and an open ocean but by artificial light, air conditioning and reams of paper. To surf like Lopez, to look like Slater, to be as cool as Curren are day dreams with which to escape the monotony of city life, an escape made physically possible by Big Friday and encouraged not more than two miles from Hammersmith, in Notting Hill, by the London Beach Store. Established in 1997, the London Beach Store, on the salubrious Kensington Park Road, is staffed by its own 'dedicated beach-life experts' and sells all manner of merchandise connected to surfing and skateboarding. That its home page at www.londonbeachstore.com is illustrated by an image of a kitesurfer could be read either as indicative of kitesurfing's own boom or of the fact that the sport – a blend of windsurfing and surfing – does not require good surf to be enjoyed. Be that as it may, there is no doubting the enthusiasm and commitment of businesses like Big Friday and the London Beach Store, nor of the ever growing dissemination of what, in surfing's homeland, is known as 'Aloha'. This, the Hawaiian philosophy of life, has begun to enter modern consciousness beyond surfing to such an extent that its primary words – *aloha* and *mahalo* – are as likely to be framed by English, French, Portuguese and Spanish accents as by a waterman on Maui. Both are words whose indigenous speakers will say need to be experienced to be understood, though a dictionary will explain that *aloha* means 'love' and, like the Italian *ciao*, serves as both 'hello' and 'goodbye', while *mahalo* means gratitude or thanks. But Gardiner – an engaging, Scottish-born surfer in her twenties who has settled in Newquay – reveals that there is more to *aloha* than understanding its phonetics. As the Big Friday website has it, *aloha* is derived from five other words:

> *Akahi* – kindness, expressed with tenderness
> *Lokahi* – unity, expressed with harmony
> *Olu'olu* – agreeable, expressed with pleasantness
> *Ha'aha'a* – humility, expressed with modesty
> *Ahoniu* – patience, expressed with perseverance

Elsewhere, I have read that *aloha* means 'the presence of Divine breath', while *mahalo* is 'may you be in Divine breath'. This is not the place for a detailed etymological analysis of the word, but suffice to say two things: Honolulu-born actress and singer Bette Midler uses the *aloha* greeting frequently on television, while those with the patience to read the credits of the cult TV series *Lost* will have noted that its final line reads: 'We thank the people of Hawai'i and their Aloha Spirit.'

Whatever its precise meaning, these days *aloha* is far from confined to Hawaii. If one of its core components is a fidelity to the sea, there is plenty to go round at Watergate Bay. The Extreme Academy's beach activities are overseen by ex-RAF helicopter engineer Carl Coombes, a waveski rider and longboard surfer, and a man whose rugged, fifteen-stone, shaven-headed six-foot presence might make him rather fearsome were it not belied by a love of the sea as euphoric as a child's. Coombes left the RAF after twenty-five years' service to take up a full-time job as sports manager at the Extreme Academy, which by then had already become his home from home. Though stationed at the end of his career at RAF High Wycombe, Coombes had established his family at Quintrell Downs, outside Newquay, and no sooner would he return home each Friday than he would be rushing to Watergate. Coombes is so readily identifiable – and enthusiastic – a presence at Watergate that sometimes it is hard to imagine the place without him. Courteous to a fault, he is also one of the more modest world champions produced by Britain, admitting that he became the World Masters Waveski Champion in 2004 as if the achievement are no more remarkable than crossing the road.

To some surfers, though, crossing the road would appear to command more respect than riding a waveski, a craft derided as a 'goatboat' and, if the lamentations of a certain vociferous minority are to be believed, ridden exclusively by kooks. As an individual whose online name is 'Chairman' wrote on the *Surfline* forum in a debate entitled: 'What's wrong with kayak surfing/waveskiing?' the reason for the antipathy stems from the belief that 'I've yet to see someone in a "boat" catch a wave and go anywhere but straight in. Do you know how much it sucks to run down a wave and then have to turn and go straight in because some big kook in a kayak snaked the wave? If you landlubbers could actually turn the damn thing and ride the wave, it might not be so bad. One last point. I can drop off my board, catch the tail, and avoid a potential disaster. How are you keeping your pickle in control in a similar situation?'

The Chairman's views meet with a sanguine shrug of the shoulders from Coombes, who won his world title in Guadeloupe by beating a field of seventy-eight waveskiers from sixteen different nations. Coombes – whose trophy was a conch – says simply that everyone is entitled to their own opinion, but that 'waveskiing today is closer to surfing than canoeing. We can pull off aerials, just like surfers. The trick is generating enough speed from a big bottom turn to get in the air. There's an amazing sense of achievement when you get it right.'

A waveski is a combination of canoe and surfboard, whose design owes much to the Tahitian canoes first observed by Captain James Cook and his men on Cook's last voyage aboard the *Resolution*. A waveskier sits on top of his board, legs outstretched, and uses a kayak-style paddle to power out through the surf. But a waveski has more manoeuvrability than a sea kayak, and in the hands of an expert like Coombes can be propelled up the face of a wave and over the top, then turned back to rejoin the face. Australian lifeguards espoused seated surfing in the 1930s, but the real forerunner of the modern waveksi was the 'Scotty Ski', invented by a lifesaver, Tony Scott, in the 1960s. Scott's board was made of moulded fibreglass, came in at 9 ft long and was narrow with a kick-up nose. It was fast but required strength rather than skill to be turned. By the mid-1970s, though, the sport had moved on with skegs added to shorter boards, allowing for much greater manoeuvrability. The first international waveski competition was held in South Africa in 1975 in conjunction with the Gunston 500, a well-established fixture on the world surfing calendar.

Waveskiing, as we know it now, had arrived, but if the criterion for being the 'sport of kings' rests upon historical precedence (a suspect construct), waveski riding is arguably more deserving of the accolade than surfing, for it was in 1777 in Tahiti that Cook's *Journals* noted 'the most supreme pleasure' to be gained from sitting atop a canoe 'driven on so fast and so smoothly by the sea'. Two years later, Lieutenant James King, serving on the *Discovery*, became the first Westerner to describe stand-up surfing when, three months after Cook had been killed in a dispute over, curiously enough, a missing canoe, he completed Cook's *Journals* thus:

> Where there is a very great sea and surf breaking on the shore, [the native Hawaiians] lay themselves upon an oval piece of

plank. They wait the time of the greatest swell and push forward with their arms. It sends them in with a most astonishing velocity, and the great art is to guide the plank so as always to keep it in a proper direction on top of the swell . . . The boldness and address with which we saw them perform these difficult and dangerous manoeuvres was altogether astonishing and scarcely to be credited.

The boldness and address seen at Kealakekua Bay, Hawaii, in 1779 has now migrated to all manner of watercraft, all over the world. Surfers, windsurfers, kitesurfers, surfboat rowers, sea kayakers, bodyboarders and waveski riders – all have come to experience that 'most supreme pleasure'. Intoxicating as the feeling of riding a wave is, it seems that often a favourite memory is not necessarily of one's best wave, but of the circumstances surrounding that wave, or the environment in which even a mediocre session occurs. Take Carl Coombes, for example: 'One of my best surfs came when I was sent to the Falklands,' he says. 'One day myself and a colleague decided to go in search of a reef break that we'd heard the locals talking about. We drove across a desolate landscape in a howling gale, and, when we found it, had to walk two miles to the water, carrying all our gear.' The pair nearly froze getting into their wetsuits, but soon enough entered the kelp-strewn, icy-cold sea complete with booties, gloves and balaclavas. 'The only part of our bodies not covered by neoprene was our eyes,' recalls Coombes. Once in the sea, the surf did not reward their determination – 'it was one foot and barely ridable' – but within five minutes they were joined by a school of dolphins. For the next two hours, the two men surfed with the dolphins, an experience that Coombes sums up thus: 'It was magical, to be in the sea, that far south, in the middle of nowhere with thirty dolphins for company.'

One of my own treasured surfing memories came at Watergate Bay in late August 2005, a few weeks after the Rip Curl Boardmasters. Arriving at the hotel on Sunday 28th – my wedding anniversary –

the surf looked tempting even though I was tired from a boxing workout in the morning. I paddled out and, sure enough, had a poor session. The morning after, I awoke to a view from the hotel of lines of sublime sun-drenched swell. I gave Karen a wedding anniversary kiss and a card, she did likewise, and then, catching sight of the date on the daily newspaper, we realized we were both out by a day. We took a walk along the low-tide beach after breakfast, the boys scampering around the exposed rocks and hunting for crabs, before climbing the path at the end and returning along the cliff-top. All the way there and back, I kept glancing feverishly out to sea, praying that the 3–4 ft perfection would last. Once at the hotel, my elder son, Harry, went off for a mountain-boarding lesson, while Karen took Elliot swimming. Cue mad rush to our room where I did my best to break the record for slipping into neoprene. Soon I had descended the steps in front of the hotel and was running across the sand, board under my arm, looking for the best place to paddle out. I opted for some right-handers a little to the right of the hotel, and found myself in the line-up among four or five other surfers. Everything fell into place: the first wave was good, those that followed were better, and even one over-the-falls disaster didn't hurt. I came in after two hours, found Harry and took him surfing. Then he was nine, and though he'd been in the sea with me on surf trips to Andalucia, this proved to be the first day that he properly stood up and surfed. The delight on a child's face as he or she surfs a wave for the first time is something that every parent should behold – an excited grin of unadulterated joy, of pure pleasure, of total absorption in the moment; it is a look that cannot but bestow happiness on anyone who sees it. Thoroughly stoked, we enjoyed a tranquil lunch on the brasserie patio, and the swell, I couldn't help but notice, was building as the tide pushed in. I opted for a scant meal, determined as I was to be back in the water as soon as possible, and paddled back out shortly after I'd eaten. By now solid 6 ft sets were pulverizing anyone who chose to go surfing, making for a 25 ft minute paddle out. Exhausted once out the back, it was all I could do to sit on the board and catch my breath. As

I did so, occasionally lying down to paddle away from rogue incoming waves, I began to grow worried. The surf had power and was as implacable as ever. As a young man spending a gap year in Australia and Bali, I'd been out on a few 8–10 ft days, but – as they say – that was then. Now I was at the limit of my comfort zone.

There were a few surfers near me, and their standard only added to my anxiety. They were easily in the good-to-excellent range, taking off fearlessly and late, cranking their shortboards so hard and low into bottom turns that getting vertical was as inevitable as the next set. Sitting in the line-up, watching, I saw the top of board after board splinter the furling white water of breaking waves, then a pair of neoprene arms being whipped round as board and surfer rejoined the face of the wave. The light offshore breeze made for the constant caress of spray, the sun and earlier exercise were wearing me down, and I was starting to feel out of my depth. Just then a set heaved into view. Cries of 'outside!' reverberated across the line-up and the frantic scratch for safety beyond the breaking waves began. I made it up and over at least four solid six-footers, and then the rest on the board began again. The question was, though: was I going to take one of these waves, and if I did, what on earth would happen?

The answer was handed to me on a plate. Surfers sit on their boards looking towards the horizon, and I knew as soon as I saw the next set that I was the man for its first wave. Not, in many ways, because I wanted to be, but because there was no choice. Waves on beachbreaks may not have the predictability of reef or point breaks, but even if, as on this occasion, you are running a little scared of taking a wave, it is a given that sooner or later the sandbars and swell will combine to put you, the reluctant surfer – the man content to sit on the shoulder and quietly slip back in unnoticed – in pole position. The other surfers around me knew this, and started to whoop me into the wave. Before I knew it a hesitant turn of the board had become a committed paddle for a glorious green-blue right-hander, the surfers' shouts and yells adding momentum to my efforts. I felt the surge of raw oceanic power, knew I had the wave and leapt to my feet. The drop seemed unfeasibly steep but I made it, bending my knees and bottom turning to race back up the face. There was no likelihood of my hitting the lip vertically, but I did tuck up nicely just ahead of the breaking crest and race back down the line. Then it was another low crouch to generate power, and back up to the lip of the wave, which now was starting to break. And then I pulled off a move I'd never even attempted before, let alone got right – a floater. If the truth be told I meant to kick out, but I was travelling so fast and at such a trajectory that I couldn't but fly up over and across the top of the white water. Once there I angled the board in to the beach, floating down the white water to return to the still-surging clean face of the wave. The sensation was one of delicious weightlessness, rather as a snowboard feels off-piste. The wave dissipated but despite the knowledge that a lot of luck had helped me in conditions that were beyond me, I turned to paddle straight back out. I wanted that feeling again.

I didn't get it, but I did have another two days of excellent surf, and later one of surfing's strange threads swung into play. I was talking to Chris Thomson, then twenty-four, who set up the Watergate Bay Surf Club in spring 2005. 'It was flat for a few days,' recalls Thomson, 'so I finally got round to getting the club going. Now we have about sixty members.' Thomson, born in Shoreham-on-Sea and brought up near the south Devon break of Wembury, is sponsored by Fat Face, Lush Longboards and the Hotel and Extreme Academy, and also runs www.errantsurf.com, a dedicated surf travel company. An amiable character, Thomson competes as a pro longboarder and runs longboarding coaching sessions at Watergate Bay. He is an inveterate surf-traveller, and as well reeling off a list of surfing's glamour spots mentioned that he'd surfed a lot in the Orkney Islands.

'The Orkneys?' I said, not so much incredulously – I was aware that there was surf there – but surprised that someone would choose to surf there 'a lot'. Is there a surfing community on the Orkneys? I asked.

'Well, my dad lives there and he surfs, and there are another couple of guys. But there's not really a surfing community, as such. The waves are fantastic, though. You know Thurso East?'

I said that I did, but only from magazine shots.

'Well, picture those long walling rights. There are waves on the Orkneys that no one ever surfs that are just as good.'

I couldn't but be reminded of my advocacy in favour of Thurso to Zed Layson, he of Surfer's Point in Barbados. 'I was telling a Bajan surfer all about Thurso a while back,' I told Chris. 'Top bloke, said he'd come over and surf it sometime.'

'Would that be Zed?' asked Chris.

'Yes, do you know him?'

'I worked for him when I was sixteen. He's a great guy. I still work with him now, with travel exchanges and trips, that sort of thing. I don't know if he'll put up with the cold, though.'

'How about you? Fancy an Orkney and Thurso trip?'

Chris smiled in his laid-back way and said: 'Sure, let me know when you're going to be there.'

I left Chris to his busy schedule at Watergate Bay, thinking that if I had to put money on which of he or Zed would ultimately make it to Thurso and beyond, it would be the man whose father was one of the Orkney's few surfers. But meanwhile, something Dave Reed had said was nagging away at me. Where was it that he had mentioned as the afternoon drew in, as his desire for one last surf became ever more insistent?

Jersey. That was it. Dave had told me to make sure I visited Jersey. It was time to hop on a ferry and see what the most populous of the Channel Islands had to offer.

PART TWO

Dogtown on the south coast: a lone surfer in his element, Brighton.

8

JERSEY JUICE/BRIGHTON ROCK

Most surfing journeys on the mainland may lead to Newquay, and in Jersey, too, they go to just one place – St Ouen's Bay. That being the case, although I knew little more than where I would be staying upon my arrival – the estimable Hotel de France in St Helier – I was reasonably confident that Jersey was of such a size that I couldn't fail to meet members of its surfing tribe. All I needed to do was take myself to St Ouen's, a five-mile expanse of sandy beach that faces due west. As such it is a magnet for the same waves that Atlantic lows drive on to the shores of Devon and Cornwall.

At just nine miles by five, Jersey is so small that the idea of the secret spot is an oxymoron. The secret spot – the cherished break known only to a few, whose whereabouts is only disclosed to those who have, through their embrace of surfing's unwritten codes and rituals, earnt the right to initiation in its mysteries – may be a physical impossibility in Jersey, but aside from this accident of geography the island has a rich pedigree in British surfing. Jersey was the home of the first surf club in Europe, the Island Surf Club of Jersey, formed in 1923 by Nigel Oxenden, whose grandsons still surf on the island today. It was the scene of the first British Surfing Championships, an event won by Watford-born, Australia-honed

Rod Sumpter in 1965 and sponsored, in what today appears to be a different kind of oxymoron, by Gold Leaf tobacco. Jersey has regularly hosted European surfing championships, has produced scores of Europe's best surfers and has a dedicated enough clientele to support a plethora of surf shops: two in St Helier under the SDS brand, the Sea Flight Surf Shop in St Peter, the famous Freedom shop (which also has a branch in Guernsey), Cloud Nine and the Laneez Surf Shop. In the 1970s Jersey residents often comprised over two-thirds of the British surfing team, and during this time, under Steve Harewood's Freedom label, the island was one of the few centres of surfboard manufacture in Europe.

Arriving in Jersey it is, initially, a little difficult to conceive of its vibrant surfing community, let alone so illustrious a history. On the evidence of its finely manicured, tax advantageous properties, the plethora of banks and well-heeled locals, surfing seems rather too disorderly to have found a niche here. But a trip to St Ouen swiftly dispels this impression. The area, denuded by the prevailing westerly winds of all but a few straggles of gorse, is wild and almost wholly unscarred by development. Many other spots on Jersey derive their charm from their sheer, simple comeliness – the beautiful bay and harbour of Bonne Nuit, the brooding Mont Orgueil Castle overlooking the Royal Bay of Grouville, the unexpected pleasure of a French country house amid the maze of inland lanes – but the appeal of St Ouen's Bay is one of sea and land meeting *in extremis*, untouched and untouchable by human influence. Roughly in the centre of the bay is the Watersplash, a popular surfers' bar, adjacent to which is the Jersey Surf School. In summer the sea is almost as crowded with surfers as the beaches of Devon and Cornwall, with much of the gently shelving bay providing perfect conditions for learners and intermediates, whose needs are amply catered for by Jersey's surfing infrastructure.

The owner of the Jersey Surf School, Jim Hughes, reckons that there are 'about a thousand regular surfers on Jersey, though as many as ten thousand will say they surf. Out of a population of eighty-five thousand that's quite a lot. It does get crowded on a good day.' Hughes himself – a 28-year-old islander who obtained a degree in surf science and technology from Plymouth University – escapes the crowds for six months thanks to a business specializing in surfing tours of New Zealand. 'I'm away during the winter, when the surf here is at its best,' he says a little ruefully. 'But hey, the surf in New Zealand then is pretty good.'

Hughes looks every inch the seasoned surfer, with his lean, tanned physique and blond hair, and has reservations about the surfing boom. 'Line-ups are getting pretty saturated and as a consequence people are getting much more territorial. Localism is on the increase, for sure. You can see people being fairly aggressive in the water.'

My trip to Jersey coincided with fine weather and an almost total lack of swell, but on the one day when there was surf I paddled out opposite the Watersplash as the tide was pushing in, creating easy, if slow, 2–3 ft beachbreak peaks. It was as crowded a line-up as I have known, and I spent most of the session sharing waves with a father and his son, the father being sufficiently hardy to be surfing in just boardshorts. I had some good waves, and around me everyone appeared relaxed and happy, enjoying the beauty of being in the ocean and catching waves. Except, that is, for one man. He was about thirty, and was a better surfer than just about everyone else. Moves such as cutbacks and off-the-lip snaps came effortlessly to him, and yet so, too, did aggressiveness to anyone in his way. Often enough those people were not actually in his way; they had not committed the cardinal sin of dropping in. They were simply *there*. And because they were there, this particular surfer felt entitled to shout at them, as if nature had decreed that he alone was favoured with the right to surf Watersplash.

This mild hint of discord was soon forgotten when I met one of Jersey's most highly regarded surfers, Mark Durbano. Now forty-one, Durbano is a builder by trade. Born and bred on Jersey, he has been sponsored from time to time as a surfer, and helps run Laneez Surf Shop with his brother Nick and his wife Karena. 'Laneez' is a nod to the long right-hander on the North Shore of Oahu known as Laniakea, a break of which the regular-footer

Durbano has cherished memories. Likewise, though, his feelings for the surf he grew up with, as I learnt over the course of a ninety-minute tour of Jersey's breaks.

'This is the first break,' said Durbano as we parked his car at St Brelade's Bay. 'It's a fun wave with good lefts and rights. It's south-facing so needs a big swell to work.' Durbano then drove me to all of Petit Port, La Rocco Reef, the Pinnacle Rock and La Pulente, then to Brucy's, Winkers, Magic Moments and La Braye, then Le Port and the Splash and finally to Cutty Sark, Secrets, Barge Aground, Goldsmiths, La Saline, Malarno and Stinkies (so-called because of its ever present seaweed). Throughout he was open, informative and enthusiastic, happy to share his exhaustive knowledge of Jersey's breaks – not because, given the island's size, they are far from secret, but because that's the way Durbano lives his life. He has no truck with aggression in the water and petty-minded localism, saying that he has surfed all over the world 'and I honestly believe most surfers don't give a damn about localism. There will always be some but these days the world is a small place, and what goes around comes around. When surfing away from home you just have to wait your turn; it might take a little longer, but the rewards might be a nice wave and maybe a new friend at most surf destinations. And if it's just too busy at a surf break there are nearly always other waves which are not so popular just around the corner.' His was an outlook which was the very opposite, it struck me, of the pumped-up thirty-year-old I'd earlier seen in the water and yet, as he explained his plans for La Rocco Reef, Durbano was clearly of vastly superior ability to the thirty-something tyro.

'There are a couple of big-wave spots, Petit Port especially, where we're planning to tow-in. But you see that white water feathering out to sea? That's where La Rocco Reef is. That's where we're looking to surf next time the conditions are right.'

I gazed out towards roughly the middle of St Ouen's Bay, and could see the white water to which Durbano was pointing. It was breaking over a hidden reef perhaps three-quarters of a mile offshore. Just paddling that far would leave many surfers, let alone non-surfers, shattered. Durbano, though, loves big waves, and has set his sights on surfing La Rocco Reef at maximum size.

'I've surfed a lot of places, Hawaii being one of them, and I know that when La Rocco is breaking it's as hard a wave to surf as any I've surfed before. It's not for the beginner, that's for sure. It gets to eighteen to twenty feet but it's not like Thurso – it jacks up really fast with a huge vertical drop. If you miss the first wave, you're going to get hammered.'

Durbano has surfed La Rocco with Rennie and Piers Gould, and another Jersey surfer, Ian Battrick, joined them once. So far at the time of writing they had paddle-surfed the break, but Durbano, with South African partner Chester, was keen to tow-surf it. 'You've got to know what you're doing out there, but I think we'll be OK,' he said and, smiling as the tour came to an end, told me to make sure I visited Big Vern's, a bar near the Watersplash. 'There's an awesome photo on the wall in there, of Grève de Lecq,' he said. 'You'll love it.'

Durbano was right. I arranged to meet Ian Battrick at Big Vern's, and while inside ordering coffee, checked out the photograph of Grève de Lecq, an old smuggling harbour on the north coast of Jersey. Of course, I was not looking at a photograph of Grève de Lecq itself; I was not admiring its sandy beach and caves, pleasingly understated cafés and amiable promenade. The recommendation, from a surfer, to look at a photograph of Grève de Lecq means none of these things. It means, instead, that I was looking at a photograph of a wave breaking at Grève de Lecq, for this, to a surfer, is what defines the place – nothing else. And what a wave it was. A barrel as cavernous and powerful as anything else on English shores, the kind described in contemporary surf-speak as 'sick'. My own sense of Grève de Lecq was informed by a rather different experience – that of coasteering with my sons there on a still and quiet summer's afternoon – but here was evidence of the kind of surf that, if you were of the standard of Jersey's finest – Durbano, Ian Battrick, Scott Eastwood – would send you to seventh heaven.

Outside Big Vern's Ian Battrick, then twenty-eight, was as cool as Tom Curren. Like the former world champion, Battrick has an economy of movement and speech that metamorphoses into an extraordinarily fluid and dynamic surfing style in the water. Battrick is also similar to the latter-day Curren in that he has nothing to do with contest surfing. Despite being sponsored by Hurley (wetsuits), Rhino (wetsuits and travel accessories), Balin (leashes), Dragon (sunglasses), Nizon (watches) and California-based Sun Prescription Surfboards, Battrick is not expected to excel in domestic or overseas competition but simply to go surfing. This suits him down to the ground.

'I was born here and grew up surfing, but when I was sixteen I realized that I could either go to the Canaries and enjoy my surfing, or go to England and surf in contests for twenty minutes. I did a few contests but that's not what it's about. Not for me, anyway.'

Dressed in blue jeans and sporting a baseball cap, Battrick's blue eyes and calm, unhurried manner add to the feeling that here is a man who is completely at ease with the life he has chosen – one that is nomadic to the core. As he puts it: 'Jobs just fund surfing. Anytime I've had a job – labouring, stone masonry, being a postman, working at the airport – I've quit them if I see the charts looking good. I'll just head off for where the waves'll be good.' Battrick's search for surfing nirvana has taken him to Mexico, the Canary Islands, Indonesia, Ireland, Scotland and Iceland. The latter is, he says, a gem – 'we scored some great waves there' – and marginally warmer than surfing the north-east coast of England.

Battrick is another of that rare breed – the surfer-boxer. He boxes at light-welterweight and has had three bouts, winning two and losing the other. Like Sennen Cove's Sam Smart, he would like to pursue his boxing, but his lifestyle doesn't make this easy. 'I'm always heading off somewhere on a surf trip. I'd love to box more but I can never give a hundred per cent to my training, because I don't know how long I'll be around.'

Perhaps the boxer in him gave a little spice to Battrick's views on contemporary surfing. Certainly, where in every other sense he exudes what certain people tend to characterize as the surfer's Zen-like state of serenity, Battrick was not inclined to pull his punches when it came to crowds: 'Surfing is losing its soul. So many people are into it now. I was surfing Thurso one time in December 2005, and there must have been at least thirty-five people in the water. Ireland used to be uncrowded but all that's changed. Here it's way too crowded and people can't just turn up and start causing mayhem. There aren't enough waves to go round and I don't think the surf schools help. Look at where they are – right in the middle of the bay, with beginners being taken out to the prime peaks. You wouldn't give driving lessons in the middle of a race track, would you?' Battrick says he sometimes prays for the wind to blow onshore to thin out the crowds, but despite his reservations Jersey remains his favourite place to surf. 'The best thing about surfing is going out on your own, or with just a few friends. You can, in winter, still have that experience here.'

I was mulling over Battrick's frustration with the hordes taking to the water each summer as I walked along St Ouen's to Barge Aground, a 1930s folly built to resemble a grounded boat. Before World War II there were many holiday bungalows along St Ouen's, but the Barge Aground is the sole survivor. It is now available as a holiday let, with its proximity to good surf highlighted as a selling point. Nearby is the Channel Islands Military Museum, a private collection of principally German military memorabilia housed in a coastal defence bunker built during the German occupation of Jersey. As I walked amid the artefacts of war I wondered what happened to Jersey's surfers during World War II. Did they continue surfing? Did the Germans try their hand at what Jack London, in his 1911 travelogue *The Cruise of the Snark*, described as 'a royal sport for the natural kings of the earth'? Or was surfing banned?

Before leaving Jersey I made another sortie to a World War II relic – the Jersey War Tunnels at St Lawrence. Excavated between October 1941 and January 1944 by the German forces (deploying forced and slave labour), the tunnels were initially intended to be bomb-proof barracks. As the Allies' victory and reacquisition of Jersey became ever more inevitable, the tunnels were converted into a sprawling, complex underground hospital. They now house the 'Captive Island' exhibition, an excellent series of vignettes of island life under the German army that ask of the viewer: what would you have done? Some islanders, it seems, plumped for appeasement rather than resistance, but given the strategic abandonment of Jersey by the British government perhaps this is of little surprise. My conjecture as to what I would have done in a Jersey islander's position was interrupted when I saw a black and white photograph of St Ouen's Bay. Faint lines of clean surf were rolling on to the clean sands, but access would have impossible – the beach was lined with barbed wire. Moreover, as one of the shop's attendants later told me, it would have been mined. There would have been no surfing, by Germans or islanders, during World War II.

> Infrequent and short duration swells, accompanied by onshore winds, typify the South Coast surf experience. The best sessions can be had with the presence of Biscay lows, or Atlantic lows below or around Land's End. Despite this grim appraisal, classic days can be had and the busy surf population, centred around the main areas of Brighton, the Witterings, the Isle of Wight and Bournemouth, is often augmented by Londoners on a quick dash away from town.

It was with this ambivalent assessment – courtesy of my *Stormrider* guide – that I made my way to Brighton to meet Pete Robinson, the director of the Surfing Museum, one cold November day. I had a board with me but, having checked www.sharkbait.co.uk, the website for all things surf-related in the Brighton area, was not holding out much hope of riding any waves. And so it proved. There was a wave, but it was lumpen and irregular. Given the cold it wasn't difficult to opt to leave the board in the car, find a bar and go through my notes prior to meeting Robinson. The notes – largely in the form of a printout from www.thesurfingmuseum.co.uk – reminded me that Robinson ran the museum out of his own funds as a not for profit organization, one dedicated to celebrating the richness and diversity of British surfing, past and present. A quote from Newquay's Bill Bailey appears on the website and sets the tone: 'Surfing is about soul, good friends and having a good time.'

Brighton's capacity for the provision of a good time was unnervingly depicted in the Grahame Greene classic *Brighton Rock* (1938), later made into a film of the same name by John Boulting. In the lead role as Pinkie Brown, Richard Attenborough brought oodles of the requisite menace to Greene's desperado of a flawed and failing gangster. Pinkie, the small-town hoodlum, orders the murder of a rival, Fred Hale, which the police initially accept as suicide. The principal doubter comes in the form of Ida, an unlikely heroine who sets out to prove that Pinkie and his gang were responsible. The innocent young waitress, Rose, can help her prove that Fred was murdered, but Pinkie seduces and marries her to buy her silence. Nevertheless, Ida maintains her pursuit, and, as ever with Greene, Catholicism's relationship with good, evil and repentance provides as much impetus for the narrative as the action. En route to the ambiguous denouement, Brighton assumes a characterization in English literature that its citizens may not always have relished, as its promenades, amusement arcades, sideshows and kiosks are seen as the vulgar facade of a place teeming with weary cynicism at best, downright malevolence at worst. The good life is an illusion, something that the crowds of day-trippers and holidaymakers force themselves to enjoy:

> With immense labour and immense patience they extricated from the long day the grain of pleasure: this sun, this music, the rattle of the miniature cars, the ghost train diving between the grinning skeletons under the Aquarium promenade, the sticks of Brighton rock, the paper sailors' caps.

Pinkie, the inveterate denizen of the town, could never leave its debatable charms, for, as he says, 'I'm real Brighton.' It is 'as if his single heart contained all the cheap amusements, the Pullman cars, the unloving weekends in gaudy hotels, and the sadness after coition'. Moreover, people don't change, hence the metaphor of the title, used subtly to denote the manner of Fred's demise but also so that Ida can declaim (in response to Rose's belief that people change): 'Oh no they don't . . . I've never changed. It's like those sticks of rock: bite it all the way down. That's human nature.'

Given that I had a little time to kill before Robinson was due to arrive I found myself recalling vignettes from *Brighton Rock*, in both its celluloid and literary forms. I had barely ever visited Brighton, arriving there once having completed the London to Brighton cycle ride and immediately turning back to London, and another time to idle on the beach for a pointless hour or two. This was unfamiliar territory, but, on a cursory glance, it seemed rather different from Greene's vision. Rather than vulgarity I perceived much more by way of elegance, and, sitting at the bar in the Old Ship Hotel, soon found that I had turned my attention to surfing rather than the town's caustic underbelly, real or imagined. Had anyone surfed in Brighton, back in the days when Greene wrote his novel? Did surfing, now part of the fabric of the town, give it an extra zest, something more wholesome than the angst, Catholic and otherwise, of *Brighton Rock*? How many surfers were there here, regularly taking to the breaks at the Piers, the Wedge and the Marina? How many scoured the south coast on big days, knowing that, say, Joss Bay and Camber Sands in Kent would be working? Further west, would the much-discussed artificial reef at Boscombe Pier in Bournemouth ever be made? Plans for artificial reefs have been a feature in the British surfing landscape for some time, but nowhere were they more developed than at Bournemouth, whose council, in September 2005, gave the green light for the creation of what will – if and when it is finished – be Europe's first artificial reef.

As I mulled over these questions, my old friend from university, Chris, popped into my mind. I'd hoped someone might have heard of him in Porthleven, but no one had. I'd hoped other surfers I met might know him, and I'd hoped I might paddle out somewhere and, lo and behold, see him sitting on his board next to me. None of this had happened, but it struck me that Brighton might be Chris's kind of place. Despite a venerable royal heritage, not least in architecture such as the Royal Pavilion, Sussex Gardens and the Regency Townhouse – all and more of which jostle for attention amid seventeenth-century fisherman's cottages, trendy bars and clubs and grand works of the Industrial Revolution such as the celebrated pier – contemporary Brighton somehow blends the anarchic with the genteel, the gauche with the glitz. It is an eclectic place, where pretty much anything, illicit or otherwise, can be found. If memory served, Chris – no stranger to eclecticism himself – had connections here. Perhaps Robinson would have heard of him? Thinking about Chris reminded me, too, of Robyn Davies. The country's best female surfer, a woman with a bright and vivacious personality, someone I had to talk to. I found Robyn's number and dialled it. As usual, it went straight to voicemail. I left a message and, just as I had finished doing so, in walked Robinson. He arrived at the bar in the Old Ship Hotel, on Brighton's seafront, clutching an outsize skateboard under his arm. He looked trim and, albeit that he was wearing casual surfwear, rather dapper. As an ex-skater I was drawn at once to his board – it was a thing of beauty, much longer than the Vision Gator I used to ride twenty years ago, and clearly not for ramps or tricks.

'Lovely, isn't it?' said Robinson, cradling the board as if it were one of his most cherished possessions, which, I suspect, is indeed the case. 'It's made by a Brighton shaper called Adam Arbeid. I can give you his details if you like. Or maybe you'd like a ride?'

That struck me as all too tempting, but we opted to talk surfing first. What was Robinson's background?

'I grew up in East Anglia and, as a child, used to swim and bodysurf on the Norfolk coast. I've been a news reporter for over two decades, fourteen of which have been with ITV. I've spent the last ten years here in Brighton. I've been very happy here – it's a great place with an embedded surfing culture. People have been stand-up surfing here since the 1950s, on wooden boards, and were almost certainly bellyboarding and bodysurfing long before then.' Robinson's enthusiasm for Brighton met its counterpoint in memories of the early days of surfing in East Anglia. 'Conditions weren't that great – the sea was so turd-filled that I guess the phrase "riding a log" took on a new meaning.' However, it would take more than a sewage-filled sea to put Robinson off surfing. 'I graduated to paddling out at childhood haunts like Cromer and East Runton. By the time I was in my early twenties surfing had become my life.'

While at the University of East Anglia in Norwich I had also made forays to the fickle breaks of the Norfolk coastline. Allied with this commonality, Robinson is naturally generous in conversation, someone in whose presence it is impossible not to feel relaxed. If ever anyone radiated a love of surfing, it is him.

'Surfing has changed my life. I've been to wonderful places and met some fantastic people. If I didn't surf I would never have met those people. The more I surf, the more I love it. It just gets better and better.'

Even on a day like this one – cold and grey, with lacklustre waves?

'I went for a surf this morning,' said Robinson. 'I keep a board and a wetsuit at work, skate to the office and if there's a wave, go for a surf. The surf can pump here as much as anywhere. It's been good these past few days, before you came – I've had some sublime surfs. The harbour walls and piers give shelter from onshore winds, and with autumn and spring swells we can get glassy, perfect waves. I defy anyone to go surfing by the derelict west pier at dawn, ride a few glassy waves and *not* be stoked by the experience.'

Something alerted me to another possible connection. I told Robinson of my Barbados trip, and as I did so watched a smile form on his alert, open face. When I'd finished he said simply: 'Zed – what a great guy.' It transpired that Robinson knew Zed Layson well. He had surfed the same lefts as me at Surfers' Point. Indeed, Zed had stayed with Robinson and his wife Bianca on a recent trip to the UK.

'Do you think he'll really come back over and surf Thurso East?' I asked.

Robinson chuckled. 'I don't know,' he replied. 'It's a long way and it'll be a lot colder than he's used to, but you never know with Zed.'

Robinson's Surfing Museum opened in March 2004, initially from leased premises on the Brighton seafront. During its initial residency in Brighton, until September 2005, the museum saw more than 30,000 visitors, before becoming an itinerant beast. Since then the collection has shown at Aberdeen, Marton near Middlesborough, Covent Garden and Newquay, each time to demonstrable popular acclaim, with visitor numbers in host museums usually trebling for the show's duration.

My own experience of Robinson's collection came at the Captain Cook Birthplace Museum in Stewart Park, Marton, on a trip to the north-east. The museum hosts a year-round exhibition devoted to the life of one of the north-east's most famous sons, and the area around Marton bills itself as 'Captain Cook country'. Cook, born in Marton, is widely credited as the first European to describe stand-up surfing, though it was, as we know, his Lieutenant, James King, to whom this honour rightfully goes.

The Captain Cook birthplace museum at Stewart Park was perfectly complemented by Robinson's collection, which he began collating as soon as he took up surfing. 'As a journalist I felt frustrated that there was no real history of British surfing,' he told me. 'I started ferreting around and discovering all kinds of stuff, curios that pre-date the 1960s. After a while I'd assembled so much material that someone said, "You should open a museum." I thought, "Well, what a good idea," and, with some help from the family of the late Ted Deerhurst, got the museum up and running.'

One of Deerhurst's boards – a 6′ 1″ twin fin fish tail – was on show at the Stewart Park centre, as was the following caption, accompanying a photograph of a surfer in thumping surf: 'Viscount Ted Deerhurst, a British Lionheart, riding his Union Jack bedecked Lightning Bolt in massive Hawaiian waves.' Deerhurst – the 'Lord on a Board' – was Britain's first professional surfer, giving it his all on the ASP pro tour in 1978. His efforts were largely fruitless – indeed, certain overseas pro surfers I have spoken to recall Deerhurst as an Eddie the Eagle figure – but notwithstanding this the aristocrat never ceases to raise a smile. Lord Deerhurst died in Hawaii, aged forty, in 1997, but his abiding devotion to surfing – and apparent rejection of all that went with his birthright – made him arguably the most charismatic surfer of his era, if also the most unsuccessful. Keith Nichol, a fashion photographer and friend of Deerhurst, told me the following story, which perhaps sums up the surfing aristocrat:

'Way back in the mid-eighties, when surfing was all hotdog boards and planks were very uncool, there was a little contest held in Newquay called the Fosters Surfmasters. Each year a carnival of top surfers would come to the west coast and try to ride the two-foot mush. The TV would give it a mention and the town would be hyped up. A long-standing friend who has since passed away was often there and it was one of the few times we would get to meet up. Ted Deerhurst was a complex character; he and I spent many hours contemplating his unsuccessful history of girlfriends. At Newquay he agreed to do an interview with me and it was later published in a little known surf mag called *Tube News*. As a gift Ted gave me his competitors' sweatshirt; it was blue and had "Fosters Surfmasters Competitor" written on the back in large white print. He and I were living out of VW camper vans, so breakfast at the Headland Hotel was a big deal. Ted and I would go there to meet the big name surfing stars whose sponsors could afford to give them a room. I soon realized that the competitors' sweatshirt was a useful way of opening doors. No one at the hotel asked, they just assumed you were part of the carnival, and so you got a free breakfast. For two weeks I ate like a king, which was a big deal to a guy living in a van with no money other than the dole. The following year I tried the trick again and it worked. It kept on working till Hot Tuna arrived and changed the competition title. There is no such thing as a free lunch but sometimes you can get a free breakfast. That kind of karma happened around Ted.'

Deerhurst was not, however, the only individual of royal lineage to surf. Robinson has unearthed the extraordinary story of the half-

Hawaiian, half-Scottish Princess Victoria Ka'iulani, which he takes up thus: 'It was in 1892, while living in Brighton, that Princess Victoria Ka'iulani, the Crown Princess of Hawaii, may have demonstrated her skills on a surfboard. Can you imagine what the local fishermen would have made of a beautiful, long-haired, dark-skinned woman riding a board to the beach? I think, though, that she started a royal revolution – King Edward VIII, Edward Prince of Wales, was taught to surf by Duke Kahanamoku on a trip to Hawaii in 1920. More recently Prince Charles had a go in Australia and Cornwall, and Prince William learnt to surf in Scotland while he was at university there.'

If royal engagement with surfing retains an air of the intangible, Robinson's collection is a living, breathing, ever expanding hymn to surfing that cannot but leave inspired those it meets. There are boards galore – from a sleek Hott Surfboards model, shaped in Cornwall by Chris Jones in 1985, and an Overlin twin fin, shaped by Tom Overlin in Santa Cruz and ridden by Rod Sumpter, to a delectable 8' 3" vee-bottomed Tiki board with the prevailing flower power imagery of the 1960s. There is a 10' 0" Bilbo longboard shaped by Bill Bailey, as well as posters, old magazines, photographs, obscure facts and a number of quirky books, including *Surf Broad*, a sixties slice of surfploitation that promised 'the naked truth about those who live only for the next big wave, a searing story of the free love, free sex, surfing generation!' There is also a copy of the now obscure, but much revered *The Natural: Adventures of a Surfing Super Stud* by Bez Newton, as well as a line that resurfaced in my mind every time I thought of the north-east: 'Almost 230 years later, if Cook were to thread his way through the reefs that litter his native coastline in the north-east, it's likely that he would sail past some rubber-clad soul paddling into a thick brown barrel thousands of miles from where this dance of grace and balance began centuries before.'

At the exhibition in Marton, Robinson had managed to arrange the loan of an historic eighteenth-century 'Olo' board from the Bernice Pauahi Bishop Museum in Hawaii. The curator of the Captain Cook birthplace centre, Phil Philo, was ecstatic about this. 'It's our first international loan,' he told me, 'and hopefully a way of getting the Captain Cook story across to a more popular audience.' His enthusiasm was understandable, given yet another royal connection: the board had been used and owned by Hawaiian High Chief Abner Paki. As Philo explained: 'Only Hawaiian royalty would have ridden a board like this. To think that it could even have been seen in action by Cook is incredible.'

This was, perhaps, a romantic, even fanciful thought, but surfing breeds such notions. Less capricious was an unfortunate fact: for all the ability and tenacity Robinson has put into the Surfing Museum, it lacks a permanent home. Robinson has tried to agree venues with various third parties, but for a variety of reasons his efforts have, so far, foundered. 'You only saw a fraction of the collection at Marton,' he told me. 'There's plenty more where that came from.' What, then, were his plans for 2007? 'I'm going to take some time out and think about options. I'll take it back on the road in 2008, but meanwhile I'm still trying to find a home. If you know of anywhere, let me know.'

Two of the stops in 2008 are Scarborough and Grimsby, towns that the casual observer might conclude have as much to do with surfing as *Brighton Rock*. But just as a spider's web penetrates even the most shadowy of alcoves, these hardy towns boast their own surfing communities. 'There're surfers there, for sure,' said Robinson. 'Especially Scarborough. Great waves round there.'

Before we parted, there were a few more questions I wanted to ask. 'Who are the key figures in the Brighton surfing scene?'

The man who has spent over twenty years collating probably the finest collection of surfing memorabilia in Europe was unhesitating. 'Cliff Cox and Jock Paterson. They're both out in the line-up regularly. Both of them are great surfers. Cliff has been a British Masters champion and Jock was Britain's first professional skateboarder. There's also Steve Darch, who runs the Filf shop in Rottingdean – another great guy, who shapes boards for the surf coast shortboard crew.' Robinson smiled fondly, before adding: 'Jock's a real character. He's Brighton's Mr Dogtown.'

I recalled Paterson's name from my former years as a skater, and smiled inwardly. I'd seen his name here and there for years, first as a skater and then as a champion longboard surfer, and here he was again, Brighton Jock, the spiritual antidote to anyone's lapse into Greene and ambivalence. Maybe the karma was of Lord on a Board genealogy. It was a long shot, but I thought I'd try one last question. I described Chris from UEA, and asked if Robinson had ever heard of him. 'I think he used to surf here, maybe?' I concluded, hopefully.

Robinson scratched his chin. 'No, I don't think I ever came across him, sorry,' was his reply. Then he asked if I wanted a go on his skateboard. This, a 'Swell' board, had a deck of high-quality birch plywood, Kryptonic Route 70 wheels and Fiberlite 135 trucks. It was hand-made, unblemished and irresistible, a longboard designed to be ridden smoothly and carved through turns. It was perfect for Brighton's esplanade. I had a quick ride, then watched as Robinson carved drop-knee 'S' turns in the winter night, deftly avoiding the few pedestrians and looking stylish throughout.

The legend inscribed on the deck of the board said it all: 'In swell we trust.'

Bournemouth, looking good in an easterly.

9

IT ONLY WORKS WITH AN EASTERLY

In *That Oceanic Feeling: A Surfing Odyssey*, the Australian author Fiona Capp describes a dream about surfing:

> I was standing in front of the Doges' Palace in Venice looking out across the lagoon towards the white dome of Santa Maria della Salute when I noticed some figures on surfboards in the grey, choppy water. There were no waves, just the wake of vaporetti and tiny peaks whipped up by the wind. Some people, I thought, will do anything for a surf. Then, without warning, a perfect, glassy wave began rising out of the lagoon like a rare, exotic beast and I knew I had to get out there.

At this point in her dream, Capp's attention is diverted by worries about what to do with her keys and wallet, a problem I had always solved by locking the car and stashing the keys either deep within the exhaust pipe or underneath a wheel arch. Capp, one of surfing's more poetical writers, wonders instead whether to bury her keys and wallet 'in the pebbles of the small beach in front of St Mark's Square', only to spend so much time fretting that this would prove an unsafe hiding place that 'I woke up before I had a chance to put a toe in the water'.

A case of *surfing interruptus*, and Capp, whose book is a reflective odyssey around what she calls 'the idea of surfing', would be well qualified to assess what this in itself means, given her interest in Sigmund Freud. *That Oceanic Feeling* is, indeed, the only book on surfing to derive its title from the man Vladimir Nabokov traduced as 'the Viennese witch-doctor'. Freud wrote of 'that oceanic feeling' in *Civilisations and Their Discontents*, describing it as that which we experience when we encounter the sublime, a word as readily deployed by the poets and writers of the Romantic era as by Captain Cook when he came to describe the pleasure of canoe surfing. Freud developed his ideas of an oceanic feeling in correspondence with Romain Rolland, a French writer and lifelong pacifist rarely cited today but honoured with the Nobel Prize for Literature in 1915 'as a tribute to the lofty idealism of his literary production and to the sympathy and love of truth with which he has described different types of human beings'. Capp's journey, from Australia to Hawaii, Cambridge, Cornwall and France, is an attempt to explain what Rolland called 'a feeling of the eternal . . . a source of vital renewal . . . like a sheet of water which I feel flushing under the bark'. Without this – 'that oceanic feeling' – there was connection, no 'contact'.

In her travels, Capp meets academic and writer Andy Martin, author of *Walking on Water*, another of surfing's literary works. Martin wrote with wit and panache of his efforts to surf Hawaii's North Shore in the late eighties, and since went on to carve out a double identity in which Freud might have taken an interest; he was perceived, as he says, as 'the surfer' in Cambridge (where he lectures in French) and as 'the academic' in Hawaii, to which he has returned regularly since *Walking on Water.* The pair discuss what Martin, in a podcast for *Surfer Magazine*, termed 'the semiotics of surfing' in the courtyard of a Cambridge bistro, and Capp learns that Martin's dreams have also been dominated by surfing:

> As a boy growing up in East London, he had a recurring dream about a freak tidal wave that would come sweeping up the

Thames and swamp the city. His parents, friends, brothers and teachers would be swept away, but he would survive by leaping onto a passing door or tree trunk and riding the crest of a gigantic wave to safety.

In common with Capp and Martin, I have also been prone to recurring dreams about surfing. Mine are arguably even more fanciful, for I was brought up on the coast of south-east Devon. My home towns were Exmouth and Budleigh Salterton. From the age of seventeen, when I discovered surfing, I would dream of huge 20 ft waves pumping across Lyme Bay to implode on the beaches of Exmouth and Budleigh. Needless to say I would be there to surf them, and in each dream the skies were blue and the seas were warm. These were boardshorts-only surf sessions, pure teenage surf-porn, and I loved those dreams. Except for one time – when the dream was that I was condemned to execute the same bottom turn, again and again, for ever – my dreams went the same way as Capp's. A black cloud would well up in my mind and something would go wrong – I'd hit a groyne, a kayaker would land on my head, my board would mysteriously disintegrate as I was riding it. *Surfing interruptus* for me, too, but I think I know the reason why. If Freud is right – that dreams are about wish-fulfilment – my conscious was kicking in at just the point when it was getting too good to be true. The reason, I think, is because in south-east Devon such dreams were much, much too good to be true.

'South-east-facing beachbreaks which only work on short-lived east swells. Best around high tide,' was the dismissive verdict of the breaks in my area in the fourth edition of *Carve*'s 'Surfing in Britain' supplement. Alf Alderson, a surfing writer based in Wales, has this to say about Exmouth's surf in his guidebook *Surf UK: The definitive guide to surfing in Britain*: 'A south-facing break which picks up big S and SW swells, but is generally a gutless wave. There are lefts and rights, best at high tide. Winds from the N are offshore. OK for beginners.' Sidmouth, further east (the next stop after the pebble beach of Budleigh), is described similarly: 'The waves here rarely have much power, and require very big swells to produce any surf at all.'

People who grow up by the sea tend to have a loyalty to their local beaches, and I am no exception. As such, it would, I confess, be satisfying to rebut such denigrations of my surfing *alma mater.* But it would also be disingenuous. And at least Alderson and *Carve* gave Exmouth a mention. It doesn't merit inclusion in either the *Stormrider* guide or in *Surfing Britain*, and the truth is that over a period of some thirty-plus years I have only ever seen Orcombe Point – at the far eastern end of Exmouth beach – once produce what could objectively be called good surf. But, in common with many other parts of the UK, that does not mean that there is not a surfing community. And it also means that surfing's close cousins – windsurfing and kitesurfing – find an embrace which is not always as warm-hearted at the better favoured surfing beaches.

In my late teens, windsurfing was all the rage in Exmouth. Legendary Hawaiian surfer Tom Blake may have put a sail on a paddleboard in 1931, christening it 'the sailing surfboard', but it wasn't until the mid sixties that windsurfing as we know it now began to appear. It was then that two Californian surfers – Jim Drake and Hoyle Schweitzer – invented what they called the 'Baja board', a free-sail system that allowed the mast, boom and sail to swivel 360° around a universal joint, itself attached to a board made from plastic foam covered with fibreglass. To give the lie to the idea that all Californian surfers of that era did little other than drop acid and hang ten, Drake was also an aeronautical engineer who worked on the B70 bomber and the Cruise missile. Early tests of the Baja board and its free-sail system were, however, failures. The board did not have a fin, and so had virtually no directional stability. Nor was there an uphaul rope to pull up the mast. One can imagine the immense frustration, mixed with excitement, of those early sessions, but the technical problems were solved adequately by 1968, when Drake and Schweitzer applied for a patent to cover their invention. Perhaps Drake had bigger fish to fry, for in 1973 he sold his half of the patent to Schweitzer for a reputed $36,000, leaving Schweitzer to bring the 'windsurfer' to the world. The sport took off in Europe when the Dutch textile company Ten Cate began importing windsurfers in the 1970s, with France and Germany emerging as the two biggest markets. The US take-up was slower but consistent, and by 1984 windsurfing was popular enough to merit inclusion in the Los Angeles Olympic Games.

But if lawyers have yet to line their pockets in any meaningful way thanks to surfing, this was not the case with windsurfing. Its rise to global popularity was accompanied by multi-jurisdictional patent litigation, with a number of individuals claiming priority in the invention stakes. One of them was Peter Chilvers, an Englishman. In 1958, he launched an ingenious craft from Hayling Island on the south coast. It consisted of a plywood hull, a Bermudan rig, a two-piece wishbone and the essential universal joint to connect mast to board. In 1984, Chilvers succeeded in domestic litigation and established, at least insofar as English law was concerned, that he was the inventor of windsurfing. Another battle was underway in the US between Schweitzer and an American from Pennsylvania, the impressively named S. Newman Darby. In Australia the courts were asked to arbitrate, whereupon they found that Richard Eastaugh was the inventor of windsurfing, given that, as a boy in the late 1940s, he built galvanized iron canoes which, once equipped with sails with split bamboo booms, he sailed on the Swan River near Perth.

My friends and I were oblivious of these shenanigans as we jumped on the windsurfing bandwagon in the mid-1980s. By then, patent disputes had been largely resolved and major manufacturers such as Mistral and F2 were producing so-called 'funboards', shorter, more manoeuvrable boards with footstraps that Schweitzer himself first introduced in 1977 thanks to the efforts of the 'Kailua Kids', Hawaiians Larry Stanley and Mike Horgan. They discovered that by fitting footstraps to the deck of the board it was not only easier to sail at speed but also to control in waves. By the time windsurfing hit Exmouth, 'wavesailing' had been born, and once we had progressed beyond the flat water of the so-called Duck Pond on the River Exe we would spend every spare moment windsurfing out beyond Pole Sands, where, in the right conditions, there are 2–3 ft waves that could be jumped and surfed back in.

The feeling of planing across the surface of the sea on a shortboard in a Force 5, and the adrenalin rush of hitting a wave face and getting 'air-time', is unforgettable. Like surfing, wanting that feeling becomes an obsession. For about a year between 1984 and 1985, I was working for the *Exmouth Journal*, and all day long, as soon as the clocks turned and I knew there would be enough time for a session after work, I would monitor the movement of trees outside the office, constantly checking them to determine the wind direction and whether it had hit the magical Force 4 (anything less was insufficient for the shortboards that I, my brother Chris and friends Elliot, Rich and Andy were sailing). We were far from alone – on weekends, all year round, Exmouth would be packed with windsurfers of all abilities. We would go out even if it was snowing, in wetsuits that were woeful compared with today's high-tech style statements, and wearing pink marigold gloves in a vain attempt to keep our hands warm. Colour, indeed, was important. Leaving aside the marigold gloves – I would have worn discreet black wetsuit gloves if I'd had any – windsurfing then was all about dayglo yellows and limes, luminous pinks and blues. The sport rapidly developed its own magazines, graced by iconic figures such as Robbie Naish, Pete Cabrinha, Angus Chater and Bjorn Dunkerbeck, all performing moves of which we could only dream and, moreover, sailing in the boardshorts-only beauty of places like Maui and the Canary Islands.

Perhaps it was its unavoidable expense, or possibly the fact that there is so much kit, but the windsurfing boom didn't last. The sport faded in the mid-1990s, as both kitesurfing came in and surfing began its inexorable march to the top of the British and Irish watersports world. As with the successive waves of interest in skateboarding, a hardcore of committed windsurfers was always there, impervious to the dictates of fashion, and now a revival is underway. Manufacturers have reappraised design and made what was in danger of becoming an experts-only sport more accessible, introducing wider, more stable beginner and intermediate boards and putting an emphasis on user-friendly rig systems, all at the same or even less cost than putative windsurfers would have faced twenty years ago.

Windsurfing never left Exmouth, and now the town is set to be at the forefront of its UK renaissance. Both its longevity and its future are due, to a large degree, to the efforts of Peter Manfield, a tuba-playing former Lance-Corporal with the Royal Lifeguards. Manfield has worked in windsurfing in Exmouth since 1986, and at the time of writing was in the midst of relocating his Waterfront Sports business from one side of the seafront to the other. For twenty years, Manfield's windsurfing centre sat next to Exmouth's old outdoor swimming pool, looking across to Dawlish Warren and, at low tide, the exposed flats of Pole Sands. Now he is looking to hop across the road to be even closer to the sea, with a building made of stainless steel and old oak proposed for ground adjacent to the Carlton Hill slipway, from which, all those years ago, I would launch a board having rushed home from the *Journal*. 'The building will have a wind turbine on its top to generate its own power,' Manfield told me. 'The retail area will be extensive, and facilities will include a chill-out zone, on-site board storage, showers and changing area. If the plans are approved Exmouth will become even better known as one of the country's best windsurfing venues.'

Manfield was the Army and Inter-Services Windsurfing Champion in 1980, and won a number of other services titles in the sport. A man of towering height and amenable bearing, he has trenchant views on the way in which watersports are encouraged in the UK. Or, rather, discouraged: 'You go to France, Spain or Portugal and people embrace beach life as if it's second nature. Here people love the sea just as much, but local authorities seem intent on making it difficult to get to the beach. In most places in Europe you don't have to pay to park by the ocean, but here it's the norm. Why? If we want people to enjoy the sea, to be healthy and active, we should be making it as easy as possible for them to have that experience. Instead, we tax them to be by the sea.'

Twenty years ago, just as Manfield was setting up his business, I was setting off for university. By then I had spent two or three years windsurfing off Exmouth, as well as Budleigh (where my father ran south-east Devon's first windsurfing business, Offshore Boards, for a while) and Lympstone. I loved the sport but, largely owing to the influence of Elliot, one of my oldest friends, found myself beginning to gravitate to surfing. Elliot was born in Australia and was a natural in the water. I don't know whether a sense of his cultural heritage motivated him, but shortly after we'd turned eighteen he began to make the case for surfing with surprising insistence given the near total lack of surf on our doorstep. We would troop back to each other's houses and compare the two sports, often calling *Surfer* and *Windsurf* magazines as witnesses.

'Look at that,' Elliot would say, of a picture of Reno Abellira gliding across the face of a Waimea Bay bomb. 'That has just got to be the best feeling on earth.'

'No way,' I'd counter, brandishing an image of Robbie Naish ripping on Maui. 'Look at that jump. He must have been in the air for ten seconds!'

These and other such arguments persisted even after a month-long trip along the west coast of France, during which we both windsurfed La Torche – one of the country's best windsurfing locations, at which Elliot broke a mast and Rich nearly drowned – and surfed a number of breaks, especially Biscarosse, a low-key spot that can be superb but which tends to close out. We would also surf around the corner from Orcombe Point in Exmouth, usually, in my case, to no avail, though on one summer day Elliot rode a wave to the sand to the admiration of one of our junior school teachers, who happened to be present.

Despite the fact that the France trip didn't convince me that surfing was better than windsurfing, Elliot's enthusiasm was wearing me down. Not only that, but watching good surfers in France, as well as overdosing on a regular diet of the likes of

Abellira, Cheyne Horan, Tom Carroll and Eddie Aikau from *Surfer* and *Surfing* magazines, was starting to persuade me that, well, at the very least surfing had to be less hassle than windsurfing. When faced with the choice between carting around all the paraphernalia of windsurfing and having to spend at least twenty minutes getting it ready before you could even venture into the water, surfing, requiring just a board, leash and wetsuit, was an easy winner. By this time, too, we had all passed our driving tests, and so began a pilgrimage known to all south Devon surfers. The trip to our own north shore, to surf the breaks of Saunton, Croyde, Woolacoombe and Putsborough.

North Devon surfers are a fortunate crew – they have this left, one of the longest in Britain, on their doorstep.

10

TIKI TIM

If the surf in south-east Devon was usually woeful, a trip to the North Devon coast could yield waves that, on their day, were of *Surfer* magazine pedigree. The focal point for surfing in the area has always been Croyde, described by Alderson in *Surf UK* as 'one of the best beachbreaks in Britain, with fast, hollow waves common around low water, especially on spring tides', but there are a number of other excellent spots, not least Speke's Mill and Lynmouth. The former is an all but inaccessible reef break for experts only, though anyone capable of finding it should, if there is a surf god, be rewarded with a wave or two for sheer determination. Lynmouth is a left-hand point break which similarly should only be tackled by experienced surfers, set at the foot of a village that appears to epitomize the quintessential Devonian idyll. The wild moorland of Exmoor seems so close as to be unwilling to relinquish Lynmouth, whose Rhenish-looking tower overlooks the ancient tidal harbour, itself sheltered from the prevailing westerly winds by a pier. In the centre of Lynmouth is Shelley's Hotel, where the eponymous Romantic poet honeymooned in the summer of 1812, and above is its sister village of Lynton, reached by a funicular railway. Two rivers, the East and West Lyn, converge in Lynmouth and enter the north-facing bay.

Two lefts break over the boulder-strewn seabed to the west of the river mouth, and at high tide a right works to the east. There are obstacles galore, such as salmon traps and marker poles, and the nagging sense of fragility that lurks in a surfer paddling out at Lynmouth for the first time can only be compounded by knowledge of events in the village in 1952. That year, on 16 August, torrential rain caused the West Lyn to burst its banks and the resulting flood, as the waters from the moor surged savagely through the village complete with tons of moorland rock and debris, killed twelve people. The chapel and the fruit shop were swept away, as was a row of cottages, the screams of whose helpless inhabitants were heard by a fisherman, Ken Oxenholme. 'We watched a row of cottages fold up like a pack of cards,' he told the BBC.

Such implacable power is mirrored in the sea not only in the manifestation of swell lines and storms, but as it surges up the Bristol Channel. The vast tidal range, moving east during the flood and west during the ebb, means that indifferent surf at low tide can improve markedly 'on the push'. As the *Stormrider* guide puts it: 'The tidal flow up and down the Bristol Channel is similar to the current in a huge river . . . The "push" effect of the incoming tide, by helping a weak swell on its way, can be significant . . . There is also a considerable difference in the water level between, say, low spring-tide and low neap-tide. This affects the quality of some of the low tide breaks.'

For many people, even some surfers, the nuances of tidal science are a mystery. Those in this category would, however, do well to heed the advice of the *Stormrider* guide: 'A local tide table is a crucial investment.'

As a group of teenage windsurfers from Exmouth in the mid-1980s, my friends and I had a reasonable idea of how tides worked, but knew nothing of the history of places like Lynmouth. The last thing on our minds, indeed, was local history. As with so many surfers who travel anywhere in search of their fix, all we were interested in was the surf. Was it going to be any good at Saunton? Would Croyde be a better bet? What about Putsborough? Or

Woolacombe? In those days webcams did not exist, and nor were there the likes of www.magicseaweed.com, www.A1surf.com, www.surfcore.co.uk and www.wannasurf.com. The surf-forecasting websites – not to mention the mobile phone, whereby surfers can alert one another the moment they are aware of good surf – have made life considerably easier, but for us to surf in north Devon then entailed a regular perusal of newspaper and television weather maps, which we learnt to understand perhaps rather better than some surfers today. But then, as now, there was one surf-check tool that was nigh-on infallible: the call to a local surf shop. For us, that meant a call to the Tiki shop in Braunton, whose owner, Tim Heyland, remains today one of the key figures in British surfing.

'I don't feel nostalgic about the old days. I enjoy a few stories around the camp fire every now and then, but that's about it. Most of the people who bang on about the old days have given up.'

So says Heyland, the man who, with Dave Smith, launched what is now Europe's largest surf shop in 1967. The Tiki shop, in Braunton, just a few miles from North Devon's premium surf breaks, is now as slick and glossy as they come, but it grew from humble beginnings. 'I turned up in north Devon with £5.00 in my pocket, a dog on a piece of string and a home-made wetsuit. I had to sleep on the beach in the early days,' recalls Heyland, an imposing man whose decision to pursue surfing meant the end of twelve generations of family service in the military. Despite his embrace of a pursuit that would appear to include little of discipline, order and institutional obeisance, Heyland appears more soldier than surfer. He is powerfully built, a testimony to early sporting prowess in swimming ('I was the fastest at my school') and boxing ('I never lost a fight') as well as a lifetime spent in the water. Now in his sixties with thinning white hair, on the day we met Heyland's concession to surfing cool was a pair of jeans and a Diesel T-shirt. In every other respect he exuded army toughness, and, so I had heard, was not a man to suffer fools. My sense of apprehension in meeting him was exacerbated when a downpour on the M5 slowed my progress, only to be turned into serious jitters when an accident on the A361 meant that I eventually drove into Braunton some ninety minutes later than had been arranged. En route, once I accepted the fact that I would be hopelessly late, I rang ahead, to be told that I needn't worry; Heyland would meet me later in the afternoon.

With time to kill I checked the surf at Saunton and Croyde, to find not even a ripple on the ocean. I hadn't been in the area for many years, but the scene was reminiscent of my stag weekend, held in Croyde so that the inevitable intoxication would be countervailed by surfing. This laudable aim had been scotched by a resolutely horizontal sea, but often in my late teens and early twenties the pilgrimage to North Devon had yielded swell. On one beautiful summer's day when we were eighteen or nineteen, Rich, Elliot and I drove into the car park at Saunton to see ruler-edge lines of 5 ft swell, furling immaculately as if Saunton had turned itself into a classic right-hand point break rather than the mellow longboarder's wave that it is. Under a clear blue sky, warmed by the sun and with relatively few people in the water, we hurriedly pulled the boards from the roof-rack and got into our Alder wetsuits, all the while watching as a surfer leapt to his feet and proceeded to carve languidly from top to bottom of a glistening, deep blue wave, barely throwing up any spray but drawing lines of pure pleasure whose seductive echo rapidly became an insistent boom in our hearts. We raced to the water's edge and paddled out; all told, probably no more than five minutes elapsed from arrival in the Saunton car park to feeling the clasp of the sea.

That and other sessions had at least occurred in perfect conditions, even if our ability was rather less impressive, but as I recalled those early days I also remembered once turning up at Saunton to find it pumping, exactly as the weather charts had suggested would be the case. Before setting out on the ninety-minute drive from Exmouth, I had rung the Tiki shop to double-check. 'Nah, mate, it's as flat as today, sorry,' came the response.

'Really? The charts look good. No wave at all?'

'A bit of chop, not worth the effort.'

Something possessed me to ignore this recommendation and make the journey. In those days if you saw another surfer driving in the opposite direction you would wave, flash your lights or make the 'shaka' sign. The latter is derived from Polynesian culture and consists of extending the thumb and little finger while keeping the three middle fingers curled. To accentuate the shaka sign, the hand is rotated back and forth. In the mid-1980s, if you saw another surfer on the road – especially one driving a VW camper van, the surfer's vehicle of choice – you would almost certainly be the recipient of a shaka sign, and if it was accompanied by a broad smile and a rotating hand, you would know that you were on your way to pumping surf. Nowadays, if you were to brandish the shaka sign in either Devon or Cornwall to someone you didn't know, you would almost certainly be derided as desperately unhip, but back then I met with at least two en route. I knew I was heading to good surf, and sure enough all the breaks in the area – Saunton, Downend Point, Croyde beach and reef – were firing, ably vindicating the writers of Ward, Lock & Co's *Guide to Barnstaple, Ilfracombe, Bideford, Clovelly and North-West Devon*, who, in 1952 – prior to the Lynmouth flood – described 'the exhilarating sport of surf-boarding' in Croyde Bay, 'the breakers being ideal'. Ideal they were, but why had I been discouraged to make the trip by someone in the Tiki shop? Now I found myself mulling over this question as I watched a group from the Territorial Army exercising on a lesser visited part of Saunton Sands. So, too, something else: twenty years ago, surfers travelled with their boards on roof-racks, but now, especially in Devon and Cornwall, the trend was for boards to be stashed inside cars. Why?

When I eventually met Heyland he cut a stern enough figure for me to resolve not to bother him with trivia. It wasn't that he was annoyed with me for being late, but more that his was such a commanding, serious presence that a venture into frippery could not but seem ill-advised. Heyland looked like a capable man who had always known exactly what he was doing – a man who had conceived a series of goals and had then, like a chess grandmaster sitting down to vanquish a novice, gone about achieving them.

Heyland was born in Bournemouth, a town that today boasts a sizeable surfing community who might, or might not, one day be lucky enough to have an artificial reef built at Boscombe Pier. He enjoyed a multi-cultural upbringing thanks to his father's job as a military attaché. His last school was in Oxford, which he left in 1963 to set off for Brazil, where he learnt to surf and collected snakes and animals for American zoos. A stint as a cowboy in Paraguay followed, and for a while Heyland worked for Linguaphone in London ('I hated being there,' he recalls. 'By then I just wanted to surf.') A true pioneer of surfing, Heyland was among the first Britons to shape a surfboard (in 1963), and set up Tiki in 1967 after he met business partner Dave Smith. 'We had a van worth £50, about £200 in capital and a few materials. That was it,' recalls Heyland, but impoverishment seems only to have fuelled his drive not least because in the late 1960s he entered a highly exclusive club. Along with Rod Sumpter he took on the formidable waves of Oahu's North Shore.

Heyland tells the story with a twinkle in his eye. 'It was 1969, the time of the shortboard revolution. I'd shaped a hundred and ten boards, pretty radical things, but Dave agreed to glass them so that I could head off to Hawaii. I'm pretty sure that I was the first Brit, apart from Rodney, to surf the North Shore. It was hard graft getting in to Hawaii, and harder still once we were there. They weren't keen on long hair. I was travelling with Mike Saltmarsh [a North Devon surfer and the owner of Croyde beach] and a friend from the Windansea Surf Club, Tom Ortner. The pair of them didn't go down well with the authorities at the airport – they were too scruffy. Ortner didn't make it in! I hid while all this was going on, and when everyone had gone I made my way outside. Within twenty minutes two girls were looking after me. The English accent worked a treat.'

Before long, Heyland had his first vision of the North Shore of Oahu in all its glory. 'I arrived at Waimea Bay and couldn't believe the size of the swell. There was no way I had the right equipment – half the North Shore was getting washed away. But we checked out Sunset, and although it was big – and I mean big – I just had to paddle out.' Heyland tuts a little at this point in the story, as if still astonished by what happened next. 'I took off on a monster of a wave, raced to the bottom of the face and started to bottom turn. Then the wave just smashed me to the seabed. The sheer force was unbelievable. I'd never experienced anything like it.'

The experience stood Heyland in good stead. After Hawaii he stayed in the fishing village of San Blas on Mexico's Pacific Coast, a place of quality surf and, in the late 1960s, a lot of what he calls 'controlled wildness. It was a big year for Hell's Angels. There were plenty of them around, a lot of girls, a big drug problem and a bucket-load of draft-dodgers. It was a bit like *Big Wednesday.*'

I doubted that immersion in a world of drugs and Hell's Angels would ever have been Heyland's scene, even if there were plenty of girls and good waves thrown into the mix, but Heyland loved the experience of being a British surfing explorer. 'It was wonderful searching for bigger, hollower, faster waves. There was a lot of respect for surfers and what we were doing. We were fit and taking on challenges that people found impressive, and we did it the hard way. I can remember turning up at one place and sleeping in a boat full of fish heads, wrapped in a bin liner. These days people charter boats with air-con and CD players. It's like being in a hotel.'

Heyland has surfed most of the major surf nations. As well as Hawaii, Mexico and Brazil regular trips have been made to Indonesia, Fiji and Costa Rica. He is known as 'Tiki' wherever he goes, and two surf spots in Indonesia bear this name. But it is in north Devon where Heyland has made his most lasting impact on surfing. He returned from San Blas in 1970, and went about building the Tiki business with remarkable assiduity. The business has constantly moved with the times, making boards and wetsuits in the 1970s and moving into windsurfing when this was all the rage. Although North Devon has a number of other surf shops and businesses, there is no doubt that Heyland and Tiki dominate the area. Tiki boards are still made and sold through the shop, as are brands such as South Point Epoxy, Anacapa by Al

Merrick, the ubiquitous NSP, Hot Buttered and Webber. Wetsuits from Tiki, O'Neill, Rip Curl and Billabong are stocked, and the fashion brands in store, for 2007, include: Animal, Billabong, Quicksilver, Rip Curl, Roxy, Etnies, Reef, Arnette, Von Zipper, Cult, Orb, O'Neill, Dekline, Calais Surf, Nixon Watches, Kaenon Sunglasses, Vestal Watches, Icon Jewellery, Sanuk and Ignite Beanies. And, of course, Tiki. All are neatly displayed in a light, airy and attractive retail emporium that Heyland's father, when aware that his son was planning to dedicate his life to surfing, could barely have imagined.

As Heyland says: 'In the first twenty years it was virtually all word of mouth with hardly any advertising. These days it's a commercial whirlpool. The top brands dominate but we hold our own.' Success has been achieved through constant hard work and innovation, and Heyland holds no brief for those who bemoan the loss of surfing's soul because of its increasingly commercial profile: 'Total nonsense. Surfing wouldn't be where it is now without commercialism. Without it, we'd still be riding tree trunks.'

After leaving Heyland I drove to Saunton to have another look at the surf. I knew that this was a futile gesture, for it was getting dark and even if the waves had improved I would only have had about ten minutes water time. But I hadn't been to the area for a while, and Heyland's curious blend of no-nonsense businessman's gruff and incorruptible passion for surfing had me hoping against hope that there might be a wave. Naturally, there wasn't, but for many people – not least Londoners, Bristolians and people from Midland cities – North Devon is a Mecca of unparalleled appeal. As Heyland says, 'It's the first place in the south-west where you can find good surf.' Save for its narrow lanes, North Devon is geared to a seasonal influx of what Devonians term 'grockles' (in contrast to the 'emmets' who invade Cornwall), and a pub such as the Thatch, in the centre of Croyde, or Marisco's nightclub in Woolacombe, will be never less than packed throughout the summer. As with Cornwall, surfing is a vital part of the Devon economy, but unlike anywhere in its neighbouring county (one that would be an island were it not for a few miles of land to the north of the River Tamar), the allure of the area has resulted in an Olympic athlete naming his son after a surf spot. James Cracknell, the gold medal winning oarsman, is so enamoured of surfing at Croyde that he named his son after the village. Croyde itself, one of the prettiest villages in Devon, with thatched cottages galore, takes its name from a Viking raider by the name of Crydda.

There are plenty of North Devon surfers, not to mention a Viking heritage celebrated each June in Croyde, to inspire the Cracknell family. Tiki sponsors local ripper Joel Fitzgerald, and current stand-outs include Adam Thornton, Andrew Cotton, Scott Rannocham, Nigel Cross and Richard Carter. Totnes-bred surfer Eugene Tollemache, a highly regarded big-wave rider and former Rick Stein chef, is another surfer to have made an impact at Croyde and its nearby breaks. There are two surf clubs – the Croyde Surf Club and the Woolacombe Boardriders – and veteran surf photographer Ester Spears is based in the area. When Croyde is working, at low tide on the push and with super-fast waves in the 4–6 ft range, Spears will as often as not be on hand to capture surfing the standard of which is as high as anywhere in Britain or Ireland. This is not a place for beginner or intermediate surfers, though few in these categories seem to realize this. One Bristol surfer and Croyde regular laments the way in which lesser surfers seem to be drawn to the hefty peaks of Croyde: 'There are so many kooks it's ridiculous. It's a great wave but it gets so crowded that you start to think the only solution is to cordon off the beach from anyone who can't surf – and I mean surf well. I know people have got to learn somewhere, and sure, it wouldn't be fair, but it would get rid of the idiots and make surfing Croyde enjoyable again. The surf schools who just take everyone out whether the surf's flat or classic have a lot to answer for. So do the webcams and surf forecasting sites.'

Ben Freestone is one target of the Bristolian's ire, given that he created the Magic Seaweed website. Freestone grew up surfing the breaks from Brighton and Bournemouth but decamped to South Devon 'as soon as I was old enough'. Magic Seaweed, now one of the most popular surfing websites, had its genesis in a personal project, as Freestone explains: 'About seven or eight years ago I used to follow the arrival of a new swell with wave buoy data I could get from the web. This was pretty novel at the time and although I don't know if it really meant we scored more waves, it seemed to build even more excitement into the wait. But knowing a bit about computers I figured that from a surfers' point of view the data was really only useful if you could see at a glance more than one buoy. Also the winds were really only relevant if you could see the whole of the UK. From this you could work out where in a pressure system we were and then figure what might happen in the next few hours. I built the software and, to give it somewhere to live, registered www.magicseaweed.com. This was really just a chance for me and the guys I surfed with to score a few more waves, and an outlet for a little creative energy.' But Freestone had opened a Pandora's Box, one which met with the deep-seated human urge to communicate. 'As the data available became increasingly more interesting and complex, I spent more time working out ways to tell me what, as a surfer, I needed. I started to share a bit of information with other surfers and a few other websites about what I was doing. Really since then what started as a personal project has grown, I guess through word of mouth, into being a pretty busy website.'

I asked Freestone what he made of the argument that sites such as his made it all too easy, that they contributed to line-ups becoming ever more crowded. His response was considered and intelligent: 'Discussion on this topic becomes so abstract and philosophical so quickly that it's hard to add much of use. Would the UK be a better place to live if only it had a quarter of its current population? I don't know the answer. I do know that the internet must have had an effect on the face of modern surfing, but that it's all too often taken as the only factor and becomes a scapegoat for a great many changes taking place in our day-to-day lives. A list of other major contributory factors would have to include the huge spend made annually by aggressive sportswear manufacturers in pushing surfing as a means of selling product, the changing face of communications technology and the ease with which the grapevine can now spread information between surfers. Look at the number of guys getting straight on the mobile to mates once they've checked the surf. On top of that there are massive advances in wetsuit technology which mean a winter surf no longer entails suffering for pleasure, the increased appreciation of outdoor leisure activity and the increase in the number of people now working flexibly and able to get to the beach at any given time.'

Freestone now lives in Churchstow, near the much-visited South Hams town of Kingsbridge as well as South Devon's premier break, Bantham. He is fortunate to have good surf within a short drive of his house, and is aware of the interplay of ethics and pragmatism when it comes to what he does for a living: 'I've never liked the "it was inevitable" argument as a way to ignore an obligation to act with integrity when creating something new,' he says, 'but one of the problems anyone taking an "anti" stance to forecasting will have is just how easy it is to do. The fact is that it's much easier to tell whether there will be surf tomorrow than whether it'll rain. Regardless of how this information is disseminated, once there were enough people interested the rise of surf forecasting was inevitable. Even the BBC now has a daily surf forecast. Eight years ago we didn't imagine building a website that everyone would use, still less that it would become a subject of debate, but one thing's for sure: change is impossible to resist. We can only ride it out, act responsibly as individuals and take advantage of the fact that some of those changes bring great benefits – like being able to grab a forecast for somewhere interesting and jump on a last-minute cheap flight out there. But the days of turning up and hoping it'll be OK are over.'

Freestone is, of course, right. But I found myself thinking of an aphorism that my mother is fond of: *plus ça change, plus c'est la même chose*. Perhaps also because of a sense of nostalgia, for me North Devon – regardless of the changes wrought by the surf schools, progress, surf forecasting or anything else – remains special. A high-rise hotel could appear at Saunton and yet I would still always remember days in my late teens when I made the journey there and returned home without a care in the world. Perhaps this came across as I spoke to Heyland, for by the conclusion of our conversation he had invited me to come surfing with him whenever I could find the time. 'Bring your boys,' he said. 'I'll have them up and riding in no time.'

Emboldened, I told him of turning up twenty years ago to find North Devon firing, despite being informed by someone in the Tiki shop that it was 'flat as'. Heyland smiled, ever so faintly. 'Must have been one of the staff desperate for an uncrowded surf,' he said.

Anyone who says East Anglia is flat should think again: natural energy
from Scroby windfarm and North Sea surf.

11

CALIFORNIA

It was dark by the time I arrived at the University of East Anglia, whose campus I had attended between 1985 and 1988. I was not there out of nostalgia but because, having not been to Norwich for so long, it was as good a place as any to rendez-vous with Mark Southgate, then twenty-eight and the man behind www.eastcoastsurf.co.uk. Southgate lived near the university and it seemed sensible to meet somewhere convenient for him and easy to locate for me. Despite this, I managed to take a wrong turn or two as I came off the A140, making for an unexpected circuit of Eaton Park to the east of the campus. Many years ago, the park was the home of a small skateboard bowl used by me and an Ipswich-bred skater called Clive Lyons. As young men in our early twenties, we were slightly older than most of the city's skaters, who favoured the town centre for the ollie-centred tricks then sweeping the country. Instead of perfecting kick-flips and all manner of ankle-breaking variations, I preferred hurtling as fast as possible over the worn tarmac on the approach to the bowl, hitting its smooth concrete at full speed and proceeding to carve 'S' turns, with frontside grinds, 360s and railslides, until exiting whence I'd come. While Clive more readily embraced the world of streetskating, I remained wedded to a form of skateboarding that while initially only ever a substitute for surfing soon became just as addictive.

I was fortunate, therefore, to attend the University of East Anglia, not merely because it was a five-minute skate from the bowl at Eaton Park but because its 1960s' architects unwittingly created a skateboarding paradise. The same can be said of much architecture of the era. The new universities and new towns that sprung up – with their endless slabs of concrete and acclivitous walls – may have been decried by the arbiters of good taste but they provided perfect arenas for skateboarding. Nowhere is this better illustrated than at London's South Bank, where for years the skateboarders taking to the sloping banks and sleek walls beneath the Queen Elizabeth Hall were perceived as an unruly menace until the powers that be realized that, in fact, they were a popular and harmless draw in their own right. Skateboarding at the South Bank is now encouraged and as much a fixture in the area as the London Eye. It was difficult not to muse on the peculiar way in which both surfers and skaters co-opt the environment, natural or man-made, for acts that are arguably profoundly unnatural, as I made my way from UEA's principal car park to its quadrangle, where I would be meeting Southgate. On the way I walked past the entrance to the student union and graduate bar, and found myself recalling many happy hours of absorption in clattering around UEA's skate-friendly surfaces when, out of the shadows, a slim man of medium height ambled towards me.

'Are you Alex?' he asked, adding, 'I'm Mark from East Coast Surf.'

We shook hands and retreated out of the cold to a nearby café. Southgate did not, at first glance, resemble the conventional image of the surfer. He wore his brown hair short and favoured understated apparel. He was courteous and friendly, and his quiet, polite demeanour reminded me more of a university scholar than what I had imagined of one of East Anglia's foremost surfers. But when the talk moved on to surfing, Southgate changed. He explained that he'd been brought up in East Anglia, an area known more for its unremitting flatness and watery fens than its surf, and had been surfing for fourteen years. He learnt in France – 'I fell in love with surfing after four months there' – and bought a bodyboard, which he first rode at Hemsby. Recalling those early days, Southgate's eyes lit up. 'I went bodyboarding every day with a friend from school. Often we'd meet out in the line-up. Hemsby's a beachbreak and can dish up some really nice lefts and rights.'

Southgate's transition to stand-up surfing came when the same friend gave him his board. From then on, he was hooked, despite the region's inclemency when it came both to the infrastructure and practice of surfing: 'There were no surf schools, no surf shops, nowhere you could rent a board and nowhere you could get repairs done. Even now we've got just one shaper, Paul Nicker. In the winter it's freezing and you can only surf for an hour, max, and that's with a 5 mm minimum wetsuit with boots, gloves and hood. The breaks here are fickle, too. We need a big low sitting between Norway and Scotland which will generate lined-up surf, but usually the wind hits and messes it all up. But then again we get a lot of offshores, and groundswells coming down from the Arctic can have real grunt. When these hit, somewhere like Trimingham can work really well as the swell has to move over deep water before hitting a sandbar. The other top spots are Cromer, East Runton and Emily's. The last one's a secret spot so don't ask me to tell you where it is.'

I had paddled out a few times at Cromer, back in my UEA days, usually to no avail. On one occasion what had appeared a promising forecast – a north to easterly swell, with light south-westerly winds – had resulted in one of the more bizarre surfing experiences of my life. I arrived at Cromer on an overcast afternoon whose muted hues were mirrored by a virtually supine sea. I was with my brother Chris and a delectable girlfriend of his, an elegant and sporty blonde from Sweden, if I remember correctly. Chris had come to windsurf and I to surf. There were neither wind nor waves but for some unaccountable reason I donned my wetsuit and paddled out next to Cromer pier. For about an hour, I sat in the chilling, murky sea on my board, a 6′ 0″ thruster whose provenance I can no longer recall, as stray bulges in the ocean ambled towards me, hinting at what they could be but not once delivering. In vain I paddled to try to catch waves that were not waves, as my brother and his girlfriend watched from the shore. Quite why I remained in the water so long I have no idea, but as a gesture in futility, this episode remains hard to match.

On another occasion, I set off with both windsurfing and surfing equipment, only to be deterred by the huge rips that seemed to be running at virtually every beach I found. This, indeed, is a problem in the area. A glance at Chris Nelson and Demi Taylor's *Surfing Britain* advises wariness at just about every break listed, owing to rips and longshore drift. Alf Alderson, in *Surf UK*, notes other problems at East Runton:

> There are three hazards to be taken into account at Runton. The first is the shingle and flint to be found littering the gully scoured out by the sea towards the bottom of the beach – this can cause cuts and bruises if you are dumped by the shore break. Next, there's the longshore current, which carries you SE on a rising tide, NW on an ebb tide. And finally, there's the sewer pipe: it's easy to surf into it or wipe out on it.

Nelson and Taylor explain the factors that affect the region as a whole:

> By all rights Cromer and East Runton should be up there among Britain's top surf spots. They sit on a part of England that juts out in the North Sea ... Hefty Arctic swells have a much greater fetch and so should be cleaner and more lined by the time they hit. They should be – if it weren't for two tiny factors, oceanography and geology. Whereas the accumulated kinetic energy deposited onto the beaches and reefs of the north comes out of deep water, by the time the swell lines pass Hull they are starting to run into shallower water. Energy is lost through friction

with the ocean floor. The waves breaking on the beaches of East Anglia are now about half the size of their Yorkshire cousins.

There might be the rub, but Southgate's enthusiasm for the surf in his locale was undimmed. He agreed that surfing in East Anglia had its drawbacks, but was adamant than on its day the breaks at the best spots could be 'as fast and as hollow as anywhere else in the country, especially between January and March. A good swell only lasts two or three days but if you're really committed you can get in the water every day if you want.' He reckoned there were about 100 dedicated surfers in the region, with the numbers dropping off to a hardcore of between twenty and thirty in the winter. There was, too, an upside to the frigidity and inconstancy of the local breaks. 'Localism is unheard of here. There are so few surfers that no one can say they own any of the breaks, if such a thing's possible. When we see someone unfamiliar in the line-up we're pleased to see him.' Were there any women, I wondered, among the small but hardy band of locals? 'Not very many,' replied Southgate, 'maybe six or seven. But there is a surf club. It's the East Anglia Surfing Association. Hopefully if we can get a surf school going more women will take up the sport.'

Southgate's optimism, as much as passion, for the future of East Anglian surfing had led him to make plans to open what would be the first surf shop in the cathedral city of Norwich. He intended to name it after his website – www.eastcoastsurf.co.uk – and had found a site in the centre of Norwich. 'There's enough business to support a shop – just,' he said. 'Clothing sales should be enough to subsidize boards and wetsuits.' As I watched him depart among the young students bustling back and forth, so many wearing the logos of the surfwear corporations with little or no idea of what they represented, it struck me that he was probably right. Just.

The following day I set off for California. Not the Edenic American state but the small seaside resort in Norfolk, some twenty miles east of Norwich. A trip to the village apparently named after the discovery of some gold coins found on the beach in 1848, around the time of the California gold rush, was irresistible because here, just a few miles from the chintz and chip shops of Great Yarmouth, there is surf. Trisha's Chippy bade me a hearty welcome once I had driven past the rows of squat chalets belonging to the California Sands Estate, and then, near the seafront, I was greeted by one of the few two-storey buildings in the vicinity, the California Tavern. It offered Boddingtons bitter and Stella Artois, and if another vice took your fancy there was also a boarded-up building calling itself 'Casino Crazy', which presumably cast open its doors to all and sundry in the summer. Now, though, it was winter – a still, calm day, the sort that can, once in a while, lend a tinge of unfathomable melancholy to surfing, as if both waves and riders are mere ghosts, given, temporarily, the freedom of the sea. Upon walking to the beach it was evident that surfing would remain wholly imagined, for there was not a wave in sight. Instead, the view was dominated by the turbines of the Scroby Sands Wind Farm, sitting out at sea like the severed antlers of an errant band of stags, occasionally glinting in the dim sunlight but otherwise appearing so static that it was hard to imagine them ever moving. The turbines would, though (so I read on notice-boards on the beach), prevent the emission of 75,000 tonnes of greenhouse gases every year and provide enough electricity to power 41,000 homes. A cat shimmied over the shingle and sand beach, oblivious to the environmentally sound derring-do about a mile offshore, as were the seagulls, yelling with typical omnipresence. I scanned the coast to my left and right and, for a second, saw some white water feathering away to my left. Was there a wave, after all?

Closer inspection yielded yet more disappointment. There was no swell, not even a hint of the large northerly required to produce surf here. It was the same story a little further up the coast, at Southgate's baptismal break at Hemsby, and the same again at Walcott, from whose fine sandy beach I had windsurfed some twenty or so years ago. I drove on to Cromer, where the weather deteriorated but not with a *quid pro quo* of discernible improvement in the swell. Here, at the formerly fashionable Victorian town, now billing itself as 'the gem of the East Coast', there was an air of vague desolation as the pier with its Pavilion Theatre and adjacent long, sloping slipway for the lifeboat, not to mention the many groynes on the beach, found themselves coated in a fine rain under a sombre sky, bereft of any human form. There was no one around, just me, looking in vain for surf, though once inside one of the many chip shops near the rather Gothic Hotel de Paris I found some builders on a lunch break, tough-looking men who would most likely have greeted a request for information about the local surfing scene with bewilderment. I retreated to my car, parked on Runton Road to savour my sausage and chips, and as I gazed out at the lacklustre sea found myself thinking of Joseph Conrad, who, according to W. G. Sebald in *The Rings of Saturn*, 'made three round trips as an ordinary seaman aboard the *Skimmer of the Seas*, a coaster that plied between Lowestoft and Newcastle'. Sebald writes that little is known of how the young Conrad spent his time in and around Lowestoft, but his fertile imagination readily conjures the Polish émigré strolling the esplanade, listening to a brass band and feeling intrigued 'by the ease with which he is absorbing a hitherto quite unfamiliar language, a language he will one day employ to write the novels that will win him worldwide acclaim ...' As I remembered these lines I tried to imagine Conrad aboard the *Skimmer of the Seas*, steaming past Cromer, the ship's bow bisecting a huge and clean north to easterly swell, one born of meteorological mayhem in the Arctic and held up by a light south-westerly, just enough to create perfect surfing waves which would rise, furl and peel beneath the Victorian pier. It was as fanciful as Phil Philo's image of Captain Cook having witnessed in action, in Hawaii, the very 'Olo' board that graced the Surfing Museum, but before long I had convinced myself that Conrad *must* have felt the rhythm of the swell, that he *must* have understood its possibilities, that surely he felt more of the sea than that it was a cruel and savage entity to be mistrusted at all times. Suitably inspired, I turned the car round to check East Runton – if there was a wave anywhere, it would be here.

Just a mile or two further up the coast from Cromer, and facing almost due north, East Runton is a small seaside community dominated by a gargantuan caravan park. The vast majority of its summer tourists will no doubt marvel at the power of the sea (for here the North Sea wreaks an all-too-visible, continuous and unforgiving onslaught on the low-lying, soft cliffs of East Anglia) but they will be unlikely to note that East Runton boasts a chalk-flint reef capable of delivering short, hollow rights and fine, longer lefts. This is the best known of East Anglia's surf breaks, and when we met on the UEA campus Southgate showed me plenty of photographic evidence of the waves to be had in the right conditions. Sadly, notwithstanding the inspirational conjunction of Sebald, Southgate and Conrad, the surf was no higher than a foot. It could, at a push, have been surfed, but the wind was freezing and the prospect simply wasn't appealing enough. Having trudged down the sharply sloping lifeboat slipway, I trudged back up to the ground level with the small parking area, and there noticed an unusually shaped, white weather vane. I had not seen its like anywhere, and for a minute could not discern exactly what it was. Then I realized – it was a surfer leaning back as if riding a tube. He or she was facing out to sea, some twelve feet above the ground, and then, as I marvelled at the depth of surfing passion that could not but have led to the strange weather vane's appearance, I realized that it was a memorial.

At the foot of its pole, nestling amid stones, which I imagine were gathered from the beach and set in concrete, there was a plaque denoting that this was the East Runton Surfers' Memorial, in memory of:

Adam Battrick	22.9.69	2.4.2000
Andrew Ayres	24.10.71	23.11.2001
Matthew Robin Smith	14.2.77	21.8.2002

Beneath was this inscription:

> Waves come and go my friends
> But your lights shine on.

I drew a blank on my East Anglia surfing odyssey, but Mark Southgate knew his market. He stuck to his guns and opened the East Coast Surf Shop on 6 February 2006, in Dove Street, Norwich. The East Anglia Surfing Association proved to be short-lived, but business at East Coast Surf was good, according to colleague Andy 'Gee-man' Goodger: 'In summer we sell five or six boards a week. There might be one week in a month when it goes a bit slack but we did really well in the run-up to Christmas. There's a growing interest in surfing in East Anglia, for sure. We've even got one guy starting a surf school this summer. We'll never have the crowds, but if you're looking to find a wave from, say, London, this place is as good as anywhere else within two or three hours of the city.'

That the time is ripe for the East Coast Surf Shop is endorsed by one of East Anglia's veteran surfers, Neil Watson. 'There have been one or two attempts to sustain surf shops before, in Cromer, but they didn't survive. Mark seems to have proved that the interest is there.'

Watson, who grew up near Lowestoft – the scene of Conrad's first encounter with English soil – has been around long enough to ring the changes. Now in early retirement, Watson started surfing on his honeymoon in Cornwall in 1969, and has kept the faith ever since. He still surfs, though not in the winters, but is keen to reject any suggestion that he is a pioneer of surfing in the region. 'No, they're other people who've been surfing longer than me. Maurice Butler, for example. His family have grown up surfing here. I think they're on to their third generation of surfers now.' But Watson's modesty belies an intricate knowledge of domestic surfing, acquired through a lifetime not only of riding waves, but also of freelance surf photography and writing. He contributed to Fuz Bleakley's *Surf Insight*, as well as other seminal UK surf magazines such as *Surf Scene* (for whom he wrote the first profile of Porthleven trail-blazer John Adams), *Tube News* and *Atlantic Surfer*, and set up East Anglia's only dedicated local surfing publication, *Ripple*. A literate, intelligent man, Watson wrote for *Wavelength* and other journals, and counts both Conrad and Captain

Cook as his heroes. His was a word to be trusted when he told me that even as far south as the Suffolk fishing port of Lowestoft there is a surfing community: 'If we get a low in the right position, we'll get a deep groundswell that'll produce good overhead waves in plenty of locations along the Norfolk and Suffolk coastline. It's the luck of the lows, I guess – there are times when Lowestoft will have a wave when the north-facing beaches are onshore and messy.'

Watson was also a man who would know the story behind the East Runton Surfing Memorial. 'It was unveiled in 2003. Adam Battrick and Matty Smith were lifeguards and friends from Sheringham, and the third surfer, Andrew Ayres, was killed in a car crash. All three of the lads were regulars in the line-up at East Runton.'

Seven surfers ride the Severn Bore at Newnham on
a sunny September morning.

12

THE LONGEST WAVE

Newnham-on-Severn was gently awakening to a perfect September morning. The tree-lined Gloucestershire village, many of whose houses overlook the River Severn, could not have appeared more peaceable if its inhabitants had all been dosed with Prozac. As it was, at seven o'clock on a warm and sunny Friday morning, a few organized souls were up and about, taking a constitutional and walking their dogs, while others were making their way to open the former Roman settlement's pleasing array of antique, porcelain, pottery, craft and book shops. St Peter's Church and the village clock tower stood resplendent in the sun, as did any number of genteel listed buildings and, beyond, woodland that hinted of the Forest of Dean, a cycle ride away. There were barely any cars, barely any sounds, barely any movement. If ever there was a village that spoke of the comfort, cosiness and allure of life in middle England, this was it.

On the river faint wisps of mist hovered over the water. Here, too, all appeared motionless. The thick brown of the River Severn seemed stagnant, its only concession to kinesis being to force the eye to squint as light fractured and bounced from the glistening surface. On the far, eastern side of the river cattle grazed in deep-green fields, and on the horseshoe bend, on an exposed mud and sand flat, a flock of birds searched for food. Amid this bucolic idyll, a man in a black wetsuit strode to the river's edge holding a huge surfboard, slipped down its muddy bank and entered the water, which, as the mist cleared, appeared so thick and so dark that it looked as if it might be comprised as much of brick and mortar as H_2O. Soon he was joined by two or three other surfers, who paddled their boards to the centre of the river and proceeded to sit on them, utterly becalmed. A little upstream the scene repeated itself as, from the car park at the White Hart pub, other surfers took to the river. One opted to stand in the shallows, with his arms folded, rather than sit on his board, while slowly, in the distance, the A48 hummed into life with commuter traffic.

An elderly man and his wife stood at the wall separating the car park of the White Hart from the river bank, gazing inquisitively at the six or seven men who had decided, for no discernible reason, to enter the River Severn with surfboards. A burly man with a suntanned face stood beside them, adjusting an expensive-looking camera. The elderly couple looked at this man, and back to the river, and back to the photographer again. What on earth was going on? they asked themselves.

'It's on its way,' said Alex Williams, the veteran surfing photo-grapher, who had been sent by *Carve* magazine to cover the strange surfing spectacle at Newnham-on-Severn. Williams pointed to the horseshoe bend in the river, at the flats occupied in tranquillity by the birds until a few moments ago. Now they were rising, taking refuge from a surging mass of white water that had appeared from nowhere. This was the Severn Bore, one of Britain's most spectacular and surreal natural phenomena, a bizarre counter-intuitive wave that draws surfers from around the world.

The Bore was late, this Friday morning, allowing for more onlookers to arrive and for two South Africans, distinguished by their red wetsuits, to enter the river at Newnham. One was Kimbell Whitfield, thirty-one, a multi-media consultant based in London, and the other was big-wave rider Duncan Scott, a man for whom the adjective 'enthusiastic' is a serious understatement. They made their way to the centre of the river in time to catch the wave, which, if truth be told, was more in the nature of a highly persuasive dribble than an ocean-born jewel. On its bubbling face they were joined by the surfers already in the river, as well as a number of kayakers who had caught the wave further downriver. All rode it for perhaps half a mile, exiting near the White Hart to scamper up the reeking river banks and rush to their cars. Again, the elderly couple, not to mention many other observers, were bemused by this sudden need for transport, but the surfers were engaging in a cherished ritual: chasing the Bore.

'Only a Bore surfer knows the feeling,' said Scott, as he and Whitfield loaded their boards on top of Scott's Volvo estate. Then they were driven by Scott's girlfriend Hannah to the Severn Bore pub, about a mile or so upriver, where they once again entered the brackish water. This, indeed, would be Scott's routine for the next four days. He would surf the Bore twice a day, come rain or shine, by night as well, chasing it upriver by car whenever he lost the wave. There were any number of entry points for Bore surfers, of whose number Scott had been a devoted member for a few years. He endeavoured not to miss any of the surfable bores, which occur perhaps twenty-five times a year. 'It's an amazing feeling,' he said, as he clambered out of the river a little further from the Severn Bore pub. Scott was fresh from taking on his home country's legendary big-wave break of Dungeons, which he surfed in the 25–30 ft region. He grew up surfing shortboards, gravitated to big waves, and yet loves surfing the Severn Bore as much as anything else. 'Where else can you cruise on a wave for so long, riding past houses, trees and beautiful fields? It's just a fantastic vibe.'

The length of rides promised by the Bore is part of its attraction, but so too is its history, one of quasi-mythological status. Thomas Harrel, writing in 1824, conjured the Bore as a wall of water that 'rolls in with a head . . . foaming and roaring as though it were enraged by the opposition which it encounters'. To surf the Severn Bore is to enter a unique club which was pioneered by Commando officer Colonel Jack Churchill in 1955. 'Mad' Jack was known for a variety of eccentric exploits, including the deployment of a longbow in a World War II battle, but earnt his unlikely place in surfing history by entering the River Severn at Stonebench on 21 July 1955. Using a homemade 16 ft surfboard, Churchill's brief ride was witnessed by a local farmer and his son. It was not replicated until 1962, when, against police warnings, travelling Australian lifeguards surfed the Bore at Stonebench for a mile. Since then, the Bore has been surfed by a dedicated crew of locals and visiting surfers, but the warnings are not made without good reason. At fifty feet, the River Severn's tidal range is the second highest in the world, meaning that an incredible amount of water is propelled up an increasingly narrow channel. Bores occur year round with spring tides, but the biggest are around the Vernal Equinox (February, March and April) and the Autumnal Equinox (August, September and October). Then, if there is also a low-pressure system and strong south to south-westerly winds, the funnel-like shape of the Severn Estuary can create a wave as high as six feet.

To add to the difficulty, another imponderable is the amount of debris in the water: tree branches, oil cans, tyres, window frames and fridges – even dead animals – are just some of the obstacles that a surfer will encounter. Another problem is exiting the river. A surfer may avoid a collision with a large floating object, but will often lose the wave, either because of a loss of balance or because it drops away as it hits different parts of the estuary. The surfer is then at the mercy of the River Severn – whose current could by then be travelling at up to 12 mph – not to mention the quirks found at various parts of the river. These include tangles of branches waiting to ensnare a surfer's leash, high cliffs and whirlpools.

Scott and the Bore regulars had nothing, though, but praise for their Friday session, which culminated in further rides at Overbridge. James Golding, a chainsaw sculptor from Taunton, and Trevor 'the Whirlpool' Stephens, a North Devon longboarder, were in their element. 'The great thing about surfing the Bore is the camaraderie,' said Golding, whose daughters Amber and Alice had on another occasion surfed the Bore with him. 'Here, the drop-in rule is out of the window. We're all in the mud together, there's only one wave, and you've got to share it. It's like the early days of surfing. There's no localism, no bad attitude – if people turn up and want to surf it, we'll give them advice. There are a couple of secret spots, mind you – Nadgell Scratcher's Hollow, and Soggy Bottom's Bottom – but we won't say where they are. The point is that riding the Bore is a surreal, wonderful experience. Once you've ridden it, you'll think of nothing else. You'll find yourself watching the moon all the time.'

Stephens was just as rhapsodic. 'Surfing the Bore at night, under a full moon – now that's something else. Everything that's incredible about surfing the Bore by day is magnified.' Stephens had, indeed, earnt his nickname thanks to a night session. 'I got knocked off one night by James, a friend who surfs here a lot,' he recalled. 'There was a ferocious current and I was heading straight to the salmon catchers at the White Hart. I missed them by about three feet but then got caught in a whirlpool further along, underneath some cliffs.' Golding chuckled and finished the story. 'So he was stuck there, and the only way out was to climb the cliffs. So he climbed a fifty-foot cliff, knowing that if he fell he'd be right back in the whirlpool again.'

Both Stephens and Golding are adamant in their conviction that the Bore has to be respected. As Stephens says: 'When it goes wrong here, it goes badly wrong. You can fall back into a whirlpool or you can snag your leash on a branch as you're trying to climb out of the river. You've got to be careful. You couldn't turn up here as a beginner and expect to surf the Bore.'

It's ten o'clock the following Sunday evening, and I'm standing on the banks of the River Severn in Newnham. The town's church bells mark the hour, and a ripple of excitement runs through the crowd next to me. In just a few minutes, the Severn's lazy meander to the Bristol Channel will be interrupted by the huge incoming tidal surge of the Bore. In the darkness, the water looks more viscous than ever. Duncan Scott arrives and, with two other surfers, enters the water. He is hoping to set a world record for the longest ride, one set originally by Rod Sumpter and, over the years, traded by Bore regulars Steve King and Dave Lawson (honours at the time of writing lie with King, with a 7.6 mile ride in April 2006). I watch Scott slide down the muddy bank, into the darkened water. He drifts across the river with two other surfers, faintly illuminated by the moonlight. The three take up position on the far side of the river, adjacent to a sandbank, but as the crowd's sense of expectation rises so, too, does a peculiar sense of anxiety. I cast my eyes upriver. Some light is given off by the White Hart Inn, perhaps half a mile away, but the near-full moon casts a diffuse, inadequate glow. How on earth will the surfers be able to see where they are going?

These reflections are disturbed by a strange hissing sound. The crowd surges forward. Sure enough, the Bore is on its way, a mass of white water spanning the river, some three feet in height. Scott, visible thanks to a yellow safety jacket, leaps nimbly to his feet. His friends catch the wave but opt to 'prone' it, lying flat on their boards, chests raised, hands holding the rails. As the Bore passes I see Scott leading the journey upriver, the Severn's flat, tranquil waters now dominated by the inexorable incoming tide. I cannot help but think: shall I give it a go, too?

Early next morning I return to Newnham. Scott had been hoping for a Bore of maximum size, but the absence of wind and high pressure has made for twice-daily tidal surges of between one and three feet. Scott will not set his record, but conditions are perfect for a Bore novice. I'm tempted, but the longest board I own is a 7′ 6″, and Scott cautions that anything less than nine feet would not do the trick. 'You need a longboard to catch the wave and stay on it,' he says. 'Do you want to borrow one?' It just so happens that he has a spare strapped to his roof-rack, and so I find myself in the River Severn at Newnham, waiting, with Scott, for the Bore on a Monday morning of Arcadian rather than oceanic beauty. Near us in the water is Steve Hislop, a local sculptor. A healthy looking, tanned, bald man, Hislop has been surfing the Bore for eight years and could, given that he lives in a converted barge on the river, be said to have structured – literally and metaphorically – his life around the Bore. Other regulars are present in the world's most unusual line-up, including Stephens and James Allan, aka 'the Silver Surfer', who is regarded as one of the best Bore surfers. The atmosphere is one of relaxed bonhomie, something I feel unable to enjoy through sheer nervousness. It is one thing to look on at sundry surfers entering a flat river, and then to see them riding what appears to be an unthreatening line of white water, but it is quite another to sit in that river, waiting for the first time for the Bore's arrival.

At last, the Bore heaved into view. It was rated a two star, which equated to about two feet of frothing white water at Newnham. I caught it and proned for a while, then got to my feet only to fall at once for fear of careering into the man on my inside, none other than Scott. Frantic paddling in accordance with his directions enabled me to catch a recycled wave off a sandbank roughly opposite the White Hart Inn, but soon enough this had faded and I was paddling across the raging Severn current for an exit point. Scott, the Silver Surfer and Stephens were ahead of me. I aimed for their exit point and Stephens helped me up the bank. Mine could not be classified as a ride, but there were smiles all round. The stoke was on, and Scott, his girlfriend Hannah and I set off to chase the Bore and find another take-off point. We tried at the Severn Bore Inn, in front of a crowd of some 200 people, but the wave backed off and we failed to catch it. So off we went, closer to Gloucester, yet further inland. Near Overbridge, we slid down the riverbank and waited. The Bore came slinking round a bend and again I caught it, as did Scott, with Hannah proning at the front of his 11 ft Tiki board. There was but a foot between the two boards, and this would be the last – and only – wave of the day, and so, again, I opted to prone. I was enjoying the feeling nonetheless, and felt sure that I had made the right decision – to try to stand up would be to risk hitting Scott and Hannah, or losing the wave. Scott, though, was having none of this.

'Stand up, Alex! Stand up!' he barked. He was right. I ought to be standing up. I stood up, and once upright was surfing past trees and fields on a brown wave face so benign that it was as if it wanted me, Duncan and Hannah to be surfing. I struggle to think of any other occasion when I have ridden a wave for so long – perhaps three-quarters of a mile before my unfamiliarity with this particular break led me to lose the wave. As we approached Maismore Bridge, I looked to my right and saw a perfect wave face, unbroken, perhaps two to three feet in height. It was impossible not to turn into it, to start to carve and enjoy its sensual curves. Scott saw this, and yet hugged the left-hand side of the river. Why?

'Turn back this way or surf over to the far right!' shouted Scott. I looked to him questioningly. 'You'll lose the wave if you stay in the middle!' I understood. The way in which the river was funnelling the Bore meant that in its centre, approaching Maismore Bridge, the wave would surely dissipate. I tried to cut back to Scott, on my left, but it was too late. The wave vanished, and I sank into the mucky water of the River Severn, whose current bore me towards Gloucester almost as fast as it carried Scott and his girlfriend, upriver and beyond Maismore Bridge, on a ride of 1.1 miles. Despite the perilous time I experienced in trying to exit the raging river (my leash, as Stephens and Golding had cautioned that it might, became tangled in some branches), this was, without doubt, one of the best rides of my life.

PART THREE

Stoked at the steel works – the Porthcawl surfing experience.

13

MR STEADY AND SANTA CRUZ

New York writer Paul Solotaroff was at his wits' end. His son Luke was one of an estimated 90,000 American sufferers of a syndrome known as 'Fragile X', a mutation of the X chromosome that results in almost complete disarray of the nervous system. Luke was floppy at birth, late rolling over, late sitting up and later still crawling. His early life was spent on a carousel of medical inquisition, for since the beginning Luke was different. So different, indeed, that by the time he was two, other children would refuse to play with him. His parents, now in the midst of a divorce, called in doctors and therapists. Though it was clear that Luke was disabled his father was determined that he would be able to delight in his body like other children, and in those early years there were occasional glimpses of improvement: at three, Luke started walking, and then a little later he could run. But each tentative step forward would be followed by several in the opposite direction, until finally Luke's diagnosis was clear. The Fragile X syndrome meant that while there would be few signs of physical disability, the absence of a crucial protein in the brain would make for a lifetime of symptons ranging from shyness, slurred and repetitive speech and obsessive-compulsive behaviour to unfettered over-reaction to just about any stimuli. By the time he was seven, Luke was still a long way from being toilet trained, ate with his hands and had no idea how to tie his shoelaces. He is autistic and epileptic, and his parents, Paul and Elaine, have no idea of his IQ because he can't, or won't, follow instructions. As his father wrote in the *Observer* in December 2006: 'Picture having to live in a video arcade with the volume and wattage up full, where everyone around you is racing past, speaking Mandarin at the top of their lungs. Your shirt feels like Brillo, your shoes like cement, and the breeze on your skin like the thwack of a soaking towel that's been left to chill in the fridge. That, in a nutshell, is my little boy.'

Solotaroff, a Brooklyn-based journalist, despaired. How to improve the quality of Luke's life? One night, having collapsed on the couch to watch TV, he came across a profile of Honolulu-born Israel 'Izzy' Paskowitz, a former pro surfer who runs a surf camp in San Diego. Izzy's father, Dorian 'the Doc' Paskowitz, practised medicine in Hawaii after World War II, where he also surfed with the likes of Buffalo Keaulana. Izzy had inherited a formidable surfing legacy from his father, and dreamt of passing it on to his own son, Isaiah. But at the age of eighteen months, Isaiah changed. He became agitated and quick to throw tantrums. He, too, was diagnosed with autism.

Izzy did not, initially, cope. He lost himself on the pro surfers' tour and drank too much. But he came back, and one day at the beach as Isaiah was in the middle of a fit, suddenly conceived of taking him surfing. With Isaiah at the front of the board and Izzy steering from the back, the pair had a blast. As Solotaroff wrote: 'Riding his first swell straight into shore, Isaiah grew calm, then exultant . . . He began again to talk, his mood improved, and his frustration lessened.'

Izzy and his wife Danielle then hit upon the idea of www.surfershealing.org, which hosts day surf camps for autistic children. Now in its sixth year, Surfers Healing has blossomed so much that Izzy and Danielle were able to hold twelve free events across America in 2006. Learning of all this, Solotaroff at once wanted to take Luke to Izzy's California-based surf school, only to realize that flying his son to San Diego from New York would be desperately tough on both of them. He therefore looked closer to home, at the mercurial breaks near New York, and soon enough found himself in contact with Elliot Zuckerman of www.surf2live.com. Zuckerman is a pro surfer on Long Island, New York, and he had a suggestion: he would take Luke for a surf, in the Atlantic just a few miles from Melville's 'insular city of the Manhattoes, belted round by wharves as Indian isles by coral reefs'. As Solotaroff wrote: 'I have my doubts – I have nothing but doubts – but Elliot Zuckerman won't hear them. "Your kid will love this. Guaranteed. Never had a kid who didn't, and I've taught hundreds."'

And so Solotaroff found himself at the beach, and watched as Zuckerman took charge of Luke in blue-black 9°C water. At first, Luke hated everything that going surfing entailed – getting changed into a wetsuit, pulling on boots and gloves, the cold, the unknown quantity that is the ocean. His father's doubts intensified and he wondered if he had made a mistake. Zuckerman, though, would hear nothing of it. 'Relax,' he tells Solotaroff. 'Next time you see him he'll be blissed.' The anxious father takes himself to a nearby jetty, the better to monitor just what will happen to Luke, how he will respond to so alien and unfamiliar an environment. His fears are understandable but, it turns out, groundless. Zuckerman, who regularly teaches disadvantaged kids, has Luke surfing for over an hour, and Luke loves every minute. His 'expression is first stricken, then shocked, [then] suddenly drops into a grin so big I see spray go into his mouth,' recounts Solotaroff. 'My little boy is surfing!'

A few days later, father and son are back for more, but this time both of them take to the water. Solotaroff's efforts are largely unsuccessful, but he has never been happier. He knows that for Luke surfing is metamorphic. 'On a surfboard Luke is instantly in all his glory,' writes his father, whose optimism for his child's future has been transformed by the experience of surfing with him. At the end of their session together, chaperoned by Zuckerman, a thought occurs as Solotaroff puts his son to bed. As he puts it:

'Carrying him off to bed then, I lower him in my arms till he's horizontal. "Lukey's surfing," I sing as we sluice the room. "My brave little boy is surfing." He puts his arms out to skim the waves and says, "Whee, whee, whee" all the way in.'

For Simon Tucker, one of Britain's most accomplished surfers, the experience of Paul and Luke Solotaroff is as illustrative of what it is to be a surfer as competition glory, riding freight train tubes or making outrageous aerials. 'There are too many little heroes in surfing, people who'd eat themselves if they were chocolate,' says Tucker, who for many years lived a four days on, four days off double life as a quality controller at British Steel in Port Talbot and professional surfer based in his home-town of Porthcawl, South Wales. 'It's so easy for people to get carried away with the image, to start thinking they're something special. And when that happens, they can start to look down on people less fortunate than themselves.'

Now, aged forty-two, Tucker has escaped the steel works to work as a rep for Santa Cruz Surfboards as well as overseeing the surf school he set up at Rest Bay in 2000, the Simon Tucker Surfing Academy. Tucker's life has been surfing, but so level-headed does he seem that John Mullin, in a piece entitled 'Big Tuesday' published in the *Guardian* on 16 March 1996, found himself drawn to Tucker precisely because of his imperviousness to the stock badges of surferdom: 'Most punters, whose bare knowledge of surfing has come through *Baywatch* or *Home and Away*, will find it difficult to reconcile the glamour of US pap and Aussie soap with the realities of our coastline. Tucker, who fell in love with surfing when he was seven, is far from the stereotype such shows inspire. No flowing locks here; no scruffy clothes; no beach-babe on either arm. He has a steady job, a mortgage, a family, and, whisper it, a Ford Mondeo (dark blue).'

Mullin's image of Tucker was not one that I had grown up with. Around the time that I was getting into surfing Tucker's rivalry with Carwyn Williams, the other great Welsh surfer of the era, was food for plenty of discussion, not to mention magazine inches. The pair featured in all the British surfing magazines of the eighties and early nineties, and I even had a poster of Tucker on my wall. It was created for the Newquay Surf Classic in May 1984. One of Wales's pioneering surfers, Pete Bounds, shot Tucker trimming down the line at Billboards in Tenerife on a hazy, almost glassy day. It was the kind of wave that I dreamt of surfing. Tucker was in a stance that signified limitless possibility. Would he come back up and hit the lip, or stall and go for a cover-up? Tanned and slim; young and dark-haired; a natural-footer eyeing up the angles: Tucker, on that wave twenty-five years ago, was the surfer I wanted to be.

This memory, and the fact that he seemed to win or reach the finals of just about every surfing contest I read about all those years ago, made me a little thoughtful as I drove along the esplanade at Porthcawl, looking for Tucker's road. It was the kind of raging, windswept wintery day that makes the idea of surfing in the UK or Ireland seem nothing but the product of a collective Walter Mitty fantasy, one sustained by those in the know for their own mysterious reasons. I turned off the esplanade, grateful to escape the wind even if, sheltered in my car, its effect was less profound than it could have been, and there, as I drove along Victoria Avenue, I saw Tucker. He was wearing a black T-shirt and light-coloured trousers, was barefoot and had a shock of black hair as unruly as the wind. Waving and smiling, he gestured for me to park outside his house. Soon enough I was inside and talking, for the one and only time in my life, to a person who had been in a poster on my wall.

The adult, mid-life Tucker is still slim, and he still surfs as much as ever. And he proved to be every bit as down to earth as Mullin's *Guardian* portrait. He explained that that he took up surfing largely thanks to David, his older brother. 'David was much more single-minded than me. He was always up for waves at first light when I'd have been happy to lie in till nine. But because of David, I got dragged out of bed. Soon I'd caught the bug myself. I was well and truly hooked. I left school at sixteen to go and live in Cornwall. We've got the waves here but that's where the infrastructure of surfing has always been. I had to go there to see how far I could push my surfing.'

For a while, Tucker lived in the Newquay house of another well-known name of the eighties, Tad 'the Guv' Ciastula of Vitamin Sea Surfboards. Ciastula was better known to me for his windsurfing – my own brother Chris was one of the first, and proud, owners of a Vitamin Sea 292, one of the first wave-jumping boards to be made in Britain – but he was also a surfer, and ran a shaping business that utilized some of the best names around: Peter 'Chops' Lascelles, Chris Jones, Martin Wright and Andy Cranston. Tucker himself was retained simply to surf, and he made the most of the opportunity, becoming the British Junior Champion in 1981, a year that was a harbinger of the good things to come in Welsh surfing, with Carwyn Williams finishing runner-up. 'By my mid-teens I realized that all I wanted to do was surf,' recalls Tucker, and his dedication and talent soon took him to Australia where he competed in the 1982 Amateur World Championships. Both his local paper, the *Glamorgan Gazette*, and the Australian media in the shape of the *Gold Coast Bulletin* rolled out the clichés in their coverage.

'Riding along on the crest of a wave', ran one pre-event headline from the *Gazette*, with the copy following suit: 'Porthcawl's "super-surfers" were in action again last week – cresting the waves in their last competition before flying to the World Championships in Australia.' The text spoke of the efforts of Tucker, Mark Schofield and Brad Hockridge in the Welsh Pro-Am Championships at Llangenwydd on the Gower Peninsula. Tucker fared best of the Porthcawl trio, with a fourth place finish, and the paper summed up his life in Newquay with an avuncular, almost indulgent tone: 'Simon is widely regarded as the best British surfing prospect for many years. He is now working for a firm manufacturing surfing gear in Newquay. They realize his potential and he spends much of his time practising for the all-important World Championships in Australia.' The *Gazette* concluded by saying: 'Porthcawl is very proud of its surfing super stars and the good wishes of the town will be with them in the

World Championships in Brisbane. Here's hoping that there will be a "World Champion" at Rest Bay this summer.'

The British team even made it into the *News of the World*, but the experience was to prove educative rather than valedictory. The *Gold Coast Bulletin* delighted in casting the British team as a collection of eccentrics whose chances of success in one of the crucibles of high-performance surfing were just a mistimed takeoff away from negligible. 'Surfers from Great Britain . . . Cor Blimey!' ran one headline, and another piece set the scene thus:

> Great Britain is famous for many things ranging from Trooping the Colour, Wimbledon, big red double-decker buses and more recently a bouncing baby boy named William.
>
> But beautiful bikini girls on beaches, warm surf and boardriders – no, somehow that doesn't fit into most people's impressions of the Mother Country.

The piece conceded that there were 'plenty of boardriders' in Great Britain and included a quote from team manager Colin Wilson: 'You never know, we might give your boys a real run for their money.' The British team included Chops Lascelles, described by the *Bulletin* as 'a former Gold Coaster who has been living in England for the past eight years', who was also doubling up as his fellow competitors' 'guide to acclimatizing to Australian conditions'. Those conditions were among the best in the world: the Gold Coast is home to excellent point breaks such as Duranbah, Kirra, Currumbin Alley, Burleigh Heads, Snapper Rocks and South Stradbroke, as well as beachbreak surf at the Spit, the Main Beach and Mermaid Beach. The principal town in the area – Surfers Paradise – can be anything but, as I knew from having been marooned there, as a penniless Pom in 1989, but there is no doubting the quality of the surf.

The omens for the British team's prospects in the World Championships did not match the waves. As the *Gold Coast Bulletin* put it: 'Aussies crush Poms in titles warm-up'. The home nation 'obliterated' the British in one-metre lefts at Duranbah, taking first and second in every heat bar one. The sole success for Britain came in the form of Tucker, who won his heat. In the main event, the British team came a creditable fifth (out of fourteen teams), with one of Tucker's principal memories being of surfing over a shark. But as he told the *Glamorgan Gazette*: 'The only way we can improve is by travelling and competing against top class surfers. We saw in Australia how the experts do it.'

The experience worked a treat for Tucker, who became the British Champion in 1986. At the beginning of his surfing life he was sponsored by Devon-based Alder, whose surfwear then seemed to resemble the apparel of the contemporary yachting set: all unthreatening beiges, soft greys and light blues, a long way from much more confrontational designs peddled by the major surfing brands today. Alder's owner, Bob Westlake, set up the SS1000, the first European Professional Surfing Tour, and Tucker threw himself into life as a pro surfer in 1988. He looks back on his time as a professional surfer with a tinge of regret: 'I could never quite get the sponsorship. I did my best but it didn't quite work out.' He even went to live in California to hone his skills and compete on the Professional Surfing Association of America circuit, but ended up living with someone who had a serious cocaine problem. 'I couldn't hack that kind of life,' he says, and soon he was back in Porthcawl, disillusioned with the one thing in life that had motivated him. But, once smitten, very few people walk away from surfing. Tucker threw himself back into the domestic surfing scene, and in 1992 held three titles: the British Championship, the Welsh and the Welsh Open. He was second to Newquay's Lee Bartlett in 1995, and, despite having given up competitive surfing in 1996, to this day remains the last Welsh surfer to be British Open Champion.

Throughout, though, Tucker held down his job at British Steel. He married Melanie, a medical rep, in 1990, and the couple had Max in 1994 and Megan in 1997. Tucker was the Mr Steady of the surfing world, a marked contrast to his principal adversary, the flamboyant Carwyn Williams. 'Carwyn was a likeable rogue,' says Tucker of the Swansea-based surfer who now lives in south-west

France. 'I was more calculating. I was never late for heats, and I didn't run around naked in a hotel with my pants pinned to a dartboard.' Williams did win the European title, and scored a memorable victory in France over world champion Damien Hardman, but, during their early rivalry at least, Tucker achieved the greater competition success of the pair. He acknowledges, though, that Williams went on to achieve a higher profile. 'Carwyn was prepared to camp on the beach if he couldn't afford a hotel, just to be able to get into a contest,' he says, looking back on those years. 'He was respected by the best surfers of his era and – who knows – could have made a huge mark if he hadn't suffered that injury.' Williams had to undergo extensive surgery on his knee after a car crash, just as he appeared to be taking European surfing by storm. He made a remarkable, if protracted, recovery, and reputedly now surfs as well as ever.

Tucker hopes that his son Max, already a good surfer, will follow in his footsteps, rather than those of the mercurial Williams. 'Carwyn had it all – so much talent and so many chances. But, to me, he's still a lost soul. With Max, it's a case of keeping his feet on the ground. If one of the major corporations wanted to sponsor him I'd be stoked, but there's also a danger that kids get too much, too easily these days. It's a tough call – I look back on my life and sometimes wish I'd had better breaks with sponsors, but then again I know that it's good to experience hardship and work for your goals.'

Tucker was by turns loquacious and thoughtful during our conversation. He sung the praises of Porthcawl – 'the Newquay of Wales' – and said that his favourite wave was Thurso East. I learnt that he had once beaten Bryce Ellis, a top Australian pro of the eighties (one of whose boards I once owned), and that he thought that localism was 'all hype'. Tucker was complimentary of his workmates at British Steel, but said that he wanted, one day, to work in the surfing industry full time. For now, he would be carrying on with the four days on, four days off routine, encouraging Max in his surfing, being a father and husband, running the surf school during the summer and getting in the water whenever he could. He was, as John Mullin said in his *Gurardian* piece, 'a conventional man in a sport of daft, so-called personalities'.

What Tucker didn't tell me about was his work with Positive Futures, a government initiative to use sport and leisure activities to help children from disadvantaged, socially marginalized backgrounds. Positive Futures works around the country and its Bridgend group approached Tucker to ask him to take some children surfing. These children are not from affluent, middle-class backgrounds. They are difficult. They come from the wrong side of the tracks. They would, not so long ago, have been readily categorized as 'problem' kids, the kind that the chattering classes read about but never meet. Moreover, it would not occur to them to go to the beach, still less to try surfing, even though many of them live on its doorstep. As Louise Williams, of Bridgend Positive Futures, put it: 'These are kids who live a few miles from the beach and yet they never go. One girl lives within walking distance of the sea and has never been in the water. Even if they wanted to, they can't afford to surf. This is why we offered them taster sessions.'

Tucker took charge of the sessions, and the kids had a ball. Williams again: 'Seeing those kids standing up on the boards was beautiful. I can't describe how fantastic it was – they were so proud of themselves, and it was wonderful for their confidence. One girl who had never surfed before and who's struggled with her weight turned out to be really good, and a lad who has difficulty using the right side of his body was in the water with the rest of them and enjoying himself. Whatever their difficulties on land, in the water there were no difficulties at all.'

Williams and the Bridgend kids could not say enough good things about surfing's Mr Steady. I later learnt that he had escaped the steel works to work for Santa Cruz Surfboards. The job was going well – Tucker was making a living out of surfing, and just surfing, for the first time in his life. He had acquired a red VW Transporter van, complete with Santa Cruz logos, in favour of the dark blue Ford Mondeo. His son Max had a deal with Quicksilver, and, at Santa Cruz's slick Kenfig offices – a part of Brad Hockridge's Double Overhead empire – Tucker was in his element. But like Elliot Zuckerman and Izzy Paskowitz, he was still finding the time to bring the surfing experience to kids like Luke Solotaroff.

The kind of reeling Pembrokeshire left-hander that can turn surfing
from a passion into a religious calling.

14

THE BLESSED CHURCH OF THE OPEN SKY

Perhaps Porthcawl's most visible surfer, today, is not Simon Tucker, nor any of his contemporaries, nor the old school nor even any of the young grommets on their way up, but a Watford-born Arsenal Football Club supporter in his mid-twenties called Tom Anderson. This is because Anderson is one the very few people – not just in Britain and Ireland but worldwide – to have written a book about surfing. Anderson's *Riding the Magic Carpet*, which recounts his obsessive quest – born out of Rip Curl's *The Search* video featuring Tom Curren – to surf the fabled South African right-hand point break of Jeffrey's Bay, was published by Summersdale in summer 2006. The book at once met with a favourable reception. Surfing and travelogue have always gone together, perhaps reaching their apotheosis in magazine form in *The Surfer's Path*, and in longer prose Anderson's contagious passion is an appealing accompaniment to a journey that begins in the Orkney Islands (where he finds some wonderful waves as well as, to his amusement, a village called Twatt) and ends at Jeffrey's Bay, via France, Spain, Sri Lanka, Indonesia and Central America. Tucker himself described the book as 'capturing the real thrill of surf travel', and this it does admirably, with a neat ending to boot. Given the buzz surrounding *Riding the Magic Carpet* – as well as the fact that the Porthcawl-bred Anderson competes in a variety of UK contests – I arranged to meet him on one of a few trips to Wales.

I wasn't sure what Anderson looked like but on my arrival at our rendez-vous it was obvious that the tall, tanned man with blond hair flopping down on to his forehead – with a board stashed inside a white Nissan Micra – was Anderson. He looked like a surfer in the way that some people look like lawyers, bankers, rugby players or private investigators. Curiously, Anderson himself had once been a private investigator but it was difficult to envisage him in this role. He appeared far too healthy and robust, not to mention good-hearted, but it was a case of needs must.

'I had to bring in some money while I was writing the book,' explained Anderson, who graduated from Glamorgan University with a degree in English and Media. 'I used to investigate insurance scams, confiscate credit cards, see if one or two affairs were going on, serve a few injunctions, that sort of thing. There was an upside besides the money. It was a great job for surfing – you could always get time off to find a wave.'

With the publication of *Riding the Magic Carpet*, it struck me that Anderson was set fair – like Tucker – to make a living out of surfing and nothing else. Would he be able to do so?

'I don't know. I think the book's been well received but I'm not going to be rich overnight, if ever. I'm thinking about my options – I want to write another book but I need to bring in enough cash to survive.'

Anderson had been diligent in promoting *Riding the Magic Carpet*, a copy of which had even found its way to Salman Rushdie. 'I was at the Hay Festival of Literature and was in a queue to meet Rushdie and ask him to sign his latest book, *Shalimar the Clown*. When I got to him I said, "Thank you very much for signing your book, here's a copy of mine in return."' Anderson told me this story as we were approaching Greg Owen's No Limits Wetsuits at Fenton Place, in Porthcawl. I raised an eyebrow and asked how the celebrity novelist had greeted so bold an approach. 'Well, to be fair,' said Anderson, 'he looked like he'd been served with an injunction.'

Anderson's direct style was mirrored by many of the Porthcawl surfers to whom he introduced me. Theirs was a world refreshingly free of artifice, in which spades were pretty much always spades, except when it might be funnier to call them something else. Just before we reached Owen's premises – which we were visiting as part of a tour of Porthcawl's surfing landmarks – I learnt, thanks to a swift Anderson anecdote, that Greg Owen was in fact known to all as Owen Owen, since this was the name under which he had been entered in the European Surfing Championships in Portugal in 1997. The mistake was made by a Portuguese official, and throughout the contest, to his increasing exasperation, Greg Owen was summoned for heats as 'Owen Owen'.

Nicknames seem to play a large part in Welsh surfing. As we stopped to view the Esp, a shallow, fast left-hand reef break on Porthcawl seafront, Anderson asked if I was planning to meet any of 'The Gill', 'PJ', 'Guts', 'Frenchie' or 'Herbie'. The names that rung the most bells for me were those of PJ, one of the UK's most respected surfers, and Paul 'The Gill' Gill, a photographer, B&B owner and shaper based in Mumbles. 'You've got to meet The Gill,' declared Anderson, as we retreated from another wind-lashed Porthcawl day to Pietro's café, a place that overlooks the Esp. 'He's the fount of all surfing knowledge, not just in Wales but all over Britain and Ireland. Europe, as well. In fact, everywhere. The Gill is the man.'

The others, said Anderson, were also all well worth talking to – not least Huw 'Herbie' John, for many years the chairman of the Welsh Surfing Federation. As we were chatting one of the café's waiters hailed Anderson, and the pair fell into a discussion about poker. Dave Daley was not only one of twin brothers known in and around the line-ups of Porthcawl, he was also a fine Texas hold 'em player. The game – 'the Cadillac of poker', according to Doyle Brunson, one of the all-time Las Vegas greats – has been sweeping the world thanks to its online boom, and some of Porthcawl's surfers have embraced it with almost as much fervour as they bring to the surf of their main breaks, those at Rest Bay, the Cove, Coney Beach, the Esp and the Point. 'If you fancy a game, you're welcome,' offered Anderson. 'Herbie plays a bit too – we could try to get him along.'

In the event, Herbie wasn't able to make the game, though we arranged to meet him later for drinks at the Jolly Sailor, a pub in Porthcawl. Earlier, neither Anderson nor I prevailed in a small stakes game held at his father's house, where Anderson still lives. In between hands, as our chip stacks diminished thanks to the unexpectedly cunning play of Porthcawl photographer Peter Britton, I asked Anderson for some thoughts on surfing and literature. Why, given the popularity of surfing worldwide, was there comparatively little written about it? If there is a surfing canon it is a small one, with American writer Kem Nunn arguably at its summit thanks to novels such as *The Dogs of Winter* and *Tapping the Source*. Eugene Burdick's *The Ninth Wave* was a slice of surf noir to predate Nunn, and there is also Fiona Capp's *Night Surfing*. Tom Wolfe, Jack London, Herman Melville and Mark Twain are literary giants who have found inspiration in surfing, and non-fiction books such as Daniel Duane's *Caught Inside*, Matt Warshaw's *Maverick's* and Allan Weisbecker's *In Search of Captain Zero* – not to mention our own Andy Martin's *Walking on Water* and *Stealing the Wave* – are also literary works. But they are notable as much for their rarity as the quality of their authors' prose. In contrast, a sport such as boxing has a vast, apparently unending literary tradition. Lest it be thought that this is obvious, because boxing was, for many years, the most popular sport in the world, the same is also true of mountaineering – a minority, so-called 'extreme' sport with a tradition of exceptional writing. What had gone wrong with surfing?

Anderson was as puzzled as I was. 'There's a preconception that most surfers aren't academic or intellectual, that they wouldn't be interested in reading, but that's not how it is, certainly not today, anyway. But you're right, when you think of how massive surfing is worldwide it's strange that so few mainstream writers, or writers who are surfers, have tackled it.' We wondered whether it might be because surfing – in contrast to boxing and mountaineering – is that little bit more enigmatic. To borrow Fiona Capp's notion of the 'idea of surfing', the 'idea' of mountaineering or boxing is simple, even to those who have never donned crampons or laced up a pair of boxing gloves. But surfing? The 'idea of surfing' is, to many people, very difficult to understand.

There was plenty to ponder but I found myself facing a heavy bet from Britton, whose surfing photography appears in a variety of magazines including *Pit Pilot, Wavelength* and Wales's own *Tonnau*. With so few chips left there was nothing for it but to call the bet and hope for the best. Britton had me drawing dead and my poker for the evening was over. I wondered what Anderson's father, Paul, made of us playing the game, given that for many years he has been heavily involved with Christian Surfers UK. Anderson senior did mention that he didn't approve of poker, correctly describing it as 'a game of deceit', but did so in a gentle, almost wry manner. Indeed, he was amenable to a fault. A religious man, his bearing in person was rather less evangelical than that of www.christiansurfers.co.uk, whose October 2006 newsletter, under the heading 'Summer Outreaches', contained a curious update on the Rip Curl Boardmasters and my suspicions about the inveterate wildness of skateboarders:

> We have been heavily involved in a number of summer outreaches again this year. These included the Rip Curl Boardmasters – which was tough, as we did not have a stall this time – and the Love Bristol Festival. One of the high points of the festival was when 34 youngsters, many of whom were skaters, committed their lives to God for the first time after a showing of the outreach movie *Kaleidoscope*. This was an incredible breakthrough and a massive encouragement to us. We then went straight on to Creation Fest and this last weekend held the Nailsea Skate Comp – which again was a real blessing to so many people. We met up with some of the skaters who had committed their lives. Part of God's long-term strategy is for us to be encouraged to reach out, to dig deep and be in it for the long haul.

Reading this, it was hard not to detect an air of sustained positive thinking, but there is no doubting the recent success of Christian

Surfers in the UK. The Jesus Surf Classic, held at Croyde, is widely regarded as one of the best surfing contests of the year, and even if stall-less for the 2006 Rip Curl Boardmasters word continues to spread of Christian Surfers' aims. They are twofold: 'to present the Gospel to surfers in a relevant and meaningful way', and 'to encourage [the] Christian growth, commitment and discipleship of surfers'. Theirs is not, though, a faith à la Tom Blake, the great early-twentieth-century surfing pioneer. Blake, whose surfing exploits are the stuff of legend, was a Romantic poet in inclination, believing that Nature was God and vice-versa. He practised what he preached in what he described as 'the blessed church of the open sky', but while Christian Surfers undoubtedly do likewise they take a more traditional view: 'We are Christians simply because we realize that we have messed up our lives and have asked Jesus to come and take control, making him the boss of our lives and our surfing too. However, we know that God is not just a myth up in the sky, and from this point, we can enjoy a radical relationship with the creator of the ocean and the surf.' Elsewhere, the group makes no bones about its evangelizing stance, but if this, to some, might be laying it on a bit thick, very few surfers would disagree with this statement on the Christian Surfers website: 'Sitting out the back, waiting for the next set, it's impossible not to be impressed by the creation around us.'

In Huw 'Herbie' John, Porthcawl and Welsh surfing has a man whose feet have only ever been firmly on the ground. Now the president of the Welsh Surfing Federation and for many years its chairman, Herbie is also the vice-president of the European Surfing Federation. He is dark-haired and swarthy, a strong and fit-looking man in his late-forties who works as a construction manager. Herbie grew up surfing in South Wales, and still surfs whenever time allows. As I learnt over the course of a few pints in the Jolly Sailor, he is a straight-talking man whose impressive natural confidence and sturdy bearing cast him readily as a Celtic version of Tim Heyland.

'I started surfing when I was eleven but dropped it for a while,' he told me, as the pints slipped down nicely later on the same cold, damp night in which Peter Britton had vanquished Anderson and me at Texas hold 'em. 'I played rugby instead and also did a lot of horse riding. But you know what it's like. Once you've surfed you always come back to it. I got back on a board when I was about eighteen, and have surfed ever since.'

Why, though, had he become so involved in the politics of surfing?

'I didn't think the Welsh were getting a fair crack. Back then, in my early twenties, surfing was dominated by all things Cornish, but I wanted to do something to bring on Welsh competitive surfing and to highlight the quality of the surf we've got here. To be fair, I think it's levelled out now. I don't think any one area is favoured more than another. Surfing has changed so much since then in so many other ways, too.'

Such as?

'It's easier. Boards are cheaper, lighter, easier to ride. Wetsuits are warmer. Websites tell everybody where to surf at exactly what time. And you can do what I'm doing soon – take a flight to the Mentawai Islands, charter a boat and surf perfect reef breaks all day long. No hassle. If anyone had told me, back in the day, that's what I'd be doing as a forty-eight-year-old surfer I'd have laughed my head off.'

When I asked Herbie if the changes were for the better, he was unusually stumped for words. Eventually he said simply: 'I don't know. I just don't know.' Then he remembered something he'd recently witnessed. 'I was driving home past Rest Bay. There was a reasonable swell and a few lads were still in the water. Then I saw a group of girls walking up from the beach, in wetsuits, carrying boards. That was a pretty rare sight in my day. But that's a good thing. It's a great thing for more people, especially women, to be getting into the sport. That's a change for the better.'

Herbie did say, though, that breaking new ground had been one of the best things about surfing as a youth in Wales: 'There was always a sense of adventure. The lads before us had started things but it wasn't all known and discovered when we came along. It was still new. I'm not sure that same sense of being a pioneer exists for people coming to surfing today. But I'd still say to a young man or woman who wants to get some great waves, you can do a lot worse than jump in a van and travel the British Isles and Ireland. You'll meet some absolutely brilliant characters.'

When pressed, though, Herbie didn't want to single any one person out. 'There are so many that if I named ten people, I'd feel bad about another fifty who I hadn't mentioned. We'd be here all night.' Eventually, though, he agreed that I was right to be searching for two particular surfers based in Wales: PJ and The Gill. 'Incredible characters, those two. But listen, there are hundreds of others. I'm lucky to have met them because of my involvement in surfing. I consider myself wealthy because of the people I've met right here in Britain and Ireland.'

Herbie also credited Dave Reed with having done a lot for surfing and did not agree with the view that the BPSA was wrong to host each of its Welsh contests at Freshwater West, a break in Pembrokeshire that will have a wave when everywhere else is flat, but which is also miles from anywhere and lacking in all but the most rudimentary facilities. As Herbie put it: 'OK, Freshwater West is a long way from Porthcawl but it's still the only logical place to host the event. It's an effort to get to but it's the only place in Wales where you can guarantee there'll be a wave.'

Fresh West, as its surfers know it, is a dramatic, exposed beach, sandy at low tide but with a mixture of sand, rock and pebbles at high water. The beach is huge, meaning that left and right-hand peaks can be found along its entire length, and it will hold waves up to 8 ft before becoming unmanageable. Nearby is the Castlemartin firing range, and if this might set alarm bells ringing that is perhaps a good thing: Freshwater West has a year-round red flag status, and its fierce rips have resulted in many swimmers getting into trouble, often to be rescued by surfers. A summer's paddle at Freshwater West can also be disrupted by the one marine creature that perennially harms bathers off British waters: the weaver fish.

At a mere 15 cm the weaver fish would appear far less threatening than the basking sharks that cruise the Atlantic seaboard. The difference is that though basking sharks can grow to the length of a double-decker bus, they feast on plankton and are wholly non-aggressive to humans. This does not mean that the experience of sitting in the line-up at, say, Sennen Cove in Cornwall (one of their regular haunts in summer) and seeing a basking shark's dorsal fin scything through the water next to you is anything less than terrifying. Scary, yes, but the weaver fish is king when it comes to inflicting pain on surfers in our waters. It is an unusual fish in that as soon as it stops swimming it sinks, which might be a factor in its decision to bury itself in the sand during the day. There it lurks, to snatch prey such as shrimp and other small fish, and if that was all that it did, no one would rue the day the weaver fish ever came to town. However, weaver fish – or, to describe them correctly, 'weevers' (from the old French word 'wiwvre', meaning serpent or dragon) – have poisonous spines on their first dorsal fin and gills. Stepping on a weaver fish, something that tends to occur at low tide during summer, is a highly unpleasant experience, and one that surfers and swimmers in Wales seem to have suffered more than most. The *South Wales Evening Post* reported on 8 August 2000 that forty weaver fish stings are recorded in the Swansea and Gower area every year, while habitués of Freshwater West remember 2003 as a year in which the fish were out in force. Once stung by a weaver fish, symptoms include nausea, headaches, itching, cramps and tremors, though there has been only one recorded death (as long ago as 1927, when a fisherman off Dungeness apparently suffered multiple stings). Lifeguards treat stings on an almost daily basis, though whether they deploy one of folklore's remedies – urinating on the afflicted body part – is doubtful. Immersion in hot water, though, is the remedy, until such time as the pain has eased.

Despite the weaver fish's evident predilection for Pembrokeshire, a visitor cannot but be struck by the beauty of this part of Wales, a landscape reminiscent of Penwith in the far west of Cornwall but on a larger scale. Designated a national park in 1952, the coastline in the south is one of lush, rolling hills and windswept cliff-tops – carpeted in spring and summer with flowers – overlooking beaches of pure white sand. The industrialism of South Wales has yet to have been left behind, however, thanks to the Texaco refinery near Pembroke Dock. Rarely a day goes by without an oil tanker hugging the horizon, but to the north, approaching St David's, the landscape changes. The coastal scenery is more rugged, houses seem to be few and far between, the industrial heartbeat of Wales a distant memory. Pembrokeshire as a whole abounds with bays seemingly facing every direction, meaning that quality waves can be found – so long as there is swell – even on the most stormy days. One of them, the beachbreak at Broadhaven, is a doppelganger for what *Tonnau*, in its second issue, described as Ecuador's 'Amplio Asilo', a heavy, murky wave on whose face Mumbles surfer Chris 'Guts' Griffiths is featured bottom turning.

Yorkshire-born freelance journalist and surfer Alf Alderson found himself sufficiently captivated by Pembrokeshire's uncrowded line-ups to move there in the late 1980s. The blond-haired, muscular 48-year-old, who skis and mountain bikes as much as he surfs, has remained a resident of Solva, near St David's Bay, ever since, and adores north Pembrokeshire's wildness as much today as he did when he first arrived, not least because of what surfing represents to its inhabitants: 'It's beautiful, remote and wild here, and you can still go surfing on your own or with just a few friends. It's one of the few places left where surfing is just one of various things that people might do. Being a surfer – having all the gear and the badges, having the look and talking the talk – counts for nothing round here.'

Alderson's joy in the ruggedness of Pembrokeshire is perhaps further influenced by his disillusion with the surfing industry. In the 1990s Alderson was the editor of a now defunct surfing magazine but he is far from yearning for a return to his old job: 'I was glad to get out of it. The backstabbing and whining within the industry – one supposedly full of "soul" and the celebration of life – was surprising and disappointing.' He is no fan of contests, either, finding them 'in most cases to be boring, crowded and over-hyped'. Now at work on an update of *Surf UK*, one of the first guide books on UK surfing, Alderson is able to apply a frank assessment of surfing's problems in relation to his own place in the sport. He says that *Surf UK* was 'a labour of love' but that it met with approval from the vast majority of surfers whose local beaches he described: 'People were, on the whole, proud of their breaks and quite happy to have them featured in the book. Whether that will remain the case when I update it remains to be seen. The possibility of being given a hard time by locals who were still in nappies when I first surfed and wrote about "their" breaks is interesting, but I guess I'll also come across the conundrum of seeing most spots busy when the swell is good and wondering: would they have been thus if I and others hadn't written about them? Then again, would today's possessive locals even have got into surfing if people like me hadn't introduced them to the sport in the first place?'

Alderson's dismay at surfing's incarnation in the early twenty-first century, allied with the fact that he was updating *Surf UK*, struck me as emblematic of one of surfing's paradoxes. Surfers crave uncrowded waves, and yet they need at least the bare modicum of information to find them. In the early days of British and Irish surfing, that information might have consisted merely of an ordnance survey map and a weather report, but as new waves were discovered the fundamental human urge to tell stories – to convey yet more information – proved as uncontrollable as the sea itself. And so to yet another conundrum: is it possible, given human nature, to experience the joy of surfing and *not* tell anyone about it? Alderson's favourite surfers made the debate all the richer: 'If I had to name anyone it would be Nick Noble and Gary Rogers of Saltburn for their undying enthusiasm. And Mark 'Yorkie' Axelby of Mumbles for his undying cynicism.'

Given Alderson's views, it was no surprise that he didn't attend the Headworx Welsh Open on 24 and 25 September 2005. It may once have been his scene, but it wasn't anymore. However, Steve Bough had asked me to write about it for *Wavelength*, and the report I filed went as follows:

After the disappointment of the Highland Open at Thurso, when a disappearing swell led to the abandonment of the contest at semi-final stage, the weather gods chose to smile favourably on the fifth event of the BPSA Tour, the Headworx Welsh Open at Freshwater West.

Day one dawned with overcast skies and a chill in the air but with reasonably clean three-foot sets in the middle of the remote bay. The event kicked off with the Men's Open and saw some fine off-the-tops from Joss Ash in a heat won by early stand-out, Irish champion Cain Kilcullen. Danny Wells and Toby Atkins were also surfing well and the huge turns made by Duncan Scott caught the eye. After round one of the Men's Open the grommets and longboarders took centre stage, in a swell dropping off as the tide retreated. Croyde's Lyndon Wake took the grommet draw and Welshman Elliot Dudley gave his compatriots cause for cheer with strong surfing to take the longboard title.

There were a few sore heads on Sunday morning after the previous night's Headworx party. Freshwater West greeted them with clear skies and balmy temperatures, but a huge and horrible swell. The wind was onshore at around force three and the paddle-out time doubled from Saturday's five minutes. The only people in the water anywhere along the beach were the pros, which gives an idea of how testing conditions had become. Some, though, were in their element – among them, once again, the 'Flying Irishman', Cain Kilcullen, who smacked the lip of a bomb of a wave and flew down the line, scoring well but not enough to prevail in his heat over Mark Harris. Harris scored an 8.5 with a great wave full of top turns and cutbacks – was this a harbinger of things to come?

Not if the big names had anything to do with it. Sam Lamiroy won his heat, as did 2004 champion Alan Stokes and current tour leader Reubin Pearce. Oli Adams was looking good and Toby Atkins bagged himself £250 for the weekend's best cutback. Richie Mullins threw in some powerful bottom turns and clearly meant business. It was hotting up nicely for the later stages, before which the women took to the water. Kay Holt had returned to competition and having won every BPSA event she has ever entered made for an intimidating opponent. But in the tough conditions of the Welsh Open, where paddling was at a premium, her record was broken by tour leader Nicole Morgan, who took the women's title.

Before the conclusion of the Men's Open Oli Adams won the Pro Junior. The swell held and the crowd was treated to an exciting men's final featuring Lamiroy, Harris, Llewellyn Whittaker and Johnny Fryer. A few people had tipped Lamiroy – who surfed well all weekend – to take the event, but the man of the moment was Mark 'Egor' Harris. The 24-year old from Newquay topped his 8.5 in the heats with an 8.83 on one wave and took home the winner's booty of £1,000.

Harris's win puts him within paddling distance of Reubin Pearce at the top of the leaderboard, with Whittaker and Adams lurking just below. Three events remain – at the Isle of Wight, Cayton in Yorkshire and Newquay – but if Harris surfs as he did this weekend, the smart money might just be on him.

I omitted two thoughts. The first, as I stood in the howling winds watching the pro surfers paddling out into a hideous sea that I wouldn't have chanced had I been paid to do so, was that Freshwater West would be a very good venue for a Christian Surfers' version of Blake's blessed church of the open sky. The place felt raw and insatiable, as if the ocean could never have enough of raging on to the soft sands, battering the nearby headland and cliffs and generally wreaking havoc. If anyone wanted to confront the sublime and experience the transcendental here was as good a place as any, provided that enough shelter from the wind could be found, which essentially meant hiding behind Anton Roberts' van and listening to him inject his amusing commentary into the elements. The second, rather more heretical thought was that this was, indeed, a destination for which the word 'far-flung' might have been invented. Arriving in the vicinity of the beach on the Friday night before the contest, it took me at least an hour to find my way around the maze of country lanes to the B&B into which I'd also booked Karen and our sons. Even in daylight the journey there, from all but the closest towns and villages, is an exercise in stoicism. Would Porthcawl – a bustling and convenient seaside town with a variety of beaches capable of working in different swells and winds – make a more user-friendly location for the Welsh Open? Among those who held this view were Simon Tucker – a former Welsh Open winner – and Tom Anderson, but Herbie's point was irrefutable: there was always a wave at Freshwater West.

Anderson's qualms about the Welsh Open's whereabouts did not stop him perennially entering the event and giving it his all. Unfortunately for him, every time he showed up at Freshwater West he seemed to fall prey to the kind of bad karma that fascinated one of his literary heroes, Jack Kerouac. The last instance was in 2006, when, once again, Freshwater West was subject to a beast of a swell.

'I couldn't enter the 2005 Welsh Open because I'd broken my leg playing football,' says Anderson, 'but I was determined to focus for the 2006 event. The buoys were registering ten-foot surf every ten seconds, and with the waves worked into a lather by thirty-five mile an hour southerly winds it was the sort of weekend that makes you want to do anything but drive all the way to Fresh West for a surf. But I was determined to banish a few demons. So far every time I'd turned up something had gone wrong, but maybe this time the lottery of the 6 ft storm surf would come to the aid of the underdog.'

It wasn't to be. Three-time Welsh Open winner Greg (or Owen) Owen was an early casualty. He returned to the shore, said Anderson, to describe conditions as 'a nightmare'. Upon paddling out, the young author soon found this to be an apposite description. 'It was unbelievably energy-sapping out there, but in the end I simply made a mistake. I didn't show the kind of commitment needed and thought too much. My demons beat me again.'

Anderson had been poised to make it through to the semi-finals, but ultimately Llangennith goofy footer James Jones would emerge as the event's winner. In doing so, he emulated his father, PJ, who had held the title decades before.

Still surfing, still smiling – Pete Jones.

15

PJ AND THE PRINCE

If Porthcawl, with its claim to be 'the Newquay of Wales', and Pembrokeshire, a place of rather more untamed aspect, represent two opposing sides of the Welsh surfing spectrum, there is no doubting its epicentre: the Gower Peninsula. It is here that Welsh surfing is at its most intense, competitive and, indeed, venerable. As Carwyn Williams put it in the *Stormrider* guide: 'The Gower Peninsula is Wales' premier surfing area, ideally located to receive swells generated by mid and south Atlantic low pressure systems. The rugged, scenic coastline offers a wide variety of breaks, most within sheltered bays providing waves which smugglers rode in on centuries ago. These bays now offer secrets for the dedicated surfer to find.' Williams added a cautionary note: 'I grew up in a spot called Langland Bay where I had to learn respect for the locals who were, by rights, the best surfers in the country. You would never paddle out onto the best breaks in the bay unless you did it early in the morning, or you were encouraged by the crew.' On the right day, the surf could be 'brilliant', but there was no escaping the prevailing weather – 'gale force winds and rain'. For Williams, though, this bred 'the hardcore element into Welsh surfing . . . We don't mind that at all so long as there's surf.' Williams concluded with a touch of self-deprecatory Welsh sang-froid: 'It's touch and go whether you'll get perfect waves if you come to the Gower, but there are a few characters to meet, the night life in Mumbles is classic – and the sheep are friendly.'

I was unable to confirm Williams' assertion about the Gower sheep, but in every other respect he was bang on the money. The infamous 'Mumbles mile' seems to have as many pubs, nightclubs and restaurants as paving stones, some of which may have been sampled by two of Swansea's most famous residents, Dylan Thomas and Catherine Zeta Jones. Mumbles itself is a quaint fishing village within a Welsh rugby song of Swansea, a city whose high street on a Friday or Saturday night is not for the faint-hearted.

The notion of 'heart' – which, in boxing, denotes a never-say-die commitment to the cause come what may – is something to which the Welsh often seem to have the exclusive rights. Joe Calzaghe, 'the pride of Wales' and pound for pound one of the greatest boxers the world has seen over the last twenty years, has it in spades and so, too, do any number of Welsh rugby teams, past and present. On my trips to the Gower or the Mumbles I would often find myself reflecting on clichés such as 'Celtic passion' or 'Welsh heart', wondering if these were lazy stereotypes of no more value than a surfboard *sans* fins. And yet every time my lukewarm response to platitudinous language would be about to rear its head, I would meet a Welsh surfer who not only confirmed the clichés but made them seem eminently acceptable. Chief among them was Pete Jones, 'PJ' to everyone in British and Irish surfing, one of the most charismatic people I have ever met.

PJ was in my sights thanks to any number of recommendations from people, not to mention the high profile he has held in domestic surfing for decades. There is a plethora of fine surfers in the Gower – from Pete Bounds, Chris 'Guts' Griffiths, 'The Gill,' Isaac Kibblewhite and Nathan Phillips to Beth Mason, Rebecca Templeton, Simon Jayham, 'Frenchie', and 'Swinno' – but PJ seems to hover above them like an amiable Buddhist, at ease with everything and everyone, a man with nothing to prove and no one to impress, because if ever someone could be said to be a 'soul surfer' it is the man from Llangennith, a village on the western fringes of the Gower.

My first attempt to meet PJ proved unsuccessful. I arrived at his eponymous surf shop on the small village green in Llangennith village, some sixteen miles from Swansea and within a couple of miles of the enchanting Rhossili Bay, on a rather lacklustre day, the kind that induces apathy thanks to the absence of anything save for a uniformly grey sky. There was no sign of life in the shop, so I popped across the road to the King's Head, Llangennith's one and only pub. Here, too, little was happening. It was out of season, and aside from the intermittent chatter of the barman and one or two regulars there was not a sound. I drove to the beach to check the surf, thinking that perhaps PJ had downed tools for some water time. Once at the bay – the first area in Britain to be designated an Area of Outstanding Natural Beauty, in 1957 – I found clean and crisp lines of swell whose contours, on the pale horizon, merged with the sky. It was low tide, and three women were carrying longboards to the sea, but aside from them and a man walking a dog, the length and breadth of the beach appeared to be deserted. To the south, the rocky outcrop known as Worm's Head was exposed, and on the sand a number of objects seemed to protrude, rather like the standing stones to be found in Celtic Britain and Ireland. I learnt subsequently that they were the oaken carcass of the *Helvetica*, a timber-carrying ship wrecked off Rhossili Bay on 1 November 1887, but initially gave these strange, distant forms little thought. There was surf, small but clean, and paddling out was irresistible.

A couple of hours later I returned to PJ's Surf Shop. Again there was no one there, not even when I tried phoning the number left on the door in the event that the shop was empty. Either PJ was on holiday or the surf elsewhere on the Gower was juicier than the complaisant waves of Rhossili Bay, but either way I decided against wiling away my time in the King's Head, though on another visit to Llangennith did precisely that in the congenial company of Kirsty Jones, a kitesurfer based on the Gower. She, too, could not say enough good things about PJ. 'He's lovely!

You've got to meet him! He's a wonderful man and a brilliant surfer.' Jones, twenty-six, has made a name for herself as an intrepid kitesurfer, and her good looks and fine physique mean that she also works as a model. Tanned and with long blond hair, dressed in casual surf-wear, Jones enlivened a damp Wales day with her enthusiasm not just for kitesurfing but the sport's forebears, windsurfing and surfing.

'I learned to windsurf first, when I was sixteen,' the Carmarthenshire-bred woman told me. 'By eighteen I'd got into surfing, but I was successful in windsurfing contests and so I went to Maui to push myself to a higher level. It was there that I picked up kitesurfing.' Prior to that, Jones had spent time at Brandon Bay on Ireland's Dingle Peninsula, where she windsurfed with Jamie Knox, another person whom she heartily recommended I meet. Despite doing well in wave-sailing events in Ireland, Jones had gone on to become one of Britain's few professional kitesurfers. The sport, which involves attaching footstraps to a slimmed down windsurfing board and wearing a harness at the end of which is a large kite, combines the speed of windsurfing with the elegance of surfing, with the extra spice of oodles of 'hang-time'. Kitesurfing goes from strength to strength in the UK, and its organizing body, the British Kite Surfing Association (formed in 1999), hosts a number of events throughout the year. My home town of Exmouth now boasts a sizeable kitesurfing community, with Stephanie Rowsell's Edge Watersports having taken up residency on the Duck Pond near the mouth of the River Exe. My old friend, Exmouthian and fellow windsurfer/surfer Elliot is now a dedicated kitesurfer, but for all that kitesurfing has as good a claim to be the 'fastest-growing extreme sport' as any, what struck me in talking to Jones – a British champion in 2002 – was how much she loved surfing.

'It's the purest water sport of all,' said the woman whose ambidexterity means that she surfs as a regular foot and kitesurfs as a goofy. 'Surfing strips everything away and you return to the fundamentals. I love it.' Jones' passion for surfing has seen her paddle out often in Ireland ('Coomeenole and Inch on the Dingle

Peninsula – just wonderful'), South Africa, New Zealand and Hawaii, and it survives even a poor session. 'Even when you feel that you've encountered nothing but wall after wall of white water you learn something. It's always invigorating, just being in the sea, and even if you're exhausted and not surfing well the experience is therapeutic.'

Jones was a fine advocate for any of windsurfing, kitesurfing and surfing, but she would agree that if there were to be an ambassadorial role within surfing, it would have to go to PJ. I turned up again at his shop on a quiet September day, having first checked the surf at Rhossili. It was flat, and on the way back from the beach to Llangennith I quickly rang Robyn Davies. For once I got through to her, to learn that she was keen to meet up. We left it that I would call her again once I'd left Wales. Suitably chipper, I pushed open the door to PJ's Surf Shop. There, sitting behind the counter, was one of the few surfers to have shaken hands with royalty. 'Hello there, what can I do for you?' were PJ's first words, uttered with a warm, friendly lilt.

I explained what I was doing, to be told that PJ himself had written a book on surfing. 'In 1978, it was,' he said, 'there was a series of "World of" books. There was a *World of Golf*, a *World of Rugby*, a *World of* a lot of things. They asked me to write a *World of Surfing*. It was a great project.'

Had the book been published?

'No, the publishers went bust. Shame. I'd written 60,000 words and the front cover was of Mark Richards doing a cutback at Off The Wall.'

There were echoes of Anderson and *Riding the Magic Carpet* when PJ divulged the upside to writing a book whose manuscript he still possessed. 'It meant I got to go to South Africa and surf Jeffrey's Bay. Amazing. Etched on my memory for ever.'

1978 was a significant year for PJ. What is now PJ's Surf Shop started then, initially as a low-key venture from the back of a van before, in 1982, establishing itself in Llangennith. PJ was freshly crowned as the European Surfing Champion, a title which he won at Freshwater West in 1977 within hours of the birth of his son

James. 'My mother rang me to tell me I had a little boy very late on the night after I'd got through the semi-final stage. To say that I was inspired when I surfed in the final would be a massive understatement.' Curiously, when I met PJ, it was just days after James had become the Welsh Open Champion at Freshwater West, making the pair the first father and son duo to hold a domestic surfing title. James himself had won the event while his wife, Lisa, was pregnant with their son Jac.

PJ was one of the original Gower surfers. He started in 1967, and never looked back. 'A friend lent me his board, a big old 9 ft log. I was a good swimmer so paddling out was no problem. I got up first time, on the white water. It was a great feeling, riding that pulse of energy, but I didn't really know anything about surfing. I suppose surfing found me before I knew what it was, but that was it. I didn't want to give the board back. It was the mid- to late-sixties, a time of great freedom, and I dropped out completely. I saw my father working in the steel works but didn't want my life to be like that. I just wanted to surf.'

And surf he did, religiously. PJ devoted himself to his new discovery with such commitment, allied with natural ability, that he won Welsh, British and European titles and surfed all over the world. Initially a shortboarder, he didn't ride a longboard until 1978, but now rides whatever board is suitable for the conditions and enters the occasional longboard competition. He wonders whether competitiveness has been detrimental to surfing's essence: 'I don't think surfing has lost its soul but the growth of the competition scene from the mid-seventies parallels a growth in localism, and that's not a good thing. Localism is a cancer in surfing but I try to engender good vibes in the water. Youngsters need to be in touch with the spirit of surfing – it's a way of life, being out there in the sea, feeling the wind and the energy of the waves. It's been my life, anyway – I've never planned anything, I've lived as if I'm riding a wave. I've just taken off to see what'll happen.'

PJ's wife, Carol, joined us, and smiled at this. The way in which the couple met is classic PJ. 'I was running along the beach, up and down the sand dunes, and was actually seeing another girl at the time. But then I saw Carol. It was love at first sight. I kept on running the same route, every day, and first she smiled at me, then she said "hi", and then after a few weeks of this I summoned enough courage to ask her out.'

PJ still surfs as much as he did in the heady days of falling in love with Carol. In fact, he says that he enjoys his surfing now more than ever. 'I can paddle out here or in Cornwall, almost anywhere really, and there'll be someone I know. There's such a spirit among the old crew. I surf today without any pressure, just to relax, to enjoy myself. There's no ego and there never was. Ego shouldn't be a part of surfing.' He has a lot of time for his son James's surfing – 'I was thrilled when he won the Welsh Open, he's a great surfer' – and for that of Sennen Cove's Sam Bleakley: 'About ten years ago I was at Watergate Bay for a longboard contest. A young kid paddled out, a lanky lad, and I wondered "who's this?" Then I saw him surfing with so much grace and style – fantastic. Real soul. The kind of thing that surfing's all about.'

It was a pleasure listening to PJ and Carol, two people whose happiness was obvious and whose joy at their son's recent success was as pleasing as the rows of pristine surfboards stacked within the shop. Moreover, PJ was the epitome of good health: lean, fit and glowing, his modest stature belied by the élan that emanated from him. It was impossible not to conclude that if surfing could bestow such well-being, both physical and mental, it had to be a good thing. This may, indeed, have been the conclusion of His Royal Highness the Prince of Wales, who, in 1978, invited PJ and other notable British surfers to a reception at Buckingham Palace.

'The Prince was the patron of the British Surfing Association,' recalls PJ. 'I think he might have tried surfing, I'm not sure. Anyway, he invited a few of us to the palace to meet him. There was me, Linda Sharp, Graham Nile, Pete Bounds, Steve Daniel, Mike Cunningham, Nigel Semmens – about thirty of us in all. I drove up with the Welsh crew in a green Mercedes that we hired for the occasion. We had our suits in the boot and got changed out of our shorts and sandals in the car park underneath Hyde Park. I put on a pair of Cuban heels that made me at least 5′ 8″, but Pete Bounds forgot his shoes! We had to leg it and buy a pair in Oxford Street. Once we were all suited up, we drove down to the palace, with Mike Cunningham at the wheel. We were waved straight through into the quadrangle, and I remember thinking "surfing has given me this experience". We were ushered into a room upstairs, very posh and elegant, and we huddled around in small groups, all feeling nervous. I was standing with Pete Bounds, a tall, long-haired bloke from Wales with a moustache, and Graham Nile, a shaggy-haired Cornishman from St Austell.'

PJ's own moustache is, to this day, one of his trademark features, and it did not go unnoticed by His Royal Highness.

'The Prince walked in, wearing a suit, and started talking to us. We were all in awe. He came up to my group and peered at us, and then said, "I notice a lot of you surfers have moustaches. Do they keep you warm in the winter?" We fell about laughing. To this day I can still recall the boom of Graham's laughter.'

PJ showed me a photograph of him, Linda Sharp, Mike Cunningham, Rawlyn Morgan, Denzil Smith and Pete Bounds taken on the Buckingham Palace inner quadrangle. The sextet do indeed look at once bemused and delighted to be wearing their suits at the British monarchy's ancestral home, though I couldn't help but observe that the picture looked more like one from a wedding reception than a meeting with royalty. 'You're right,' said PJ, 'it looks like Linda and I have just got married.'

As I was chuckling over one of the more unexpected of surfing's *tableaux*, I caught sight of a postcard next to the counter. It was of a blond surfer in boardshorts arcing his body through the mid-section of a cutback. There was something familiar about the surfer, though when I scrutinized it more closely I couldn't determine who it was. On the back, though, were the words: 'Featured surfer: Zed Layson'.

As I drove away from Llangennith, one of the prettiest, most peaceful villages in the UK, my thoughts turned back to Porthcawl; specifically, to the woman standing next to PJ in the

Buckingham Palace photograph, Linda Sharp. On a day of good surf and constant rain I met Sharp, fifty-three, a surfer from Aberavon who is arguably the most successful amateur in British surfing history. Sharp has won the British Ladies' title ten times, the Welsh Open nineteen times, and the European title twice. She was so good a surfer that in the mid-seventies she would often enter men's events, only to have her progress curtailed at the semi-final stage if she was doing well ('they needed to have an all-male final so that they could pick teams,' she told me, recalling with complete equanimity the fact that she would then be disinvited from continuing to compete). Sharp started surfing at around the same time as PJ, and has lived with Huw 'Herbie' John for many years in Porthcawl. We spoke in the couple's Porthcawl house, as their charming, lively daughter Angharad endeavoured to control their even livelier terrier, a determined dog whose occasional banishment to the kitchen left me with at least a couple of moments in which to gaze at the model ships on the mantelpiece and, above them, a Gordon's Map of South Wales Coalfields hanging on the dining room wall.

Like PJ, Sharp has seen the world thanks to surfing, and, like him, she regards her European successes as among her most cherished memories. 'At Seignosse in France, in 1975, my proudest moment came when I won the European title for the first time. The day couldn't have been better. It was glassy, six feet, the sun was blazing and there wasn't a cloud in the sky. Over the loudspeaker system I could hear Santana's 'Samba Pa Ti' playing. It was like surfing in a film. I kept taking the left-handers and each time I'd surfed them in, caught a rip that took me straight back out to the line-up. All the other girls kept taking the rights. Everything came together that day. It was wonderful.'

Also like PJ, Sharp never planned anything in her life. She became a PE teacher after completing a teacher training course in Kent ('I was wave starved,' she recalls. 'We surfed Joss Bay and Sandwich Bay but they were horrific. The sea was filthy and it wasn't anything like Wales'), but never set out to become the person she now is: 'I had no idea I was any good at surfing. I just did it. If that meant being told to turn up in Biarritz for a contest, I'd do it. I'd go to the train station, ask for a return to Biarritz and jump on with a board under my arm. I didn't even have a wetsuit or a boardbag. My whole life has been like that.'

Sharp recalls Eden Burberry and Arlene Maltman as the best female surfers of her era (a long one, spanning her first British title in 1975 to her last in 1994), and rates Robyn Davies as the best of the current crop of women. 'I surfed against her when she was only twelve. She was so tiny that she had more wetsuit than body. But she had perfect timing and great style. I told her afterwards to keep going. She had it all – the drive and the ability.'

In 1976, Sharp competed in California in what was the second, and last, Hang Ten Pro for women. 'I was invited because I was the European champion but I was hopeless,' she says, with typical modesty. 'I came fiftieth out of eighty entrants but the thing is, because of the heat system, you couldn't come further back than fiftieth.' This taste of professional surfing was enough for Sharp. 'I didn't like it,' she says. 'It was far too cut-throat.'

Sharp rarely surfs any more owing to knee problems, but her love of surfing is undiminished. Moreover, she didn't have a bad word to say about anyone, and would nod and grin at the names of surfers I mentioned I'd met. Not least, when Peter 'Chops' Lascelles' name came up. 'Chops, now he's a character!' she said, something with which I was able to agree readily. Then, though, Sharp surprised me. 'Do you know he's related to royalty?'

That was news to me – how so? 'Yes, he's related somehow to the Queen. He's probably in line for the throne! Or his sons are.'

If this were true, perhaps it gave another reason for Lascelles' decision to abandon the Gold Coast for St Agnes. I would have to ask him sometime. What was certain was that talking to Linda Sharp was a perfect counter to a sodden Porthcawl day, one which I recalled as I drove along the M4 as slowly as possible to avoid yet another speeding ticket from the many cameras that the Welsh authorities seem to enjoy placing on this stretch of motorway. I recalled what Linda had described as her best surfing experience, when she and a few friends were surfing a remote bay at the end of the Cape of Good Hope in South Africa: 'We'd only been there two days and had found this beach with a good swell coming out of the Indian Ocean. We'd just paddled out to the five-foot peak when we saw a pair of whales and their young. The young were suckling on their mother. None of us could surf – we were spellbound by the sight. It was absolutely incredible. Was it luck or karma that gave us that experience? I don't know. But on that trip we also surfed perfect J-Bay. Sunshine, surf and whales . . .'

Sharp's normally ebullient voice trailed off, and she looked at once wistful and serene, as if the whales had swum in among the charcoal lines of Gordon's Map of the South Wales Coalfields and never left.

Proving that Brandon Bay is one of the best windsurfing locations in the world –
Francisco Goya, back looping at Dumps.

16

DUMPS

Ryan's Daughter – 'a story of love, set against the violence of rebellion' – met with an unfavourable critical reception upon its release in 1970. The consensus appeared to be that the film's director, David Lean, had created a sprawling, self-indulgent piece of cinematic ephemera, one that may have co-opted the plot of Gustave Flaubert's *Madame Bovary* to the Dingle Peninsula in Ireland but which regrettably failed to attain the depth of the French writer's subtle and provocative prose. Lean's epic was undoubtedly ambitious, for he set a classic Flaubertian tale of *ennui*, repression and infidelity against a backdrop of the Easter Rising. In 1916, between 24 and 30 April, militant Irish Republicans used force to seize key locations in Dublin and declared independence from British colonial rule. The Rising was suppressed, and its instigators executed, but it presaged the Anglo-Irish War and led to partition with the creation of the Northern Ireland Parliament in 1921 and the foundation of the Irish Free State in 1922. Lean set *Ryan's Daughter* in an unnamed village on the Dingle Peninsula, the most westerly point of the Republic of Ireland and, indeed, Europe. Here, geographically isolated, on the fraying edge of British rule, an unfulfilled Rosy Ryan abandons her school-teacher husband (played by Robert Mitchum in a role that was the antithesis of his evil preacher in *The Night of the Hunter*) to have an affair with Major Randolph Doryan, the British Army's commanding officer. Dingle's locals are hostile enough as it is to their British rulers, but when the affair is discovered tragedy is inevitable. It comes, ultimately, when Doryan finds a cache of arms on a beach, arms which have been recovered from a wrecked German ship and hidden by the Irish. The guilt-stricken, compromised Doryan commits suicide by detonating the explosives.

Upon its re-release on DVD, *Ryan's Daughter* underwent a reappraisal. Lean's film was, in some quarters at least, proclaimed a masterpiece, one wholly in keeping with his other great works, the likes of *The Bridge over the River Kwai*, *Brief Encounter* and *Doctor Zhivago*. Whether the man who was married six times, to be divorced five times, would have much cared is open to doubt, but one thing he might have been interested in is that, along with a select few, he is a director who, wholly accidentally, made a film that appeals to surfers.

Well, perhaps not all of it. The score by Maurice Jarre is often suffocating, the film is too long and its principal characters unsympathetic. But Freddie Young's cinematography is sumptuous, and, better still, the Oscar-winning cameraman homed in on the beaches of the Dingle Peninsula. Many of the most affecting scenes in *Ryan's Daughter* were shot at Coumeenole and Inch Strand, but any surfer who watches the film will find that it is impossible to concentrate on the dialogue. The backdrop – of endless sands at Inch and diaphanous surf at Coumeenole – is simply mesmerizing.

I arrived at Coumeenole on a brittle, sunlit April day, having first checked the surf at Inch. Lines of swell were making their way on to the three-mile stretch of white sand, but unfortunately in keeping with the beach's name. This was not the kind of surf once ridden, according to Celtic myth, by Finn McCool, the urbane giant whose most famous legacy is the Giant's Causeway on the Antrim coast. At Coumeenole, however, there was a wave. There were also a number of American tourists, who found the thought of anyone going surfing in such chill air – let alone water – incomprehensible.

'Can I take a photo of you?' said a lady with a New York accent as I zipped up my wetsuit. 'Isn't it cold? How do you do it? You Irish must be mad!'

I refrained from pointing out that I was English and let her take her photo. She and her friends were on a *Ryan's Daughter* pilgrimage, and I sometimes wonder if back in New York they unveil their pictures of this exquisite part of Ireland and encounter an image of me, standing at the top of the gravel slipway that winds its way down to the sands, to say, 'And guess what?! There was this guy, going *surfing* there! Can you believe it? Those Irish, they're crazy!'

But, of course, it isn't crazy to surf at Coumeenole. The beach is at the apex of the Slea Head Drive, a circular route that starts in Dingle Town and takes in the world's largest collection of 'clochans', or beehive huts. Similarly there are plentiful 'dunta', or ring forts, bearing witness to the fact that the Dingle Peninsula – or Corca Dhuibhne – has been inhabited for 6,000 years. Beyond Coumeenole lie the Blasket Islands, whose last inhabitants upped sticks in 1953, saying that life there was too remote and harsh. All around are the green fields of the Kerry countryside, whose dry-stone walls sweep down to the cliff-tops. As I entered the crystal-clear water a solitary surfer was riding in on a nice two-foot left-hander. He was ginger-haired, about thirty, and was all smiles and goodwill. We greeted each other as I began to paddle out. He exhorted me to 'Have a great session', adding that it was 'gorgeous out there', and he was right. Sitting in the line-up, looking up at the Kerry fields, which were deserted save for the occasional dwelling – some derelict, some inhabited – I wondered if this was the most beautiful place in the world that I had ever surfed. There were just a handful of tourists on the beach, and a local mother with her two young children. The waves arrived so predictably, so courteously, so delicately, in such clean water under so cloudless a sky that I thought of a line from Marina Tsvetayeva's poem, 'A Kiss on the Head':

A kiss on the head – wipes away misery.
I kiss your head.

Even the mild sense of dissonance when I returned to the beach to encounter a group of leather-clad bikers – who, from the line-up, looked like a gaggle of over-sociable and upright seals – seemed somehow right.

The attractions of the Dingle Peninsula remain relatively unexplored by surfers. Most of those on an Irish surfari tend to head north, to Lahinch in County Clare or to the breaks of Counties Sligo and Donegal. The peninsula does, though, have a number of quality breaks, as well as the Finn McCool surf shop run by Newquay-bred Ben Farr. 'We've got beach and reef breaks here, and given the shape of the peninsula there's usually somewhere that's got a wave,' says Farr, whose business blends easily with Dingle Town's hotpotch of brightly coloured shops, cafés and restaurants. Moreover, custom is good: 'We set up here in 2001. It can be quiet but we're making a good living. Surfing is on the up here, for sure.'

Dingle is also home to the man who wrote the section of the *Stormrider* guide devoted to its waves – Jamie Knox, a former professional windsurfer and highly experienced surfer. Knox set up home at Brandon Bay, near the small and scattered village of Castlegregory, in 1990. In this windswept place, in the shadow of Mount Brandon, Ireland's second-highest mountain, and the Connor Pass, its highest pass, Knox runs Jamie Knox Watersports, a windsurfing and surf hire business dubbed by the *Sunday Times* as being in 'the number one windsurfing location in the world'. Life has not always been easy for Knox, a vicar's son who built his business from nothing, but behind his somewhat gruff exterior is a man with heart, kindness and remarkable ability in the water.

'I came here after about nine years on the pro tour,' Knox told me on a typically blustery Brandon Bay afternoon. 'I'd had enough of life on the circuit, living out of a suitcase. I knew that conditions were as good as it gets. I wanted to settle, have a family, and not have to travel anywhere again.'

I had arrived unannounced to find him welding metal behind the house that he built and which now doubles as his home and accommodation for visitors. The Jamie Knox Watersports Centre is open year-round, with the majority of its visitors being Irish and English. There were times when Knox regretted the decision to set up business in an area which, to many people, would be classified as on the edge of the middle of nowhere, but Knox has made a success of it, thanks both to the excellence of local conditions and his commitment to teaching beginners. A practical man, Knox hails from Poole in Dorset, and while at ease when working with his hands is not readily loquacious. He did not, initially, seem predisposed to chat, but the conversation took a turn that created a bond between us. As I eyed up all the windsurfing kit I told him that I used to windsurf, but that I'd lost my nerve many years ago after an injury off the coast of the Canary island of Fuerteventura. Knox nodded and looked a little unenthused, so I rambled on.

'Yeah, must have been in 1990 or 1991. I was off Corralejo in cross-shore force five to six. The surf was good, about four to five feet with bigger waves outside. There were some great windsurfers out that day – they were filming Bjorn Dunkerbeck, I think.' Dunkerbeck was a windsurfing world champion, and Knox would have known him from the pro tour. He became more attentive, perhaps because of this but also, I suspected, because he could well envisage the fun to be had in jumping such waves and surfing them back in, which was precisely what I did for a few hours. Until, that is, disaster struck. I told Knox how I'd been venturing further and further offshore, towards the island of Los Lobos, when a turn on a wave known as a carve gybe had gone wrong. At the crest of the wave, once I'd got the board parallel with its face, I was about to flip the sail round when a suddenly rearing lip slammed me against the rig. My right shoulder, which had already been dislocated five times thanks to skateboarding, was wrenched again out of its socket. Familiarity with the pain did not ameliorate a rather difficult situation. There was no way I could waterstart, let alone clamber on to my board and somehow paddle it in, and the shark-infested waters of Los Lobos seemed all too near. Thankfully, an Italian windsurfer happened past, saw my plight, sailed back in and told people on the beach. After about an hour of bobbing around in the sea with my shoulder hanging loose, I'd been rescued and was back on dry land, trying to get the shoulder to go back in and making a resolution: nearly drowning while windsurfing wasn't worth it.

Knox listened to this tale and then confounded me with five words that I did not expect to hear: 'Yeah, I remember that happening.' It transpired that he had been windsurfing with Dunkerbeck on the same day. 'Yeah, we heard about it. We were talking about the poor English sod whose shoulder had gone in the bar that night. So you haven't windsurfed since?' I confessed that aside from half an hour on the unruffled waters of the River Teign a couple of years ago, I hadn't been near a sailboard. The idea of windsurfing at speed, at sea, in surf, seemed certain to result in another near-drowning.

'How's the shoulder?' asked Knox. 'Has it come out again?' In truth, it hadn't. Indeed, plenty of upper body exercises ever since – on doctor's orders – had probably made my shoulders stronger than they would otherwise have been. This, to Knox, was the green light.

'You should give it a go again. The kit's way better than in your day. It'll be like riding a bike.'

Knox is hefty man with close-cropped hair, the kind who might, in different circumstances, be described as 'hard-looking'. He has what might be mistaken for an intimidatory aura, a stern, taciturn demeanour which, to me, is born of his lack of confidence with words. In contrast to Knox, I am utterly incompetent when it comes to hammer and nails, and so, in situations where my practical abilities (or, rather, non-abilities) come under scrutiny, I tend to an over-compensatory folded-arm stance. Knox is dyslexic and, I think, a similar process happens to him where language is concerned, perhaps in conversation with people he doesn't know or when articulacy is at a premium. But he is a good man who exudes confidence, and so when he suggested I lay my windsurfing demons to rest and try the sport again, the only answer was 'yes'.

My reacquaintance with strong winds came later, in May. I returned to the Jamie Knox Watersports Centre at the same time that 2000 World Wave Champion Francisco Goya and 2005 World Wave Champion Kauli Seadi would be demonstrating their skills thanks to an event hosted by Knox, O'Neill and Goya. By then I had familiarized myself with Brandon Bay sufficiently to agree with Knox's belief that it offers 'some of the best windsurfing and surfing spots in Ireland'. Knox had practised both sports all over his adopted country, but raved about conditions on his doorstep. 'Brandon Bay picks up swell from every direction. There's nearly always wind and you can find somewhere to launch where it'll be cross-shore. Because the bay is horse-shoe shaped, there are often surfing spots that will be sheltered from the wind.' Knox had a quiver of some seven surfboards, and rated Garywilliam Point as the best wave around. 'It's a real Pipeline wave, a fast and hollow right-hander that'll break your board. Not just that, it's broken-arm territory. Unless you really know what you're doing, you shouldn't go out there.' But there were plenty of other, less forbidding spots. 'Kilcummin, Gowlane, Stradbally, Stony Gap and Sgraggane are all great beginner to intermediate waves,' he said, an assertion I could vouch for having surfed Stony Gap on a day that looked challenging only for the waves to be pleasantly forgiving. All of these breaks, as others such as Mossies – named after the farmer who first saw surfers at this spot – and Dumps, were good for windsurfing in the right wind, too. 'We've got everything here,' said Knox, and so it was that I found myself windsurfing in a force four, gusting to five, at Sgraggane.

One of Knox's instructors, Sam Robbins, came out with me, and soon enough I found that windsurfing again after so long a layoff was indeed like riding a bike. I didn't make a single carve gybe but the sensation of planing across the sea was, thanks to Knox, something I enjoyed again some fifteen years after the last dislocation of my right shoulder. My hands were red raw from holding the boom without gloves, but later that afternoon, as I watched Knox and Robbins sailing with Goya and Seadi in conditions that were strikingly similar to those at Corralejo in

Fuerteventura, I vowed to return to County Kerry in south-west Ireland, to surf at Coumeenole and windsurf at Brandon Bay, to idle in Dingle Town and to gaze at the sea from the Connor Pass. And I understood why Knox had settled in the Dingle Peninsula. Even if *Ryan's Daughter* continued to await universal valediction, there could be no doubting the raw beauty of the peninsula's setting, a place where the sea is alternately grey and metallic and pulverized by the wind or left in peace to deliver sweet, clean and enchanting waves, waves like gypsies bearing the most highly prized bounty before once more vanishing on their travels.

Mike Morgan, deep inside a County Donegal green room.

17

CHARLIE DOES SURF

If Ireland was once a surfing destination known only to a minority, its surf is now celebrated worldwide. Mike Morgan, the 2005 Irish Open winner, is unequivocal in his assessment of the quality of surf on his doorstep. 'The stretch of coastline from Bundoran to Easkey in County Sligo has the best surf in Europe,' says the compact, 21-year-old goofy footer, whose sister Nicole was the Irish Ladies' surfing champion in 2003. Indeed, Morgan, a surfer since the age of nine and now sponsored by O'Neill, goes further. 'There are only two places *in the world* that are better – Indonesia and Hawaii.' His confidence in the quality of his home surf is not misplaced. Morgan's stamping ground of Bundoran, the most southerly town in County Donegal, is home to several contenders for the title of Ireland's best wave.

In the *Stormrider* guide, Roci Allen described the area as 'one of the few places in Europe to warrant the title of "Surfers' Paradise",' and he is not far wrong. Bundoran is a cold water, and less tacky, twin to the eponymous town on Australia's Gold Coast. There are two surf shops on its main street – long time local hero Richie Fitzgerald's, and Aidan Browne's more recent arrival, the Bundoran Surf Co. Fitzgerald is well known as a surfer around the world, having travelled extensively and been a regular in the Irish surfing team. His shop is crammed with surf wear and gear, photos and memorabilia, while Browne, who set up the Bundoran Surf Co. in March 2005, runs a surf lodge as well as selling equipment and offering lessons. Bundoran itself is a curious mix of the threadbare and the elegant, once dubbed 'the Brighton of Ireland' because – thanks to the Great Northern Railway which ran between 1866 and 1957 – it was easily accessible to inhabitants of Belfast and Dublin. The opening of the new Bundoran and Ballyshannon bypass in 2006 has helped cement the town's position as Ireland's pre-eminent seaside resort, as have its golf course, water slide (the fastest in Ireland), adventure centre and six-screen cinema. But it is the town's surf that is its major draw. Bundoran is Ireland's surf city.

'There are waves here that make you never want to leave,' says Aidan Browne, a Bundoran resident since the age of thirteen. 'The Peak is one of the most consistent reef breaks in the country, an A frame producing a long walling left and a short right. It's best at low tide and can hold up to eight feet. It's for experienced surfers only but there are good intermediate waves as well, like the Sandbar on the main beach. Further up the coast Rossnowlagh is great for learners, while at Tullan Strand there's pretty much always a wave even if everywhere else is flat.' There is also Pampa Point, a wave that made it into Chris Nelson and Demi Taylor's *Surfing the World*, a selection of the best eighty waves in the world culled from interviews with leading surfers. As Nelson and Taylor put it:

> Pampa Point was brought to the attention of the surfing world in the movie *Litmus*. When the Aussie pro Joel Fitzgerald charged huge, gaping lefts here in the 1990s it really opened people's eyes to the potential that lies around the Irish coastline. Pampa was named after the PMPA Insurance sign that stood near the break – and good insurance is probably a wise thing to have at this ledgy point that offers some fast, challenging and hollow lefts. As the size increases, so does the danger level of the wave. It can be transformed into a race for survival . . . Pampa is a serious wave for

serious surfers, not the kind of spot to paddle out at if you haven't racked up some serious time at some serious reefs. After all, at a surf spot named after an insurance company, the only thing you want to claim is the barrel you just pulled out of.

Pampa Point may be an exceptional wave, but there is one thing that perennially disrupts Irish surf: the wind. As with the UK, the best waves arrive between autumn and spring, but they are frequently accompanied by howling gales. Fortunately, Sligo and Donegal are home to beaches facing a variety of directions, meaning that, with the right swell, good surf can be found at one spot while another will be blown out. There is, though, no escaping the cold. Surfing in Ireland in winter is an act of commitment with which the country's still highly religious population would, one hopes, empathize. A session in a full 6 mm wetsuit, complete with hood, boots and gloves, will not feel too taxing while in the water, but once back in the car park or on the beach the cold sets in with body-numbing ferocity, not least thanks to the wind chill, as I found when I surfed Strandhill in County Sligo early in 2006.

I had checked various spots along the coast, including Easkey right and left, two waves further west on a wild and Spartan stretch of coast. Easkey was sufficiently wind-blown for windsurfing rather than surfing to be the order of the day. The surf was large and lumpy, messed up by the wind, but there was more than a hint of the power and form that had led Barry Britton, one of Ireland's surfing godfathers, to name his daughter after the place. Easkey Britton herself has more than amply fulfilled what must have been her multi-talented father's hopes for her (Britton senior is a pen and ink artist, sand-etcher of glass, architect and interior designer as well as a surfer), having secured sponsorship deals with the likes of Etnies, Alder, Nev Surfboards and Animal as well as representing the Irish Ladies team. Neither she nor any other surfers were in the water when I arrived at the rather desolate but beautiful reef set-up that had so inspired her parents, and having checked one or two other spots I was giving up any hope of a surf until I doubled back and found myself at Strandhill. Here the wind was not so formidable and reasonably clean 2–3 ft waves were breaking on sand that bore a grey and weary look, one not shared by a woman in her twenties who was emerging from the surf as I made my way to the water's edge. She looked contented, if cold, and stopped to talk.

'Wow! That was great!' she declared, in a rich Sligo brogue. I told her I was from England and unfamiliar with the break, but she told me there were no rips to worry about and to 'get out there and have a blast'. Her enthusiasm was all the more remarkable given that her cheeks were starting to turn blue and her teeth to chatter. She was so talkative – so happy with her surfing and eager to share that happiness – that the sea's evident frigidity, allied with the near-hypothermia that seemed about to possess her, receded in my mind so that what was admittedly a decision to go surfing full of misgivings turned into an urgent desire to get out there. I said that I'd better not detain her anymore and that she should go and get warm.

'Oh, no, don't be silly!' she said, as if my suggestion were one of the utmost foolishness. 'I'm just walking along the beach to go back out over there. Look, I think the waves are handy over there.'

Sure enough, they were, but so too did they look good enough where we were talking, our feet lapped by the icy water. We bade each other farewell and I paddled out to enjoy a decent session among six or seven other surfers. Two young teenage males dominated proceedings, taking off late, whacking the lips of the waves and nearly making aerials (which they seemed to attempt on every ride), and the atmosphere was friendly throughout. Soon, though, the cold started to gnaw at me. After just an hour I came in, and the moment I started walking up the beach the wind chill hit me. As for getting changed and drying off in the car park, only a masochist could have found the process enjoyable. As I was shivering and considering if it would be possible, one day, to be warm again, I caught sight of the Celtic Seaweed Baths and, upstairs, the Sligo Surf Club. Inside the seawater and seaweed-filled baths, on the Strandhill esplanade and facing the Atlantic, an end to worry and stress was promised: 'Imagine relaxing back into a big bath full of hot seawater and seaweed. The heat releases all the seaweed's rich, silky essential oils so your body feels smooth, buoyant and luxurious. Tiredness, tension, aches and pains slip away. Feel your eyes close and your whole body sigh with sensuous satisfaction.' After the cold of the surf, this was all too appealing, but instead professionalism prevailed and I asked the attendant, Mark Walton, about the Sligo Surf Club, whose doors were looking decidedly shut.

'Yeah, that'd be right, it's closed at the minute,' said Walton, a surfer for fifteen years who was born and raised in Sligo. 'It's going great, though. Really busy in the summer. At least sixty members, I'd say.'

Walton was an affable, kindly man who treated visitors to the baths with an abundance of courtesy and respect, qualities whose absence in some of Ireland's line-ups he lamented.

'The waves round here are tough. They're reef breaks and a lot of them will consistently break your board. If you can't surf, you shouldn't be here – not on the reefs, anyway. But we're getting a lot of people coming over who aren't up to the quality of surf we've got. They're just not experienced enough for waves like Easkey or Kilcummin Harbour. But you know what the worst of it is?'

I wasn't sure, but Walton enlightened me.

'I hate to say it but the worst thing is the English and Welsh who come over here and think the waves are theirs. Also some of the Aussies and overseas surfers. We Irish are a mellow crew and you won't find any localism from us. All we want to do is have fun and enjoy the sea. We're friendly by nature and that's how we go surfing – with a good attitude, to meet people and enjoy each other's company. But what's starting to get to me is paddling out at Easkey, or another wave that I've been surfing all my life, and being given the eye by some guy from Cornwall. Someone who's come here once a year for a while, who sees the crowds, and wants to claim the wave as his before he goes back home. They've no business turning up with so much attitude. I don't understand where it comes from but it's a real shame.'

Walton is one of life's good people, and he expressed his qualms quietly, as if reluctant to admit that there might be a problem. I bought some Connemara Shores moisturizing cream for Karen and a bottle of water for myself, and began to wonder: was surfing, for some people, a form of colonialism? Was it the case that if localism did exist in Britain and Ireland its development was not to be laid at the door of, in this case, Sligo's surfers, but with those from the UK and Europe who felt that they had 'discovered' surf spots and, as such, were entitled to preserve them, pristine, for their occasional return journeys? If this was the case, it was a mode of thinking that seemed to owe much to the colonial imperative that led to the Spanish and Portuguese sweeping the globe from the fifteenth century onwards, thence to be replicated by the British, French and Dutch from the seventeenth century. Perhaps, indeed, Francis Ford Coppola's *Apocalypse Now* revealed the logical conclusion of colonialism in surfing. The film, an adaptation of Joseph Conrad's *Heart of Darkness*, sets Captain Willard (Conrad's Marlow) on a quest upriver to the depths of Cambodia in search of the renegade Green Beret Colonel Kurtz. The film is set in the Vietnam War and Willard's mission is to 'terminate [Kurtz] with extreme prejudice'. One of *Apocalypse Now*'s most unforgettable scenes is that in which Lt Colonel William Kilgore, played by Robert Duvall, leads a Wagner-accompanied helicopter strike on a supposed Vietcong village, essentially so that Kilgore, a surfer, can surf its perfect point break. As he says in John Milius' script, upon learning about its surf: 'Why the hell didn't you tell me about that place – a good left. There aren't any good left slides in this whole shitty country. It's all goddam beachbreak.'

Kilgore's underlings (one of whom, Lance Johnson, is a famous Malibu surfer) doubt the wisdom of attempting to surf at the village. As one of them says: 'That's where we lost McDonnel – they shot the hell out of us. It's Charlie's Point.' To Kilgore, though, 'Hunting up Cong, and going surfin' is about as fine a combination of pursuits as there is. He exhorts his men to pick out a board for Lance and get ready for some water time. Again, though, one of them has doubts: 'I don't know, sir . . . It's hairy in there. It's Charlie's Point.'

To this, Kilgore says: 'Charlie don't surf.'

The surfers among Kilgore's 9th Cavalry regiment proceed to surf a head-high swell as warfare rages around them. Carnage is omnipresent but Kilgore is immune. He orders a huge napalm strike in the adjoining jungle, leading to the climax of the battle and, one imagines, the end of this particularly gnarly surf session. As he says to Willard: 'Do you smell that? Napalm, son! Nothing else in the world smells like that. I love the smell of napalm in the morning.'

Apocalypse Now finds time in this scene – inspired by Milius' background as a California surfer – to demonstrate the logical outcome of fascism in surfing. Charlie don't surf, and he never will either, because the colonialists have got there first. Their effect is one of total decimation.

In Ireland, Charlie does surf. And thanks to the likes of Mark Walton, the country remains the land of '*céad mile fáilte*' (a hundred thousand welcomes). The surfing colonialists might do well to preserve the *céad mile fáilte* philosophy lest one day they find that Charlie doesn't want them in the water anymore.

And then the wind died – John McCarthy tasting heaven at Aileens,
County Clare, as tow-in partner Dave Blount heads for cover.

18

THE CLIFFS

The scarred, black cliffs, which rise a sheer 700 ft out of the ocean, were away to my left. The mid-October day was unusually windless, and ahead of me, a third of the way down the shale and sandstone path that leads to the foot of the cliffs, was Al Mackinnon, a 27-year-old surf photographer. Despite the weight of his camera equipment and the likelihood that a slip would have bone-breaking or even fatal consequences, Mackinnon skipped nimbly down the path. With his bright orange kagool, habitual faded beige shorts and tousled blond hair, he looked for all the world as if he were off for a summer's Sunday afternoon's ramble in the Cotswolds. The bright sunshine only added to the sense that we were two gents out for a balmy constitutional, as did Mackinnon's commentary.

'Down there you've got the shorebreak,' he said, gesturing some 400 ft beneath us. A 6 ft surge of white water crashed on to the boulder-strewn shore, its sound echoing up the cliff face. 'Some of the guys scramble all the way down there and paddle out. Big climb back up if you ask me!'

I dreaded what was coming next. Thanks to the sheer scale of the Cliffs of Moher, which dwarfed me, Al and everything in sight, I was feeling distinctly vertiginous. I have climbed mountains in the Alps, Russia and Romania, but never had I felt so dizzy as when I stood in the shadow of the vast, pitiless Cliffs of Moher, one of Ireland's top tourist destinations. On another visit I had wandered the five-mile stretch of land on top of what the locals refer to simply as 'the Cliffs', at virtually the highest point of which stands a tower built by Cornelius O'Brien in 1835. O'Brien built his tower as a tourist draw, convinced that visitors to the breathtaking Cliffs would boost the local economy, and today hundreds of daily visitors bear witness to his foresight. The Irish, various European races, Americans and, on my first visit, a coach-load of Japanese come in their droves to O'Brien's tower because of its magnificent views of the Aran Islands, the mountains of Connemara and, below, 'Breanan Mor', a sea-stack hewn from the cliffs by the unceasing, elemental power of the Atlantic and home, in spring, to guillemots, kittiwakes, shags, choughs and puffins. The wind on top of the Cliffs is relentless and this, coupled with grandeur of the landscape, leads easily to speculation as to just what an extraordinary race the Celts – the area's early settlers – were. But the conventional pilgrimage to the Cliffs is, at least, safe. Unless you were possessed of a bizarre urge to clamber the wall that forms a barrier between the green fields and a vertical drop to certain death, you will feel suitably awestruck (if a little wind-blown) after a stirring but circumspect tour and more than happy to spend some money in the nearby visitor centre. This was precisely my reaction, though once inside, as I was ordering my coffee and cake, I overheard an Australian male discoursing on surfing in Ireland.

'I've heard they surf off those cliffs,' he was saying to his companion, who greeted this information with understandable bewilderment.

'What?' she said. 'Where? How on earth could anyone go surfing down there?'

'Beats me,' said the Australian. 'It's probably some kind of media myth.'

But surfing at the foot of the Cliffs of Moher is no media myth. It is all too real. Hence, in the company of Mackinnon, on a subsequent visit I found myself some distance from the fenced-in safety of O'Brien's tower and, instead, halfway down a sketchy old cliff path, dizzily attempting to keep pace with Mackinnon and meet his jaunty comments in kind. As we stopped to contemplate the shorebreak, I feared that a suggestion that we clamber all the way down, the better to observe its formidable power, was in the offing. Given my nervousness and conviction that continuing our descent would lead to nothing but the utmost peril I was racking my brain for something with which to distract Mackinnon when he stopped and, wide-eyed, scanned the horizon.

'Amazing, isn't it?' he said, swivelling his head to take in the sea, the cliffs, the sea-stack and, in the foreground, on the deep blue ocean, a fishing boat which was bobbing in the swell. From this vantage point, it was impossible to determine the size of the waves, and would only become more difficult the further we descended in the direction of the shorebreak. Mackinnon knew this. 'Let's forget about going to the bottom and head over there,' he said, pointing to an outcrop of crumbling rock that looked about as stable as a skateboard on top of a serac. Full of yet more misgivings, I followed him, only to find that he'd stopped just beneath a decaying pinnacle with a concerned look on his face.

'Damn!' he said, and as I followed his stare I saw a lens cap bouncing down the cliff, a journey which would surely end with it gently plopping into the azure sea.

'Hang on a minute,' said Mackinnon. Within minutes he had clambered so far down the southern cliff-side – a mixture of grass, gorse and stone – that I could no longer see him. What would I do if he didn't reappear? If he slipped into the Atlantic? I would go after to him, but then what? How on earth could I help him if something went wrong here? Again I looked at the black and menacing Cliffs of Moher. To some, they 'stand sentinel' at the edge of Ireland; to others, they are fully deserving of their Irish name, 'Aillte an Mhothair', the 'Cliffs of Ruin'. To me, then, they looked simply terrifying.

Mackinnon returned, lens cap in hand, just as I was steeling myself to go and look for him. Breezily, as if hopping around on ruinous cliff-sides was his favourite pastime, he took himself to the extremity of the nearby outcrop, there to gaze with an uninterrupted view at the break known as Aileens. 'Aill Na Searrach', to use its Irish name, is an ultra-serious reef break just a few miles north-west of the County Clare surf town of Lahinch. Thanks to the exploits of a local crew for whom the word 'hardcore' might have been invented, as well as some high-profile visiting surfers, Aileens has, in the last two years, become a world-famous big-wave location. Mackinnon has photographed this and many other cold-water big-wave spots in Britain and Ireland, and was giving me an up close and personal view of Aileens. Halfway down the cliff, the wisdom of agreeing to this had become a distant memory.

'Come over here, you can get a great view!' declared Mackinnon, lying upon the rock edge and taking photographs. A fall would lead to certain death, and the rock face above him was so weathered that it looked as if it might give up its wearisome battle against the wind and sea salt at any moment, to collapse and send him hurtling to the broiling sea below. Tentatively, I inched towards him. I kept saying to myself that vertigo was just the title of a book by one of my favourite writers, not a condition that was afflicting me, there and then, with increasing urgency. I peered over the ledge for my best view yet of Aileens. What I saw astonished me.

The surf was not, according to Mackinnon and a group of spectators whom we had left at the top of the cliff, 'Aileens at its best'. Far from it. It was big – perhaps in the 15 ft range – but it was not breaking cleanly. The swell direction was not quite right, and only one in seven or eight waves could have been ridden, and then only for an express train drop and brief ride to the right. But the sound was immense as wave after wave detonated over a slab reef the size of a tennis court, and the big-wave perfection possible at Aileens was obvious.

Pictures published in Issue 85 of *Carve* magazine with the front cover teaser 'British and Irish Surfers 'Ave It Large' illustrated just how good Aileens can get, with surf that is easily Hawaiian in scale, whether measured from the front, back or anywhere else. A group of surfers including Dan Joel, Sam Lamiroy, Russell Winter and Duncan Scott are pictured riding mean, moody and monstrous waves, waves that would convince even the most sceptical denizens of the North Shore that there is world-class big-wave surfing to be had in Ireland. For any big-wave surfers for whom excess danger is the prerequisite for kudos, Aileens has it all, as Al Meenie, a surfer present during the *Carve* 'H$_3$O' session featuring Joel, Lamiroy, Winter and Scott as well as Andrew Cotton, Spencer Hargreaves, Dave Blount and Ian Battrick, told the magazine:

> It looks so similar to Maverick's [the Californian big-wave spot]. The water's so dark with a big nasty-looking peak. It brought back so many memories. The only difference is that Maverick's breaks out at sea, and it breaks on rocks not cliffs, so in terms of safety, Aileens is more dangerous.

Likewise, Sam Lamiroy:

> I would like to go back but I wouldn't like to surf it much bigger because the inside wave was just a nightmare. I wouldn't like to go back and surf 40 ft waves there because I don't think that it would deal with it. It's one of those places where if it goes wrong, it goes really, really wrong. If someone knocks themselves out or snaps a leg and gets washed in then no one could get you on a jet ski. It's not like a wave breaking in the middle of the sea likes Cortes Bank – if something happened there you know that you could physically get to them. It's a bit of a nightmare scenario and it if was any bigger I think I'd have to decline.

When I visited the Cliffs with Mackinnon, Aileens was not providing the surfing jewels that have drawn surfers of the highest calibre. 'It's a shame,' said Mackinnon. 'Nearly good enough but not quite. It would have been great for it to be working and for you to be out in a boat watching from the water.'

Mackinnon's enthusiasm for this idea was prompted by the

arrival of a small outboard containing two men and surfboards. They had launched from Doolin Pier – the nearest access point for jet skis or boats, a few miles up the coast – to see if Aileens was, after all, surfable. As we retreated up the cliff path I heard another thunderous wave smashing on to the reef at the foot of the cliffs, and caught site of a sign that I hadn't noticed before our descent: CLARE COUNTY COUNCIL – EXTREME DANGER – CLIFF FALLS CONTINUING was its unambiguous message. I stumbled on up the path and sincerely hoped that the swell did not improve. Just being on the cliffs was scary enough, and the last place I wanted to be was out in a boat when Aileens was in its full glory. As for going surfing there – a place where one's fragility in the sea is only emphasized by the adjacent landscape of ancient and mocking cliffs – to do so was surely insane.

Carve's H_3O project was conceived to 'push the boundaries of cold-water big-wave surfing'. Dan 'Mole' Joel was credited with surfing the biggest wave of the day during the session featured in Issue 85, one which was comfortably eight times his height. *Carve* assembled a crew of some of the top surfers in the UK and Ireland for the O'Neill-sponsored project. As well as Joel, Lamiroy, Winter, Scott, Meenie, Battrick, Hargreaves, Cotton and Blount, other surfers on standby for the H_3O included Gabe Davies, Richie Fitzgerald, Danny Wall, Cain Kilcullen, John Buchorski, Ben Skinner, Russ Granata and Jack Johns. 'Special guests' for the 2006–07 winter-long mission would be internationally renowned big-wave surfers Carlos Burle and Rusty Long. The H_3O would not be confined to Aileens but to other Irish and British locations. Any 'local chargers up for the challenge' would be welcome to join the surfers, all of whom were working in tow-teams using state-of-the-art Kawasaki jet skis capable of travelling at up to 60 mph.

The sight of Aileens breaking at size would be enough to scare the living daylights out of the majority of surfers. There is one local charger, however, who can't get enough of the place. That man is John McCarthy, a Lahinch local and the first man to ride the giant surf of Aileens. On a bright afternoon I met McCarthy, thirty-one, in Joe's Café, an airy, relaxed establishment no more than fifty yards from the clean lines of swell that were breaking on Lahinch beach.

Inside the café a poster for a local event featured McCarthy bottom turning at the foot of a 25 ft Aileens wave. This prompted Morgan Phillips, a South African bodyboarder who had hitched to Lahinch from Ennis, to draw breath. 'Jeez,' he said, 'that's awesome.' Turning to McCarthy, who was sitting to the side of the poster, he asked: 'How'd you survive a wipe-out on a wave like that?'

McCarthy grinned and, almost shyly, said: 'I don't know. You just try your best.'

The Irishman's calm, leisurely bearing is mirrored by life in Lahinch. The town's population of around 1,000 swells to more than 10,000 during the summer months, with visitors drawn to the perfect beginners' waves off its sandy main beach. Many will hire boards and take lessons through the Lahinch Surf School, which is owned and run by McCarthy. Small it may be, but Lahinch boasts a total of three surf shops, all within a stone's throw of one another. The first to arrive was 58-year-old Tom Buckley's Lahinch Surf Shop: 'I set up here in 1989, and my family thought I was mad,' Buckley told me. 'Back then it was very quiet here. If there were twelve surfers that was it, and you'd know everyone in the water. Now, even in the winter, if conditions are good there will be a hundred people out there.'

The worldwide boom in surfing also supports Ollie Welsh's Ocean Scene, just above the beachfront. Across town, opposite O'Looney's pub, is the Green Room, whose name derives both from its owner, Stuart Green, and the mystical 'green room' into which surfers disappear when they are inside the curl of a breaking wave. The Green Room was set up in October 2001, making Welsh the new kid on the block. Having surfed in County Clare for fifteen years, Welsh has no doubt about the quality of surf in the Lahinch area: 'I used to travel a lot looking for paradise. But I realized that paradise was here all along.'

McCarthy agrees. A born-again Christian, surfing, for McCarthy, is imbued with religious significance. 'One time I was surfing Aileens on a medium-sized day. The surf was in the twenty feet range. I pulled in to this immense barrel, about one and a half times the size of this room. I'd never been so deep inside a wave before, so far inside all that relentless energy. It's the most blissful feeling you can have in this world. A taste of heaven.'

McCarthy's conversion to Christianity occurred in early 2006 but it was not motivated by a catastrophe or ungovernable inner demons. Far from it, for McCarthy seems to have been unusually blessed with talent, ability and popularity. After graduating from the Waterford Institute of Technology aged twenty-one as an electronics engineer, he went to Japan and worked in various parts of the IT industry. He speaks not only Japanese but also Spanish and French, is a handsome man and has a welterweight's physique, one which is elastic and supple, without a hint of excess weight. As he says, he had 'an amazing first thirty years. I made money, I had a beautiful house, I was popular with girls, I could travel and I had surfing.' Despite this, he always felt that 'there was a terrible void in my life', and in March 2006 came the moment that he decided to devote his life to God.

'One morning I was staring at the bay, thinking how amazing it is, what a beautiful sight, and I asked myself, "What do you want your life to be?" I knew what the answer was. I'd already read a lot of the Gospel over a month in Indonesia, and I'd been struck by my ignorance. There was so much I didn't know. So I resolved to study the Bible more. I went to a couple of Christian Surfers conferences in Devon, and during a sermon at one of them experienced an epiphany, a moment when I knew I had the opportunity to forget pride, ask for forgiveness and accept God fully into my life.'

The sincerity of McCarthy's convictions – which he amplified later that evening in Pat Ahern's Cornerstone Bar – was obvious. He talked passionately of the consequences of surrendering to the Lord: 'Only Jesus lived a sinless life but once you accept this, once you accept that he died for us, once you surrender to God you become empowered. The Holy Spirit heals you.

Desire disappears.' McCarthy's innate charisma means that an evangelism that might be a little too insistent in a lesser individual posits an intriguing, not to say appealing, way of life, one in which he is liberated from undue anxiety about the surf school or other aspects of the quotidian such as leases and building work on his house. Was this how his fellow Lahinch surfers saw things? 'I'm not sure. But it doesn't matter what other people think. It's about the daily acceptance of God.'

Over the course of a few days in Lahinch I watched as McCarthy surfed some secret spots down the coast near Spanish Point (whose name derives from the fact that survivors from wrecked Armada ships swam ashore here), as well as the rather more public Crab Island, a break further north near the village of Doolin. Often he was joined by Oisin McGrath, an air corps pilot (who has been known to scour the coastline for good surf from the air), Peter Conroy, a fireman, Marty Cullinane, a surf shop owner from Tramore, Andy Burke, a musician, and Gavin Gallagher, a wedding photographer and documentary maker. Not once did I detect any sense that McCarthy had alienated himself thanks to his conversion, and throughout there was an exceptional *esprit de corps* among the Lahinch surfers. They were tight-knit but welcoming, capable but not arrogant, exuberant, generous and modest. Thanks to Gallagher, their lives and waves should soon appear on celluloid, in a DVD whose title is a nod to the nemesis of surfing in Ireland: *And Then the Wind Died*.

Gallagher's documentary contains wonderful footage of the first time Aileens was surfed, on 15 October 2005, when McCarthy and Blount were joined by Californian big-wave surfer Rusty Long. It was, as Gallagher says, 'a magical occasion . . . Aill Na Searrach has been breaking here for thousands of years, exploding perfectly, untamed and unridden. How many jaw-dropping monstrous waves must the cliffs have faced? If a wave breaks in the ocean but nobody hears it does it still make a sound? On this day she gave up her secrets and allowed the privileged the honour of surfing her.'

I did not see Aileens being surfed, though I did end up in a boat at Crab Island to witness a tow-in session first-hand. The boat, an inshore surf lifesaving craft known as a Zapcat, was driven by Welshman Steve Thomas, who has been living in the Lahinch area for the best part of a decade. With Mackinnon taking photographs – not easy, given the constant motion of the sea – we watched as McCarthy was towed into Crab Island waves that were not quite materializing into the 'very frightening tubes' of the *Stormrider* guide's section on County Clare ('Great wave but few capable of handling it!' is the cautionary assessment). It was a sunny, cold day, but if Crab Island's barrels were less than perfect, the rainbows on the back of the breaking, opaquely green waves were exquisite.

Early the following Sunday morning Lahinch high street was bathed in light and, once again, the main bay was being blessed by perfect clean lines of 3 ft swell. The brightly coloured shops, pubs and restaurants were closed as a great many people worked on recovering from the previous night's craic. The Cornerstone was shut, so too Kenny's (the official home of the West of Ireland QPR Supporters Club), O'Connor's Amusements Bar, The Old Cuban Cigar Shop, the golf store and the book shop. The newsagent was open as, I think, was Mrs O'Brien's Kitchen, but I walked on to the beach, past O'Looney's, the pub on the esplanade. The surf was as inviting as possible, a world away from the outsize tubes of the Cliffs or even the many experts-only reef breaks of the area, Crab Island especially. Three women were in the car park, already getting changed out of their wetsuits after an early morning surf.

Eilis Ni Dhuill, 31, Claire Burke, 32, and Patricia MacEoin, 30, regularly drive from Galway to surf Lahinch beach. They spend the day there, probably have a light lunch at O'Looneys, and then go for a surf again. None of them put themselves in the expert bracket – 'we're strictly amateurs' – but all are devout surfers and have seen how Lahinch has been gripped by surfing. 'Surfing has taken off here so much in the last three years,' said Pat, whose Monday to Friday existence sees her working as a criminal lawyer. 'There are as many women in the water as men now.' Eilis, a fine art student, and Claire, a physio, agreed, and had their own views on why surfing is so popular. 'It's the feel-good factor, and not having to conform – that's what brings us here,' Eilis told me, while Claire had a rather more wry take: 'It's not having to go shopping.'

In the distance, the Cliffs of Moher shimmered benignly in the sun. McCarthy would surf the Cliffs again, soon; so too would some more local chargers and members of the *Carve* H_3O Project. Ireland's reputation as one of the world's foremost surfing destinations would continue to grow as, oblivious, the tourists braved the wind to scurry in the shadows of O'Brien's tower. Gallagher would complete his documentary and beginners would flock to the Lahinch Surf School. McGrath, Conroy, Cullinane and Burke would shred the reefs up and down the west of Ireland while Eilis, Claire and Patricia would keep on coming to Lahinch Bay, maybe soon to progress to its own heavier reef breaks, the Left, Cornish Reef and Shit Creek. All were united by one thing, a dedication to the experience of riding a wave, that which McCarthy said was 'a taste of heaven. You glide on the sea's momentum and experience the purest freedom on earth. It's the most blissful feeling you can have in this world.'

PART FOUR

One man and his board: Jesse Davies outside his Tynemouth home
with his custom-made Dick Brewer gun.

19

IT'S GLASSY UP NORTH

In *Get Carter*, Mike Hodges' 1971 film, Michael Caine plays Jack Carter, a London gangster who journeys to Newcastle on a quest to find his brother's killers. Caine oozes viciousness even as he sits impassively on the train that takes him from London to the north, the viewer's sense of foreboding only marginally deflected by Roy Budd's much-admired up tempo jazzy score. Carter appears every inch the (rogue) urban sophisticate and is at once perceived as *outré* upon his arrival in Newcastle. His Cockney accent jars with the Geordie sounds of the locals, and Hodges' nihilistic film portrays the north-east as a bleak, windswept land of council estates and redbrick houses, one with a sordid underbelly in which women are at the mercy of an array of unattractive, violent men. Carter duly discovers how his brother was killed and by whom, and embarks upon a merciless campaign of vengeance. There is nothing redemptive about his actions, nothing to suggest that he is a better man than his adversaries. He is merely more effective, a cold-hearted, dangerous man operating with total detachment in a grim landscape in which people are as easily dumped in the sea as slag from the coastal collieries.

Carter's journey takes him from one metropolis to another and, finally, to the sea. His last act of vengeance is to force one man implicated in his brother's death to drink the entirety of a bottle of whisky before beating him senseless. He places the character, known only as Eric, in a skip which operates as part of an aerial flight system used to carry coal waste from an unidentified colliery to the ocean. Eric is dumped in the freezing North Sea, and Carter laughs, dementedly, as his quest comes to an end. Just as he is about to hurl his shotgun into the water, an assassin takes up position in grassland above the beach, and executes him. He is unidentified (though connoisseurs of *Get Carter* point out that he is seen in the opening scene, reading on the train). Carter lies dead on the beach, his black shoes, overcoat and suit lapped by the gentle waves, his shotgun by his side.

Get Carter is widely regarded as one of the best British films ever made. Its existential despair is of a piece with Albert Camus' *The Outsider*, but like the French–Algerian's novel, its unremitting bleakness can be as depressing as it is affecting. However, every time I watch *Get Carter* – a film that surely endorses the flippant cliché 'It's grim up north' – loomings toward depression are averted by the final scene, not because I rejoice in Carter's death and interpret it as a moral statement of some kind (which it most definitely isn't), but because every time I look at the beach and its waves, I am convinced Carter meets his end on a surfing beach. And so, rather as with *Ryan's Daughter*, I find myself wondering just how good the surf gets on that particular beach, wondering if anyone surfs it, and thinking that, one day, I will go and visit it. And this, despite the remorseless nihilism of *Get Carter*, always cheers me up.

Jesse Davies, a Tynemouth local and highly regarded big-wave surfer, had seen *Get Carter* but couldn't recall its final scene. When I told him about it and asked if he knew where it had been filmed, his brows furrowed and he seemed on the brink of remembering, only to say, 'No, do you know what, I don't know where that is.'

My own research had led me to believe that it may have been filmed at Blackhall Rocks, a beach not far from Hartlepool that is now part of a nature reserve and picnic site. Was it also a surf spot as good as many of the other top-quality limestone reef breaks between Newcastle and Scarborough?

Davies couldn't tell me, but he was living proof of the *Stormrider* summary of surfing in the north-east: 'Hardened by cold weather, polluted and freezing seas and inconsistent swells, the local guys are some of the keenest, most competitive and yet friendliest surfers anywhere, and define the term hardcore.'

Davies is a slightly-built man in his mid-30s, the eldest of three brothers all of whom surf. His middle brother Gabe is the best known, having carved out a successful career as a pro surfer in which he has been a British Senior and a British Masters Champion. Gabe now lives in France where, with Joel Gray (another north-east stalwart) he runs a surfing vacations business. Younger brother Owain is a student at Falmouth University, but Jesse has remained a fixture in the north-east. Over a mid-winter lunch in the Copper Kettle in Tynemouth, I asked him just how good the North Sea surf could be.

'It can be as glassy as you like, and as heavy as you like. It's not like Cornwall, where you can find a wave somewhere just about every day if you're that keen, but when we get a good swell, with the wind in the right direction, the geology of the coast here means that we get perfect surf.'

Good swells for the north-east are born of bands of low pressure sitting between Scotland and Scandinavia, which, with winds from the west or south-west, will create offshore walls of water at many of the breaks between Saltburn and Berwick-upon-Tweed. One of them, the Cove, is a secret spot whose incredible left-breaking barrels have reputedly prompted declarations from figures of the stature of Kelly Slater and Tom Curren that they would like to surf it. Overseas surfers are, though, a rarity in the counties of Northumberland, Tyne and Wear and Durham. Likewise further south, in Yorkshire, where Scarborough has a thriving surf scene, and in Whitby – one of the settings for Bram Stoker's *Dracula* – a port which is now as notable on the right day for its young surf dudes as for its ruined abbey, tall ships in the harbour and itinerant devotees of all things Gothic. These areas are known among British surfers for their waves, but while the surfers of France, Spain and Portugal will have heard of surfing in Devon and Cornwall, Ireland and Scotland, few of them will associate a Lincolnshire seaside town such as Skegness with the sport of kings. And yet even here there is a vibrant surfing community, as Matt Strathern of Lincolnshire online surf shop and resource centre www.extremehorizon.com says: 'Lincolnshire is often ignored by the surfing masses – which sometimes isn't a bad thing – but there's a small, hardcore band of surfers here who surf year round. The North Sea can be fickle and often flat but when it turns on the surf can be great.'

Strathern first surfed in Malibu in 1991, and has been longboarding ever since. As he puts it: 'I got trapped in corporate London for a few years but moved back to Lincolnshire in 1994 and set up Extreme Horizon to design, manufacture, distribute and retail surf hardware. I first saw the surfing potential in Lincolnshire after a visit to California to see relatives in the late 1980s. Driving along the coast I saw a small number of surfers out in super-clean four-foot offshore surf. I couldn't believe there was such potential on my doorstep.' Strathern, who regularly contributes to *Wavelength* and to the newest of all the UK surfing publications, *Drift* (an online magazine with an emphasis on environmental issues), even muses over whether Alfred Lord Tennyson – born and bred in Lincolnshire – had in mind the miles of surf in England's second largest county in *The Lotus Eaters*. 'Think of the second line – "This mounting wave will roll us shoreward soon" – is it a reference to the feeling of riding a wave? It's a nice thought.'

Strathern told me that, remarkably, there was a surf club in Grimsby in the late-1960s. 'It was formed in 1968 and lasted three years. Then in the 1970s, as kids, we used to bodyboard on the forerunner to the boogie-board, the cheap styrofoam or plywood planks which were purchased from a Spa shop or tacky seafront souvenir shop. But it wasn't until much later that I became aware of a surfing scene here.' That scene is probably about as underground as any in the UK or Ireland: 'Lincolnshire as a surfing destination is still pretty much unknown,' says Strathern. 'Other than the occasional passing mention in some UK surf guides and reference to certain spots on surf internet sites, Lincolnshire doesn't seem to register on the UK surf map, which is strange given that we have a huge coastline running from the Humber in the north to the Wash in the south. Not all the coastline is surfable but there are miles of untouched beachbreaks and almost unlimited space.'

As Strathern admits, Lincolnshire does suffer from some drawbacks. There are only beachbreaks, and 'the North Sea also has a relatively short fetch, which combined with a shallow sea and long gently sloping beaches produces fairly short period swells that lack real power.' The best swells arrive in mid-winter when the sea and air temperatures are, as Strathern puts it, 'Baltic'. Against this, prevailing winds are from the south-west, making for offshore conditions in decent swells. Moreover, the three main surfing areas – Mablethorpe, Sutton on Sea and Skegness – are served not only by Extreme Horizon but by the Coogee Surf Shop, and both were recently joined by a new extreme sports centre in Skegness. The opening of the centre on the North Parade car park will, says Strathern, 'attract more locals and groms into the water and provide a hub for Lincolnshire surfing. I know that Lincolnshire is never going to hit the world surfing map as a top-class surfing destination, and the WQS and WCT aren't going to fight over hosting contests here, but if you're dedicated, keep a close eye on the weather charts and own a thick wetsuit there are some great waves to be had.'

Outside the Copper Kettle the wind was blowing so fiercely that I feared that Jesse Davies might be spirited away. The surf was utterly destroyed by the gale force winds, which were blowing cross-shore with such force that, on the beach, sand was being whipped up into my eyes. The Tynemouth Surf Co. shop, on the seafront, was shut – no surprise given the inclement conditions and time of year. Despite the freezing cold and howling winds, a lone surfer strode across the sands to enter the sea. En route, his board was all but snatched from under his arm by the wind. I watched as Davies retreated to his house, a short distance from the Grand Hotel and the ruins of Tynemouth Castle. The surfer walked to waist depth, then lay on his board and paddled out into what might have been a line-up had there not been such relentless wind. He slipped from his board a couple of times as he tried to sit on it, suggesting either that he was a raw beginner or that the wind was even more vicious in the sea than on the beach. I didn't see him catch a single wave, but it was impossible not to admire his dedication.

Likewise that of Davies, whose nine-stone frame would not at once be associated with big-wave riding. The conventional image of the big-wave 'hellman' is of someone in the North Shore hero's mould of a Ken Bradshaw or Laird Hamilton, men with perma-tans and square jaws, sculpted 6 ft plus physiques and deep macho drawls. Davies does not conform to the stereotype. He is a quietly spoken, modest man who runs a surf school in Tynemouth and studies yoga. Having graduated with a geography degree from Plymouth University, he took a postgraduate diploma in hydrographic surveying and worked on offshore survey ships around the world. This was a source of income rather like Tom Anderson's stint as a private investigator in that it allowed the time and money for surfing: 'I'd be on a boat for months and so could save enough money to go surfing. Also we'd be in some amazing places and I'd go surfing when we got to them. I did a lot of surfing in South America thanks to working offshore. I even made it to Easter Island for a surf thanks to that job.' But it is closer to home that Davies has made his mark. He is one of the UK's foremost 'chargers', a surfer known for his seemingly total absence of fear.

As a north-east local, Davies has North Yorkshire's premier secret spot, the Cove, on his doorstep, as well as Tynemouth's very own rivermouth left-hand reef break, the oft-polluted Black Middens. The latter is a 'great wave', according to Davies, whose enjoyment of it no doubt owes more to its breaking congenially for his goofy footer's stance than the industrial waste that lends an even blacker tinge to the North Sea surf which, even at the best of times, is almost always a thick, soupy brown colour. Davies, whose academic father Peter had a hand in the commissioning of Andrew Gormley's immense Angel of the North sculpture at the entrance of Tyneside, has surfed the Cove at 'three times overhead', and when he says this, in his quiet, self-effacing fashion, there is a distinct sense that in fact the Cove might have been rather larger. Davies was taught to surf by the late Nigel Veitch, a man who pioneered surfing in the north-east rather more than the man who is technically the area's most famous surfing son, Martin Potter. 'Pottz', as he was known, is Britain's one and only professional surfing champion, winning the ASP title in 1989, but though he was born in Blyth he learnt his craft from an early age in South Africa. It was Veitch who took the Davies boys into the frigid North Sea at Tynemouth and then, once they were ready, to the Cove and – a rite of passage for many north-east surfers – to Thurso East in Scotland. Today Davies will be in the line-up at Thurso and its surrounding breaks whenever there is a good swell, and he has also spent plenty of time exploring the similarly dynamic reef set-ups of the west coast of Ireland. He has surfed Waimea Bay, Sunset Beach and other breaks on Oahu, but counts the Spanish break of Menakoz as possibly his favourite. 'That, or La Santa Right in Lanzarote. I was out there on a 7′ 8″ once when it was five times overhead. It was sketchy, for sure, but, man, it was fantastic too.'

Davies is devoted to surfing waves such as the formidable La Santa Right in the same way that many of his fellow Geordies swear blind by Newcastle United FC. 'Round here it's all football and a fair bit of drinking. That's the way life is. But as soon as I could stand up on a board I just threw myself into surfing. And then as I got better big waves became my focus. I love big waves because they're more challenging, it's all about making the wave and survival. I did a few contests but I'm not into surfing in two-foot waves to impress judges. I like surfing in small waves, yeah, but I won't go looking for them. And in the right conditions we've got classic set-ups all along the coast here, waves that are serious and demanding, waves that will take you to your limits. The Cove is as perfect a wave as you'll find anywhere. They're right when they call it one of the best left-handers in the world.' Moreover, Davies eschews the world of tow-in surfing. 'I'm not interested in going out with a jet ski. There are environmental issues connected with tow-in surfing and it's not such an act of commitment as paddling in to big surf. If you can paddle out into a line-up in a serious swell then paddle in and make the wave, you've experienced surfing at its purest. More than that – you've experienced something fundamental to life, something that makes you feel more alive than ever.'

I had ample time to ponder Davies' words as I embarked upon a tour of Captain Cook country. My first visit to the north-east coincided with Pete Robinson's Surfing Museum being on show at the Captain Cook Birthplace Museum in Stewart Park, Marton, and in the vicinity I marvelled at the beauty of this region, one which in the triumvirate of Newcastle, Middlesbrough and Sunderland had its fair share of industrial monoliths but which was worlds away from the vision of *Get Carter*. There seemed to be any number of ruined castles on windswept headlands, whose stark silhouettes, illumined by the wintry sun, would make for one of the more beguiling of views from the line-up. Davies told me that surfing was booming here as much as anywhere else in Britain or Ireland: 'People are starting to realize how good the waves are here. More and more women are getting into it, too.' His belief was endorsed when over 5,000 spectators turned up in October 2005 to witness the O'Neill British Nationals in Tynemouth, an event won by Newquay's Alan Stokes (the 2006 event was much anticipated and would have resulted in deafening applause on the beach given that it was won by another Tynemouth-bred surfer, Sam Lamiroy, but owing to poor conditions had to be held in Devon). Phil Philo, the curator of the Captain Cook Birthplace Museum, could not have been more enthused by the arrival of surfboards and memorabilia at Stewart Park, and Robinson's collection was enhanced by an exhibition of photographs of another strong north-east surfing community, Saltburn-on-Sea, by locally based photographer Ian Forsyth. Once I had absorbed the image of a tattoo bearing the legend 'The Cove' between the flexed shoulder muscles of a surfer named Nathan Robinson – not to mention some of Robinson's collection of 1960s surf literature (*The Girl in the Telltale Bikini* and *Freaked Out Strangler* seemed to be two especially striking works of surfploitation) – I headed along the coast, to Saltburn, hoping against hope that the wind might have dropped so that, despite the cold, I could go for a surf.

The Victorian resort town looked splendid, and not merely because of its strange street names. Saltburn-on-Sea was founded by Victorian entrepreneur Henry Pease, whose glittering vision of a heavenly town in place of Old Saltburn led him to bless what is now the North Sea's most popular surfing destination with streets called Ruby, Emerald, Garnet, Pearl and Diamond. Pease, whose family owned the Stockton and Darlington Railway, had his vision one night before a family dinner in the nearby coastal community of Marske. He informed his brother, whose reaction does not appear to be known, that he had walked to Old Saltburn and that 'seated on the hillside he had seen, in a sort of prophetic vision, on the edge of the cliff before him, a town arise and the quiet unfrequented glen turned into a lovely garden'. Pease duly commissioned a series of impressive buildings, not least the Zetland Hotel and the world's oldest water-powered cliff lift. There remains a grandeur to Saltburn, with its immense headland jutting out into the North Sea, wide, sandy beach and its old Victorian pier, the last still standing in the north-east, but, if anything, the wind had grown yet more remorseless. I wandered down on to the beachfront, there to notice that the Saltburn Surf Shop looked decidedly, and quite reasonably, shut. Upon peering through the window I saw that there was, though, someone inside. It turned out to be the proprietor, Gary Rogers, he whom Alf Alderson had commended for his 'undying enthusiasm'.

Would there be any surfing today? I asked Rogers, with no little irony since the answer was clear. He smiled wryly and gestured at the mass of white water in front of us. 'No chance,' he said. 'Not until this wind drops. If it ever does.'

Rogers was about six feet tall, had a weathered face and looked lean and fit. The British Masters Champion in 2004, he set up the Saltburn Surf Shop in 1986 having initially run a surfing business from the back of an old Ford Luton van with Nick Noble. Now Rogers is in sole charge of the shop, while Noble concentrates on Saltburn Surf Hire. 'There was a surf club here as far back as 1963,' he told me, as we sheltered inside the shop out of the wind. 'Now the club's got up to a hundred members, maybe more. Nick runs a BSA-approved surf hire business and we're pretty much always busy. Except days like this.' The day of my visit was, though, one of the few in which Rogers had not been surfing: he keeps a diary recording where and when he surfs, and takes to the sea easily in excess of 200 times a year. He concurred with Jesse Davies about the strength of the surfing community in the north of England: 'There are as many women taking up surfing as men, and though a few years ago we were regarded as aliens, people in the north-east have got used to surfers. We're part of the furniture now.' And, if I wanted to find the icing on the cake of my tour of Captain Cook country, he pointed me a few miles down the coast, to the tiny village of Staithes. 'It's beautiful,' he said. 'You can get a real sense of what Cook achieved there.'

Rogers was right. Just ten miles north-west of the Transylvanian romance of Whitby, Staithes, once a thriving fishing town, is the site of the cottage in which Cook lived for eighteen months from 1745. Cook was then a young man in his teens, and as the various monuments to the great seaman in Staithes make clear it was there that he received his first taste of maritime life when he worked as an assistant to William Sanderson, a merchant. Cook's cottage overlooks the tiny harbour, and, beyond, the often raging North Sea. Nearby is a restaurant named The Endeavour, and, on Church Street, the Mission Church of St Peter the Fisherman. High cliffs overlook the village, and beyond, either side along the Cleveland Way, is yet more evidence of the mining heritage of the north-east. Staithes now is accessible only by foot, and its charming, colourful and almost labyrinthine streets are much visited not least by those, like me, who are in search of the background to the man who sailed the seven seas and, incidentally, became credited as the first Westerner to witness surfing. As I ambled the cobbled streets I wondered whether Mike Hodges had visited Staithes, perhaps by way of some light relief from the intensity of the filming of *Get Carter*. And just as always happens when I watch the last scene of *Get Carter*, before I left Staithes I looked out to sea and, for a second, envisaged outlandishly perfect, gleaming and addictive barrels, the kind of waves that Cook must have seen when he reached Hawaii.

Australian surfer Glen 'Micro' Hall on a Hebridean wall.

20

COLD RUSH

Derek Macleod looked more like a boxer than a surfer. His forearms were almost as huge as his biceps, and additional evidence of great physical strength – a taut neck with pulsing veins, bulging pectoral and latissimus dorsi muscles – was on display thanks to a tight-fitting orange T-shirt, this Macleod's concession to the cold along with a faded pair of blue jeans. Outside the Corner Tapas Bar, the storm that had been raging on the Outer Hebridean Isle of Lewis since I arrived continued to batter the streets of Stornoway. Once inside anyone choosing to emulate Macleod's minimalist sartorial style would still have felt a nip in the air. But while the restaurant's other customers were wrapped up in jumpers, with their scarves, hats and raincoats hanging in the cloakroom, Macleod alone was wearing a T-shirt. He seemed wholly impervious to the elements, and bore the aura of a man who might have been a prize fighter in a former life.

But surfing is Macleod's thing, and he loves it unconditionally. The 40-year-old was born and bred on the Isle of Lewis, and ever since he witnessed surfing on television at the age of twenty-nine he has been in thrall to a pursuit that he says 'is a release from society, something that gives you a feeling of absolute freedom'. I had heard about Macleod from a number of people, not least

Huw 'Herbie' John, Tom Anderson and Al Mackinnon. All had counselled that a visit to the Outer Hebrides was a must: I would almost certainly find good surf, and, in Macleod, would encounter a man who was the living embodiment of the word 'hardcore'.

As a child, I had been fascinated by stories of the pure white sands and clear waters of the Hebrides, a 150-mile-long island chain on the far western fringe of Europe. I recall my old friend Elliot's father, a Scotsman, telling us that our decision as 18-year-olds to undertake a surf trip to France could have been bettered had we opted to point our converted Ford Transit van north and make our way to the Hebrides. At the time I knew, as a windsurfer, that islands such as Tiree and Coll offered excellent year-round windsurfing conditions, but Elliot's father also offered a perspective on the surf: 'If it's Atlantic rollers you're after, you can't go wrong with the Outer islands.' I asked Macleod how true this was.

'I'll surf every day if I can, that's how good it is here. There's always a wave somewhere. It's just a case of finding the time to get in the water.'

Macleod's fervour for surfing convinced me that he would find the time more often than not. After his televisual glimpse of the artistry of wave-riding he ordered a Nigel Semmens 6′ 8″ pintail gun from a surf shop in Bournemouth and set about learning how to surf. 'The board was tiny and way too thin,' he recalls. 'It wasn't suitable for a beginner.' Despite constant batterings and barely getting to his feet, Macleod is not the kind of man to quit and his perseverance was eventually rewarded when a teacher on holiday with his son lent him a mini-mal. 'I was on the verge of giving up but then this gent turned up and lent me his board. It was a 7′ 4″ and had the extra volume I needed. I paddled out and a shoulder-high set came through. I caught a wave, jumped to my feet and was up and riding for nearly two hundred yards. I was flying! The feeling blew my mind. I ordered my own mini-mal, kept paddling out and got better and better.'

Macleod's reputation as a surfer had preceded him – was it true that he would surf just about any swell, no matter how big?

'I've been in some big stuff, aye,' he said. 'The thing is, round here we get such massive surf that often the only surfing you'll be doing will be in big waves.' For Macleod, though, it was a case of the bigger the better. He owns a boat and will take anyone up for the challenge out to Lewis's hidden reefs and points. 'If they've got the balls,' he adds.

Macleod had been a commercial fisherman for many years and agreed that his experience in the open ocean helped his surfing, both while he was learning and as he got better, so that he felt relaxed in larger swells. He now runs a surf lodge and says that Lewis and its neighbouring island of Harris often see travelling surfers. Word of the quality of the surf in the Hebrides and especially that of Europie, the most north-westerly beach in Britain, has spread far and wide, not least because of what was dubbed 'The Hebridean Surfing Festival', an event conceived by Macleod. Excerpts of the festival appear on north-east filmmaker Mark Lumsden's celebration of surfing in Scotland, *Cold Rush*, and look every bit as good as Macleod's description: 'There are waves here that are as big as Aileens and as fast and critical as Pampa Point. I wanted the international surfing community to realize just what we've got here so I got in touch with Derek Hynd.' At the time, Hynd, a noted surf journalist and former pro surfer, was keen on developing an alternative to the ASP Tour. Thanks to Macleod's determination Hynd finally flew from his base in Australia to visit Lewis on a reconnaissance mission. He was, says Macleod, 'blown away'. The pair collaborated to host the Hebridean Pro-Am in 2001, in which local and British surfers went head-to-head with internationally known surfers such as the USA's Hans Hagen, South Africa's Frankie Oberholzer, surfing pioneer Skip Frye and, remarkably, three-time world champion and icon of the Rip Curl search, Tom Curren.

The festival coincided with the 9/11 terrorist attacks on the World Trade Center in New York. 'The tragedy happened on the first day of the contest,' recalls Macleod. 'The Americans were in a terrible state. We all were. We held a remembrance service for the victims at the Callanish Stones.'

I had visited the Callanish stone circle earlier. Thought to date as far back as 3,000 BC, the stones are as haunting and mysterious as any in Britain or Ireland. There are thirteen upright stones with a huge megalith at the centre marking a later burial cairn, but yet more curiously the overall layout of the Callanish stones is in the form of a Celtic cross. Local folklore suggests that Lewis's native giants refused to convert to Christianity only to find that Saint Kieran, whose missionary zeal they ignored, turned them to blocks of gneiss stone as a punishment. Exactly what the prehistoric inhabitants of Lewis had in mind when they painstakingly erected the stones is impossible to determine, but the island is certainly now one of the most religious places in Britain. It all but shuts on Sundays, and an air of reverence and respect is present in the Outer Hebrideans, a hardy people whose daily experience of the elemental is as unchanging as the Callanish stones.

'The service helped bring us all together at a very traumatic time,' says Macleod, and the Hebridean Surfing Festival went on to be a great success. The small local surfing population was delighted to watch surfers of Curren's calibre riding their waves, so too to be competing against them, eating and drinking with them, talking to them. Perhaps inevitably, Curren won the event, but the result was not what mattered. 'We all met some great people and shared some wonderful experiences,' says Macleod. 'I'm still in touch with a lot of them and hope to see them here again. I lost money organizing the event, but it didn't matter. It was really touching.'

Macleod is a tough-looking man who does not appear readily given to expressions of emotion. He is, though, 'just the best', according to one of the waitresses in the Corner Tapas Bar, a young Canadian woman with the apposite name of Cherish Dinner. Cherish had recently arrived in the Hebrides and loved the islands. Macleod was giving her surfing lessons. 'He's a great teacher, really athletic, always enthusiastic, almost like a child the way he's so keen. His passion rubs off and he keeps you motivated. He's got such a great spirit.'

In this, Macleod is not alone. He is the Hebrides' most well-known surfer, but his zest and energy are shared by the twenty or so natives of Lewis who surf. Despite being cursed by incessant rain and conversely, albeit that it was in October, not being blessed with a single wave, my trip to Lewis and Harris (technically, a single land mass rather than two islands) was notable for the warmth and hospitality of the locals. As one of them, Mark Maciver, put it: 'We're always happy to see new faces here. The types of surfers who come through have made a lot of effort to get here – it's not cheap or easily accessible – and they're the kind who respect the environment and people they meet.'

Similar views were held by another of life's men of integrity – Rodney 'Cheggs' Jamieson, a long-time Lewis surfer and key worker with children with learning difficulties. I arranged to meet Cheggs in a bar in Stornoway on the fourth successive day of ceaseless rain, though before he arrived found myself discussing Lewis's 'bridge to nowhere' with London barrister and surfer Tim Kevan. *The Times* had called me about an article I'd recently filed, and, one thing leading rapidly to another, it transpired that Kevan – who had also just written something for the newspaper – was at that moment on a surf trip to the Hebrides. Strangely enough I had noticed a hire car containing books on ornithology and surfing outside the bar, and, once I'd been alerted to the fact of another *Times* contributor's presence in Lewis, had a notion that Kevan might be in the very bar in which I was due to meet Cheggs. As I was scanning the room searching for a likely figure, I noticed a blond-haired man dial a number on his mobile phone. My own phone then rang. 'Hello, my name's Tim Kevan,' said Kevan, who was sitting perhaps three yards from me but gazing out of the window onto the bedraggled Stornoway streets. He explained how he had got my number and who he was. 'Yes, I know,' I said. 'I'm sitting just behind you.'

Kevan joined me before the arrival of Cheggs. He adored the Hebrides and was making his second trip to the islands. Having been brought up in Minehead, he was familiar with the same North Devon breaks that I surfed in my late teens. He raved about the surf on Lewis. 'There are world-class waves here, with a backdrop of outstanding natural beauty. The wind can be ferocious but you've got the heavy beachbreak surf at Europie, the friendly reef break at Barvas and a lovely long left at Braggar. There are loads more – they're just a few of the spots.'

Kevan warned me, though, of being tempted during the course of any island odysseys to try and cross Lewis's 'bridge to nowhere'. Not because it would give way, but because of what was on the other side.

'People happen upon it, see the sign saying 'The Bridge to Nowhere' and think 'Oh, I'll drive across and see what's there.' The trouble is that there's nothing there. They get stuck in the nowhere bog and a farmer has to come and tow them out.'

Cheggs appeared and grinned at the story of the Bridge to Nowhere. A tall man aged thirty-four, Cheggs grinned at most things. He was kindly, courteous to a fault and, like Macleod, learned to surf the hard way. 'It was about fifteen years ago that I first went surfing, with a friend called Saul,' he told me. 'It was a February, I can remember that because I can remember the cold. Saul had a 6′ 8″ pop-out and had been surfing a few times at Tolsta, a mile-long beachbreak on the east coast. We only had one wetsuit between us, a 3.2 mm [a summer wetsuit]. Saul would go surfing while I waited on the beach, come in and take off his wetsuit, then I'd put it on and give it a go. We'd take it in turns. We had no boots, no gloves, no hood. It had to be the coldest system for learning to surf ever invented. I didn't even get to my feet and my hands were so cold I couldn't get the keys in the ignition. But I loved it. I never looked back.'

Cheggs went on to grow up surfing with Macleod and the Hebrides' small but fanatical surfing community. His view of surfing's burgeoning popularity is not protectionist: 'We just want to treat people in a way that we'd want to be treated ourselves.'

Cheggs was also a windsurfer and says that there was quite a windsurfing scene on Lewis. The past tense is operative because, in a horrific storm in January 2005 (one which killed a family of five who were swept into the sea after fleeing their flooded house on the island of Benbecula), the entire kit of the Stornoway Windsurfing Club was lost for ever. 'It was stored in a metal container,' says Cheggs, 'but the wind was up to 120 mph and as strong as a hurricane. The container just got blown over, split in two and then all the gear was strewn first all over the island and then out to sea. We didn't recover any of it.'

Hebridean weather can, as I found, be merciless. My trip was accompanied by incessant rain and wind, and when I visited Europie, the 'Hossegor-like' beachbreak on the north-west of Lewis, I felt as if I had reached the most desolate place on earth. There was nothing, and no one, there, merely a huge, uncontrollable sea smashing on to the sand under a black sky. The maddened, maddening wind made it barely possible to walk on the beach, and the children's play area, adjacent to the sands, looked utterly forlorn. The rain lashed in and within seconds of leaving my car I was soaked through. As far as the eye could see, looking towards the ocean, there was nothing but a heaving mass of white water. Its violence made me yearn for a pub with a warming fire and a pint of Guinness, but there are barely any houses near Europie, let alone any pubs. I retreated to my car and drove to the Butt of Lewis, where there is a redbrick lighthouse originally built between 1859 and 1862. To look north from the lighthouse, out to sea, is to contemplate the next stop of the Arctic, while to the west is Newfoundland. While both looking and contemplating I was able to confirm that the Butt of Lewis deserves its official recognition (in *The Guinness Book of Records*) as the windiest place in Britain.

And yet I know that on its day the Outer Hebrides can have waves as sweet and Edenic as those that I beheld were malevolent and crude. Californian Skip Frye, then sixty and renowned in world surfing for his graceful, fluid style, speaks of them in *Cold Rush*, as well as the place that he says is 'what most of us would regard as a perfect world'. To scenes of deserted beaches of shining white sand, unostentatious houses amid peat valleys and deep blue, perfectly formed waves, he says 'we'd all like to live in a more rural world' if we could, one with 'a house here, a house there'. For Frye, a devout Christian raised in San Diego, it was 'really refreshing' to visit the Hebrides, a place of such 'peace and quiet'. Elsewhere, Frye has said that the surfing festival conceived by Macleod truly 'promoted the Aloha spirit'.

In keeping with that spirit Frye left his quiver of surfboards on Lewis, to be used by the locals.

The charts looked promising. It seemed that a hefty northerly swell was within days of descending on Britain's most northerly islands. This was just as well, since the vagaries of existence as a freelance writer and family man meant that rather than drop everything and travel whenever good surf would be guaranteed, I frequently found myself having to pre-select a given few days, then set off and hope for the best. As with the Hebrides, this could lead to frustration, and one or two other pre-booked trips also turned into exercises of hope (and stoicism) over experience. So when I came to organize a trip to the Orkney and Shetland Isles, destinations rarely visited by travelling surfers since most get as far as Thurso East and remain there, transfixed by its long, walling rights, I was pleased to note that it looked as if decent surf would coincide with my arrival.

The plan was that I would make a quick stop in Thurso before heading north via the Orkney-bound ferry from Scrabster. Then I'd take another ferry to Lerwick, the capital of the Shetland Islands. I'd heard that there was surf on the Shetlands, and I knew that there were waves on the Orkneys. I recalled that Watergate Bay's Chris Thomson was interested in a return trip to Orkney, not least to see his father, so dropped him a line. He said he was keen to come on the trip, and with a north swell looming everything looked good. I got in touch with Zed Layson and told him that my travels were nearing their end and that it looked as if I might be spending some time at Thurso. 'What dates are you talking about?' was his reply.

I sent Zed the dates, and wondered if he would leave his Caribbean paradise in favour of Scotland in January. I had a feeling I knew the answer, and it came through a few days later. 'I've been trying to get my stuff together for this trip but I can't make it,' he wrote, wishing me all the best.

I wasn't put out. After all, had I really thought that Zed would sacrifice the warm water of Duppies, Freights and the Soup Bowl for Scotland? In January? Anyway, the charts continued to look good, and I was excited enough about the trip as it was. Then, almost on its eve, Thomson announced that he couldn't make it either. I had been due to drive to Scotland with him in his van, so this created a problem. After much last-minute wrangling, there was a new plan. Jesse Davies had always wanted to check out the surf on the Orkney and Shetland Isles, and if I could get myself to Tynemouth he'd do the driving. We'd take a ferry from Aberdeen to Kirkwall on Orkney, spend a few days there then take another ferry to Lerwick. There wouldn't be time for a detour to Thurso. Perhaps it was just as well that Zed hadn't booked a plane ticket from Bridgetown after all – not least, as I was to find, because our new itinerary would culminate in the Shetlands' world-famous Up-Helly-Aa festival.

This celebration of the Shetlands' Viking heritage proved to be more taxing than a three-hour session in overhead storm surf, but Jesse and I were blissfully unaware of its rigours as we drove up the A1 from Tynemouth on a fine, if brisk, January day. Jesse pointed out various jewels of the north-east surfing coastline, none of which was surfable, before we eventually arrived at Aberdeen with an hour's light remaining. With time to kill before the ferry would depart we checked the surf on Aberdeen beach. To our surprise grey, well-formed 1–2 ft waves were appearing from a misty horizon and being surfed by one bodyboarder and one surfer. 'Always take a wave if you find one,' said Jesse, a rule that he applied on surf trips as much as the travelling surfer's other oft-repeated mantra: never drive away from pumping swell. Swiftly, we changed into our wetsuits, mine a freshly-purchased O'Neill Mutant 5.4.3 mm, one of the new breed of Velcro-less, near-zipless, hooded and flexible suits that make old wetsuits (by which I mean those made only a few years ago) feel like sacks of Hessian cloth. I hadn't been able to bring any boards owing to the last-minute change of plan, but fortunately Jesse had a selection. Unfortunately, however, they were all performance shortboards. It seemed that there wasn't a longboard or even a mini-mal in sight, though as I peered inside Jesse's van I noticed one outsize board bag. It housed a 9′ 6″ custom-made Dick Brewer gun that Jesse had yet to use. 'Want to try it?' offered Jesse. With its extra length the Brewer seemed a better bet than any of the shortboards, and so, with Jesse being kind enough to allow its baptism in the chill waters off Aberdeen, I picked it up and strode to the water's edge.

Brewer is another of surfing's legends, a man who hails from two generations of engineers but who chose to forsake a conventional life in favour of Hawaiian surf, which he first discovered in 1959. He is renowned as one of the best surfboard shapers in the world, having accrued years of first-hand experience of surfing the monumental waves of Waimea Bay and Sunset Beach. Jesse had asked Brewer to sculpt him a 'gun', an elongated shortboard specifically created for serious surfing in serious waves. The narrow width and vee bottom of a gun enable a surfer to plummet down the face of a large wave with the risk of 'spinning out' – losing control – minimized.

An hour later we were back on dry land. Despite my agreement with Fuz Bleakley's concern about metaphors in surfing, the most appropriate summary of Jesse's surfing is to say, simply, that he ripped. Time and again the nose of his board was thrust vertically beyond the lip of the breaking waves, to be snapped stylishly back on to the face, where Jesse would continue to ride again before setting himself up for another move of exceptional athleticism. He may be a man who lives for big-wave surfing but it was a pleasure to watch Jesse surfing the small Aberdeen surf, a view evidently shared by sundry passers-by given that a crowd formed on the esplanade, staying to watch in the light rain that had by then begun to fall. My own efforts – first to get used to a Hawaiian big-wave board and secondly to surf it in such small surf – were rather less impressive and I emerged from the water feeling rather frustrated. I was not to know, though, that seven days later I would be pleased even to have had a poor session.

Lying off the northeastern tip of Britain are the Orkney Isles, an extension of the wonderful slabstone geography of the Caithness region and a world-renowned danger to shipping since humans first took to the sea. Add to this the fact that the islands pick up more swell than the mainland and you have a place of amazing surf potential. Mainland Orkney has some excellent slab and boulder reefs and points that go unridden every day . . .

So say Nelson and Taylor in *Surfing Britain*, and with high hopes of tapping into the Orkneys' amazing surf potential, Jesse Davies and I met up with Al Mackinnon on the quayside in Kirkwall. Mackinnon had been on the Orkneys' principal island, Mainland, for a couple of days but had bad news for us.

'The charts aren't looking good, guys. I don't think that north swell's going to appear after all. And if it does, it'll be destroyed by the howling westerlies.'

I queried this, not because I knew any better but out of pure optimism: 'There must be a wave somewhere here. Look at the set up of the islands. There just has to be a wave.'

'Dude, I've spoke to The Gill,' replied Mackinnon, pausing to let the full import of these words sink in. I looked at Jesse, who was appropriately downcast. For good measure, Mackinnon added: 'If The Gill says we're not going to score, we're not going to score.'

Jesse confirmed that he had been on surf trips with The Gill, and that the man's ability to predict swell was uncanny. 'Ah well, if that's what The Gill says . . .' was all he said, his words trailing off with the wind. As we were contemplating the likelihood of our surf-free fate a well-set man who looked to be in his mid-thirties approached us. He had a brown dog with him. It looked like a Labrador but I wasn't sure. Mackinnon greeted both man and dog. 'Shaun and Sancho,' he said, 'what's up?'

'Just taking Sancho for a stroll,' said Shaun, in a West Country accent. 'There's no surf, that's for sure.'

Shaun lived in a van with Sancho, and intended to stay on the Orkneys for the next few months. If he needed money he would busk, playing the bagpipes for money on Saturdays. He had surfed both the Orkneys and the Shetland Isles previously, and

Mackinnon would often meet him when he himself was living out of his van, photographing the surf along Scotland's north shore. 'He's not a fan of society,' explained Mackinnon subsequently. 'He thinks that humanity has become corrupt and tries to get away from it as much as he can. That's why he's here.'

'Blown out and nothing going on,' said Shaun on the day we met him at Kirkwall harbour. He had earlier checked Orkney's two best-known waves, the left point at Skara Brae and the right-hand point known as Skaill Point.

'Thought so,' said Mackinnon. 'No real swell and what there is will be getting hammered by a westerly.'

'That's about it,' said Shaun.

Nevertheless, we couldn't resist a drive to Skaill Bay. We loaded a couple of boards into Mackinnon's VW Synchro and made our way across Mainland. On the way we drove into Stromness, the Orkneys' other large town whose rivalry with Kirkwall is not quite as intense as that between the 'Uppies and Doonies' in Kirkwall itself. The two sides compete in an annual game of street football known as 'the Ba' with the Doonies' goal being the sea, while the Uppies must round Mackinson's corner at the junction of Main Street with New Scapa Road. The Ba itself is a leather ball filled with cork and there appear to be no rules as such. Tradition dictates that if the Doonies win there will be good fishing, while a victory by their marginally less nautically inclined brethren, the Uppies, will bring a good harvest.

This ancient and maniacal-sounding game, comprising upwards of 500 burly Orcadians and played to see in the New Year, was difficult to imagine amid the quiet quays of Stromness. It is a charming place, running for a mile along the shore of Hamnavoe, an inlet of Scapa Flow, with one main street that seems to wind around with a will of its own. Given that we doubted we would be losing surfing time it was easy to decide to take time out to meander its peaceful streets. Roughly in the centre, in Graham Place, is the J. L. Broom bookshop, an Aladdin's Cave of bookselling in which I found an edition of Knut Hamsun's *Hunger*, a book I had always wanted to read. I complemented Tam

MacPhail, the owner, on his excellent stock and as we talked detected an accent that was not solely Orcadian.

'No, I was born in Honolulu,' said MacPhail. I asked him if he had surfed in Hawaii, and though he hadn't he seemed to be aware of surfing on Orkney. 'Aye, there've been a few surfers here in recent years,' he said in a mellifluous blend of Orcadian and Hawaiian-American.

I took the fact that a Honolulu-born man was at the helm of one of the finest bookshops I have ever visited as a good omen, but none of Orkney's breaks were working. Mackinnon, Davies and I scoured the coastline but at each potential surf spot the story was the same. Everywhere we went a severe westerly wind was annihilating the waves, which were not born of our longed-for north swell but were the meagre offerings of the wind itself. We found Twatt, the settlement that had amused Tom Anderson, and, like him, we did some island-hopping. Unlike the Welshman, we encountered nothing but appalling weather and a complete absence of surf. We did, though, meet two of the Orkneys' very few surfers, Steve and Dan, both of whom were Englishmen abroad. Steve was a gargantuan though fit-looking man from Axminster, Devon, and ran one of Orkney's swimming pools. Dan, from Manchester, had been on Orkney for nearly five years and worked as a commercial diver. Steve was thinking of returning to the south-west one day, while Dan – of slighter build and a more surfy look – had no intention of ever leaving Orkney. 'I love it here,' he said. 'It's quiet and beautiful and the surf is out of this world.' Both, however, agreed that the charts weren't looking good for our trip. Their firm conviction was that Nelson and Taylor were right – there was cracking surf to be had given a propitious alliance between swell and wind – but that the only way we were likely to get wet was in a rainstorm.

Mackinnon duly checked again with The Gill. Steve and Dan were right. A propitious alliance was unlikely for at least a week, if not longer.

On the ferry to the Shetland Isles I came across plenty of old sea superstitions in Ernest Walker Marwick's *An Orkney Anthology:*

Selected Works. Marwick (whose name is also that of one of Mainland Orkney's best reef breaks) was a self-taught and highly distinguished Orcadian writer and folklorist, and the *Anthology*, edited by John D. M. Robertson, is a wonderful collection of writing that attains a meditative quality through its simplicity. 'If a ship was experiencing ill-fortune, and it was discovered that some Jonah on board was the cause, the only way to change the luck was to draw a picture of him and burn it,' wrote Marwick. 'Sometimes, if the luck was extremely bad, two or three pictures had to be burned.' Elsewhere, he describes the refusal by fishermen to count boats before they put to sea ('if this was done one would not return'), and how 'old whaling skippers were most unwilling to leave port just after a bird had flown between the masts'.

Marwick shared my fascination for seal stories, recounting that of a young seaman who went to sea in the 1850s only to be unwilling to part with his pet seal. His mother insisted that the seal be disposed of, saying, 'I almost fell over it last night, and it may learn to bite people.' The skipper of a local ship took the seal and put it into the sea to the west of the island of Hoy. Next day, the seal returned to the seaman's house at Knockhall. This and other examples of the folklore of the *selchie* abound in Marwick's work, but as I was reading this tale one word prompted my thoughts to take a different direction. That word was 'Hoy'.

In *Feeding the Rat*, Al Alvarez's testament to Welsh climber Mo Anthoine, the poet, writer and critic describes how he and a band of five other climbers (with a collective age of 264) climb the Old Man of Hoy, a sea-stack that rises 'like an admonishing finger of God' from the Atlantic on the north-west coast of the Orkney island of Hoy. Hoy is the exception to the paradigm of the seventy or so low-lying, fertile and gently sloping skerries and islands on the Orkney archipelago, being high and rugged with steep cliffs falling vertically into the sea, rather as a smaller, but no less forbidding, version of the Cliffs of Moher. Alvarez succeeds in climbing the Old Man of Hoy (a serious climb graded 'Hard Very Severe') on the kind of squally, wind-lashed day that Davies, Mackinnon and I had cause to bemoan, and the episode affords another glimpse of Anthoine's character. This is a climber of prodigious ability, great character and discreet intelligence, a modest man who has survived numerous expeditions to the Himalaya and whose essence remains as incorruptible as the mountains he scales. He is down to earth, always prepared to help his friends and yet, for all that he appears possessed of a profound, if indefinable, inner tranquillity, something drives Anthoine to keep pushing himself, to take risks, to keep going and to embrace ever more dangerous expeditions. His explanation is that he has to 'feed the rat' that lurks perpetually within him:

> The rat is you, really. It's the other you, and it's being fed by the you that you think you are. And they are often very different people. But when they come close to each other, that's smashing, that is. Then the rat's had a good meal and you come away feeling terrific. It's a fairly rare thing, but you have to keep feeding the brute, just for your own peace of mind. And even if you did blow it, at least there wouldn't be that great unknown. But to snuff it without knowing who you are and what you are capable of, I can't think of anything sadder than that.

Anthoine, apparently indestructible, suffered a brain tumour in his late forties, and yet within ten days of consequential major surgery he was skiing black runs. Three months later he went to the North-East Ridge of Everest, prompting Alvarez to wonder how he would fare at such high altitude so soon after brain surgery. Alvarez records that a mutual friend, Ian McNaught-Davis, shrugs and says: 'Better to die on a mountain doing something he loves than rot in a hospital bed.'

In surfing, big-wave surfer Mark Foo once told a journalist that he wasn't afraid to die because 'if you want the ultimate thrill, you've got to be prepared to pay the ultimate price. To me it's not tragic to die doing something you love.' Foo died, aged thirty-five, while surfing an 18 ft wall of water at the Californian cold-water big-wave break Maverick's, a place surfed by local Jeff Clark on his own for over a decade before it was lauded by the surfing world as 'the new Waimea'. Anthoine, defeated by Everest, succumbed to a recurrence of the brain tumour and died in Wales shortly after his fiftieth birthday.

As the ferry docked in Lerwick, I put away my books and hoped that the wind might have dropped. I could do with a surf after unexpectedly wandering amid the ambivalent psychological contours of surfing and mountaineering. I made my way from my cabin to the car deck, there to find Mackinnon and Davies. Mackinnon looked out of sorts but, before falling ill for the remainder of the trip, passed on a message.

'The Gill says we're out of luck. There's even less chance of a north swell now than there was when we were on Orkney.'

Being out of luck was starting to be the common denominator of every surf trip I made to Scotland. On another occasion I scoured the breaks between Losssiemouth and Fraserburgh for a wave, only to draw a blank. Well, not completely. At the austere town of Fraserburgh I met a surfer called Jamie Christie as he was coming in from an early morning session. The tide was retreating but it looked as if the Broch – Fraserburgh's main break – might have had a decent wave. Christie, a 24-year-old mechanic who had a couple of boards stowed in a converted Ford Transit van, confirmed that conditions had been surfable an hour or two earlier. He noted, though, that this, the Moray Firth stretch of Scotland's coastline, was well populated by seals and that they weren't always the cuddly *selchie* of Marwick and Thomson's books: 'One bashed my leg at West Point. They come up spluttering and jumping and can be a bit of a worry.'

As I left Fraserburgh I recalled that someone had told me that surfing had arrived in this hard and grey town thanks to Willie Tait, a fisherman, who returned from a voyage with a Malibu board from California. Today Fraserburgh still boasts a large fishing fleet but also a sizeable surfing community whose needs are met by the Point North-East Surf Shop. The set-up at the Broch clearly offered good beachbreak surf, and as I inched my way east towards the 'Scottish Riviera' town of Lossiemouth, I could discern a number of nearby surfable breaks, most notably at Pennan, Banff and Sandend Bay, all of which, in facing due north, made for rather shadowy seaward dwellings.

Eventually I found myself in Lossiemouth, where, at last, there was good 3 ft surf near the rivermouth. Even better, the wind was offshore. I paddled out and within seconds of reaching the line-up, the wind direction shifted. The water was the coldest I have ever been in and what had been nicely lined-up, if rather brown, waves had turned into odious onshore mush. It was so cold that there was no consolation to be had in staying in the sea, and afterwards Ed Borrowman, a local doctor, surfer and man of direct if occasionally mysterious pronouncements, volunteered this diagnosis of surfing along the Moray Firth: 'The first lesson about surfing here is that if you expect anything you will be let down. There is no surf here. Anything you get is a bonus. Don't move here to surf.'

That sounded rather discouraging, but there were upsides. 'There are some breaks round here that may not exist but which can be fantastic. Also, the vibe is good. The surf community is small and friendly, you'll recognize everybody in the line-up and it's still the case here that we're genuinely pleased to see other surfers.'

Borrowman's words were jostling with thoughts of *Feeding the Rat* as Jesse Davies and I toured the Shetland Isles. It was January, and the sea was sure to be cold, perhaps not as cold as that along the Moray Firth (given that a hint of the Gulf Stream permeates the sea around Shetland) but still severe enough to induce hypothermia within five minutes if anyone was unlucky, or foolish, enough to take to the water without a wetsuit. In Jesse's van we covered the nooks and crannies of the main island (which, like its near neighbour in the Orkneys, is called Mainland), but as on Orkney we met with a ubiquitous westerly wind blowing at a force six to seven. The eastern side of Mainland would be sheltered from the wind, but any hope of finding a wave there depended on the elusive northerly swell or a fresh southerly to take its place. Neither was on the cards. Feeling rather despondent, our spirits improved when a message came through from The Gill, a man I had yet to meet but who, from his home in Mumbles, seemed to know more about what was happening in the far north of Scotland than we did.

'Get in touch with the local butcher,' said The Gill, 'a young lad called Martin. He's a surfer. At least if you find him you can talk to the locals. I don't think you've got any hope of finding a wave, though.'

Martin Sanderson was all exuberance and welcome when I tracked him down to one of the three Lerwick butchers listed in the Yellow Pages. He commiserated and laughed by turn, and suggested we meet for a drink in Lerwick that evening. He cautioned that it would be a busy night in town, since Up-Helly-Aa was due to start the next day. Many Shetlanders warm up for Up-Helly-Aa with an appetizer or three the preceding evening, but, said Martin, we would still be able to find somewhere quiet to talk. 'I'll bring some photos and prove that we've got surf,' he promised, adding that he would see if Vince Attfield, the original Shetland Islands surfer, was around.

The topography of the Shetland Isles was enough to convince me that there had to be surf here. Shetland is a chain of over 100 islands stretching ninety miles from Muckle Flugga in the north (on the same latitude as Greenland) to Fair Isle in the south. Sumburgh Head, the most southerly point of Mainland, is ninety miles from Caithness in Scotland and 210 miles from Aberdeen, to which we would be returning by ferry after Up-Helly-Aa. The Shetlanders make much of their Viking heritage. Though there is evidence of settlement at a much earlier date, the arrival of seaborn Scandinavian pirates in longships in around 800 AD has left an indelible mark. Norse names abound, Viking houses have been excavated and elements of the Norse legal system survive to this day (under 'Udal law', landowners held land themselves and not, as in feudal law, in obeisance to a king. I was told that Udal law still applies to ownership of the foreshore and salmon fishing rights, to the chagrin of politicians in Edinburgh).

As Jesse and I made our way into Lerwick, there was ample evidence of high spirits among the town's 8,000 inhabitants as they geared up for Up-Helly-Aa. Little wonder, for Up-Helly-Aa is reputedly the world's biggest fire festival. It is held on the last Tuesday of January and marks the climax of a year's work in building a Viking galley. The climax comes in the destruction of the galley by fire. Up to 1,000 'guizers' – men who have dressed up in accordance with the Shetland tradition of 'guizing' – march through Lerwick at night, the town lit only by their torches. The guizers are divided into squads, with the chief squad being that of the organizing committee, the Guizer Jarls (or 'chiefs'). The Guizer Jarl, like his squad of fifty men, dresses in Viking apparel, while the other forty-nine squads dress in whatever takes their fancy. The squads tow the galley in their wake, singing a variety of traditional songs, and eventually deposit it in a park in the centre of Lerwick. There, in the culmination of festivities that have gone on all day long, it is burnt as each of the 1,000 torches is hurled on to the galley. Thereafter the squads and majority of people on the Shetland Isles repair to one of several halls to be greeted by a host and hostess. Vast quantities of alcohol are consumed over a night that, for those who have the stamina, ends at 10.00 the next morning. Throughout the night the various squads tour the halls and perform skits of one kind or another to an increasingly impassioned audience.

'It's cracking,' said Martin, when we met in the evening. 'It's such a laugh. I'm the squad leader of Squad Number Eighteen. Look out for me and say hi!'

With him was 38-year-old Vince Attfield. Vince smiled at Martin's enthusiasm but would not, this year, be taking part in Up-Helly-Aa. If, however, outsiders might consider the Up-Helly-Aa festival to be an exercise in 'controlled mayhem, with a lot of madmen running about' (the view of one man I met in the Orkneys), Vince was used to being perceived as being eccentric, at the very least, by his fellow islanders.

'Oh, they think we're barking mad to surf here. When I first started surfing people would see me in the water and call the coastguard. They just had no idea what I was doing. A lot of them still don't.'

Was there a surfing community? Any shops? A longboarders versus shortboarders debate?

'No, there aren't enough of us,' said Martin. 'Vinnie started it all off but we're still in a very, very small minority. We're mostly all shortboarders anyway.'

Vince agreed. He started surfing in the mid-1990s simply 'because it was something I fancied doing'. He reminded me of Derek Macleod, with his light-coloured hair, medium height and powerful build, and the parallels didn't stop there. Like Macleod, Vince had surfed in the Shetlands on his own, in all conditions. He had made his first board – 'I think it was about three-foot long, I didn't know any better' – and learnt the hard way, by trial and error. Moreover, the Shetlands was not conducive to beginners: 'We've mostly got points and reefs. The beachbreaks tend to close out and don't really work all that well.'

Martin interjected, though, that those points and reefs were capable of producing great surf, which he proceeded to illustrate via a series of photographs. Thick, cold-looking water was barrelling left and right, and in one shot there were at least three surfers paddling into position in a swell that was comfortably double-overhead. 'That was a killer session,' said Martin. 'Greg and Rusty Long came over and stayed for a while.'

Aside from the Californian duo, travelling surfers were a rarity. Indeed, of the Shetland Isles' total population of some 22,000 people fewer than ten of them were surfers. This meant that Vince and his fellows (there were no female surfers) could guarantee uncrowded surf sessions. Vince showed me a map of the Shetlands against which he had marked an X for all the places he had surfed. There must have been 100 Xs. 'We don't get world-class waves but what's on my doorstep is good enough for me. I don't need to travel anywhere, there's so much here. You can usually find a wave most days because there are so many different-facing spots. The cold's not a problem – it's about six degrees C in winter and twelve degrees C in August. That's fine. We can get our gear from Rick's shop in Thurso or order it online.'

According to Martin, if it was communing with wildlife that you were after, the Shetlands had it all. 'You'll never surf with so many seals as here,' he told me. 'They come and look at you and flap and spray you with saltwater then swim off.' Vince agreed. 'You get a lot of the young seals following you when you paddle out. They jump out behind you then disappear, come back and do it all over again.'

'We get dolphins, too. And sea otters,' said Martin. 'They pop up to see what's going on. They look at you as if to say "Who the hell are you?" then vanish. But they're fine. The only problem is the whales.'

Whales?

'Yeah, we get the big whales in the summer, minkes and humpbacks, but it's not them you need to worry about. It's the killers. I think some of them live here, isn't that right, Vince?'

Vince concurred. 'I was surfing Quendale one time and there must have been a pod of six killer whales next to me.' He seemed, suddenly, lost for words, and I remembered that on the Hebrides Cheggs had told me a similar story. Everyone else had seen the whales and paddled rapidly for the shore, leaving Cheggs alone in the line-up. 'I thought, "Why are they leaving me here? Don't they like me?" Then I looked round and saw the fin of a killer whale and thought "Jesus!"'

This was Vince's reaction, too. 'They're huge animals and it's scary when they pop up, no doubt about it.' But Vince would keep paddling out, rather as Jeff Clark had surfed Maverick's alone and with all its risks for years, because he loved surfing and lived for its joys. He had also read – to his relief – that killer whales have not been known to kill humans.

Jesse and I did not abandon hope of finding some surf in the Shetlands, despite increasingly dreadful weather and daily updates from The Gill to the effect that there was no swell for miles. We took ferries to Yell and Unst, we smiled at the 'Dunna Chuck Bruch' imprecation adjacent to a wastebin outside the Wind Dog Café, we discovered Boddam and the Boat Ramp, we looked at the strange refraction wave at St Ninian's Isle, but all was in vain. The wind was like a shot-blaster unleashed for eternity. We made it as far as Skaw, Britain's most northerly beach and the scene of its most northerly inhabited house. The roof of an outhouse is the hull of a boat, but aside from this notable example of architectural creativity Skaw was a disappointment. There was almost a wave as a gentle, intermittent series of bulges broke on the coldest beach I have yet to visit. Most, though, were closing out, providing very little that could be ridden. Jesse and I wavered, decided to go in, then, as we were walking to the van to get changed, thought better of it. During our return jouney to Mainland to prepare for Up-Helly-Aa I made a mental note to tell Tom Anderson that there was also a Twatt in the Shetlands (and, indeed, to tell him that way down south, back on the balmy English Riviera, there was yet another 'TWAT' – the Torbay Wave Attack Team).

The spectacle of Up-Helly-Aa did, however, go a long way to compensating for the absence of any surf. The sight of 1,000 torches being held aloft and marched through Lerwick by squadrons of Vikings, Toms and Jerrys, swag-men, British constables and all manner of other quixotically dressed individuals was at once primeval and surreal, but the festivities in the halls were yet more remarkable. The Saturnalian tradition was alive and well as virtually the entire population of the Shetland Isles engaged in controlled mayhem, drinking, dancing and carousing with surprisingly few, if any, untoward incidents. Jesse and I failed to last the course, calling it a night early at seven in the morning. We returned to our base at the Herrislea Hotel where the owners, Gordon and Marjorie Wallace, had put on a 'survivors' breakfast'. This I devoured as manna from heaven while Jesse reflected on our Orkney and Shetland odyssey.

'They've got some good set-ups here and Vinnie knows what he's about. He's a cool guy. But we were unlucky. That's how it goes. Hey, would have been good if we'd scored at Skaw, eh?' I chuckled over the concept of scoring at Skaw and wondered if, just for the hell of it, we should have paddled out into its 2 ft close-out waves.

'No,' said Jesse. 'If we hadn't got in the water at Aberdeen, maybe. But we did. And thank God. You see – never turn away from surf if you find it.'

Scotland's North Shore regularly serves up waves like this: Russell Winter in a
Brims Ness barrel, on his way to victory at the O'Neill Highland Open.

21

59 DEGREES NORTH

Love Hodel was impressed. 'Man, when it's on that wave is pretty damn perfect,' said the 34-year-old Hawaiian, his blue eyes lost in awe. 'Maybe not as powerful as Hawaiian surf but good, really good.'

Thanks to the O'Neill Highland Open, Hodel was undergoing his first experience of the surf at Thurso East. Hodel was one of 144 professional surfers drawn to the freezing northern fringes of mainland Scotland for what was a five-star WQS event. WQS events have a rating according to the quality of their waves, from six star down to one. The higher the rating, the more points – and prize money – are up for grabs. O'Neill put up a prize pool of $100,000, and Thurso's reputation as a quality wave meant that it was easily given five-star status. Vital points could be accrued in the quest to finish in the top sixteen of the WQS, meaning promotion to the pro surfer's Holy Grail, the WCT. That this was a serious contest, with some serious spoils, was underscored by its location: at fifty-nine degrees north, the O'Neill Highland Open could justifiably claim to be the world's coldest ever international surfing contest.

Hodel was one of twelve Hawaiians to make the mammoth journey to Thurso, Scotland's most northerly mainland town. Other competitors came from Australia, South Africa, Brazil, America,

Britain and Ireland. They were in Thurso to surf its super-fast right-hander, the same wave that I had read about for over twenty years, the same wave that I had raved about to Zed Layson, the same wave that a number of surfers I had met on my travels described as the best they had ever surfed. The organizers had chosen to host the event in April, which, aside from autumn and winter, is just about the best time for swells to hit northern Scotland. The water would still be cold but if ever there was going to be an opportunity to see world-class surf without having to fly overseas, this was surely it.

Sam Lamiroy, who had won the Independence Pro in Barbados a few days before I met Zed, was in Thurso for both the Scottish leg of Dave Reed's BPSA Tour and the WQS event. I arrived just as the BPSA event was finishing to find that it been been won by Russell Winter (himself a victor of the Independence Pro in 2006) and, moreover, blessed by pumping surf. Lamiroy had no hesitation in agreeing with Hodel: 'In surfing terms this place has iconic status,' he told me. 'It's a world-class break.'

The town of Thurso itself is remote, exacting and rather more understated than its surf. Its houses are pebble-dashed in dour browns and greys in an attempt to cope with the near-constant wind and rain, and its roofless, once-grand castle, overlooking the reef break of Thurso East, appears as a duly admonished subjugate to the Old Man of Hoy, visible to the north. Thurso's congeniality to surfing arises because it is exposed to the full force of Arctic swells that are driven irresistibly on to its flat, kelp-covered reefs. Nearby is the Dounreay nuclear reactor, which, since 1955, has been as much a source of local employment as controversy. Dounreay is now subject to a decommissioning programme set to last decades after a number of safety scares. Plutonium particles were found to be leaking from the plant and have been seen at Dounreay's nearest beach, Sandside Bay – 'a classic/reef set-up' according to the *Stormrider* guide and reputedly now the home of one of the first people to surf Thurso East, Pat Kieran. Also, evidently, a place that carries a health warning. The spectre of Dounreay hovers uncomfortably over life around the beaches and fields of Caithness, and was yet more unavoidable when

I realized that my arrival in Thurso coincided with the twentieth anniversary of the Chernobyl disaster. Any thoughts that this might be a bad omen were swiftly countered not merely by the excellent waves but also by a remarkable conversation with Love Hodel.

Perhaps anyone whose brothers are named Peace and Joy, and whose sisters are Fauna 1 and Fauna 2, would have a diverting effect. Certainly, Hodel brought a dash of colour to the gritty hues of Thurso. He told me he was conceived in the sea at Pipeline and that his 'surfer dad/hippie chick mother' named him I Lêo I Holo Kai, which means 'he who freely rides the sea'. He had recently got married and would be calling any children conceived by himself and Amy, his wife, Justice (if a boy) and Nia (if a girl), the latter translating as 'dolphin'. Of his siblings he was the only surfer, starting at age four and turning pro at twenty. He had been in the top fifty of the WQS but the WCT has thus far eluded him. The Highland Open was a chance to boost his ratings, and he was enjoying every minute of being in Thurso, a town whose daily rhythms bore as much resemblance to life on the North Shore of Oahu as those of a train station in Tirana.

'It's so cool to be so far north for a surf contest,' he said, as we ambled the streets towards Gary Reid's Riverside Fish Bar. On the way there young Scottish girls cooed at Hodel, whose piercing blue eyes, blond hair and bronze complexion obscured a rather more unnerving past.

'You've heard of the Black Dahlia, right?'

I had indeed. Elizabeth Short was a 22-year-old brunette waitress in Los Angeles who, on 15 January 1947, was found dead on wasteland in the Leimert Park section of L.A. The murder became notorious because Short's body had been both drained of its blood and severed at the waist. The two parts of Short's naked body were found as if in a presentation, her arms above her head like a dancer's. A number of precise incisions had been made to deface the body and face. The gruesome and horrific killing baffled detectives and to this day has not been solved.

Or had it? 'My mum, Tamar, was the daughter of the Black Dahlia murderer,' said Hodel. I choked on my chips as he continued: 'The murderer was a man called George Hodel. My granddad. The case was solved by his son, Steve.'

Hodel said this with complete equanimity. Reid brought us our fish and chips but my appetite had vanished. Apparently Steve Hodel, a former cop, had spotted a photograph of Elizabeth Short in his father's photo album. Hodel senior died in 1999 but his son began to suspect that his legacy was more disturbing even than the known charges of sexual abuse against his daughter (George Hodel was tried and acquitted of charges of molesting Tamar in December 1949). The result of Steve Hodel's suspicions was a book called *Black Dahlia Avenger*, which suggests that George Hodel – a medical man, misanthrope and art lover – committed the murder as an artistic *acte gratuit*.

'My mom has a radical life story,' said Hodel, just as Reid wandered over from his fish 'n' chips counter to ask us if we were in town for the surfing contest. 'Yes,' I replied, and asked him what he thought of surfing in Thurso.

'It's fantastic and it's what this town needs,' he said. 'It's great for the kids. This can be a tough place to grow up but surfing can give them a focus.'

Hodel talked readily with Reid about life in Thurso and the extent to which its 11,000 inhabitants might themselves freely ride the sea. His remarkable background was forgotten in a twinkle of his blue eyes as Reid and I learnt that he had recently taken Olympic oarsman James Cracknell surfing. 'Yeah, he wanted to know what it'd be like to be out in fifteen-foot surf. So I took him out at Phantoms, a heavy break on the North Shore. I think he enjoyed himself.'

I asked Hodel how he kept himself occupied when the surf itself became rather more revenant than real. After all, he and his fellow competitors were on and off planes travelling the world for most of the year, but as often as not they would arrive for an event only to be cursed by a flat sea. What did they do then?

'Play poker, mostly,' said Hodel. 'I love the game. Do you play?'

Shortly before I arrived in Thurso work took me to London. I was staying with a writer friend in Brixton, and the conversation inevitably turned to our various projects. When he heard that I was writing about surfing in the UK and Ireland, with a trip to Thurso looming, Barney jumped up, grabbed a notepad and wrote down a name and number. 'Speak to Kirsten. She's a friend of ours. She knows heaps about Thurso.'

I duly caught up with Kirsten MacLeod, a Scottish documentary-maker living in Brixton, to learn that she had completed a dissertation on surfing as part of an MA in Archaeology and Social Anthropology in 1991. MacLeod had spent months with Thurso's surfing community in 1990, travelling with them to Easkey in Ireland and surfing the beginner and intermediate waves in Thurso (essentially, its beachbreak and a friendly reef break known as the Shit Pipe) as well as those along the Caithness coast. Kirsten's face lit up with memories of her time in northern Scotland. 'It's such a beautiful area. You're lucky to be going,' was just about the first thing she said. She told me of a hardy local crew who 'weren't part of the regular surf scene', which she clarified as follows: 'Surfing in Thurso isn't about image and hype. At least it wasn't when I was there. It was about surfing itself – the love of it and the doing of it. It was elemental. There was no side to anyone there – they just surfed for surfing's sake, not to pose and say they were surfers.'

Kirsten appeared wistful as she contemplated her time in Thurso. 'God, I wish I was going,' she said. 'You should go to the café on the corner and see if the 'Details' graffiti is still there.'

What was this?

'Remember the old slogan – "Surfing is life, the rest is details"? It was used by a surf company in its advertising, I can't remember which one. There's a café there and in the backroom the locals scrawled the graffiti on the wall. They left out the surfing bit and just put "Details, the rest is details". I always liked that. It got to the point where they'd just say "Details" in response to any given situation that they considered meaningless or unimportant, anything that didn't involve surfing.'

Kirsten gave me another vignette of life in Thurso over fifteen years ago. 'There was a boy called Gourlay who sprayed graffiti on the harbour wall. Some of the other lads questioned him about his choice of location. He said he was making a point of spraying the wall and not the rocks beside it. He explained himself by saying "The rocks are part of the sea – and that's surfing. The wall is just details."'

I looked for the 'Details' graffiti and couldn't find it, but Andy Bain, Thurso's long-time local surfer, remembered Kirsten. 'Aye, she was a nice lass. Wrote a PhD or something didn't she?' Bain, or Bainers as he is known to everyone, is a tall, long-haired and quietly spoken man who was working as a beach marshal for the duration of the O'Neill Highland Open. He knows as much about surfing in Thurso as anyone, being a surfer since 1994 and born and bred in the town. 'I went away for a while,' he told me, 'but came back and stayed for the surfing.'

What did Thurso's citizens make of people like Bainers going surfing in the middle of winter?

'They still haven't got used to it. They still think we're mad. If you consider the history of the area you can see why.'

Bainers was referring to Thurso's location on the edge of the Pentland Firth. The channel between Caithness and the Orkneys is some six to eight miles wide and through it, twice daily, huge tides surge between the Atlantic and the North Sea and back again. Currents can reach up to 12 knots and countless ships have been lost in this, one of the most dangerous stretches of water in the world. Captains would often prefer to make lengthy detours north of Orkney or south by the English Channel to avoid the notoriously treacherous eddies and whirlpools of the Pentland Firth.

'People in Caithness have long memories,' said Bainers. 'They still associate the sea as a place where people have died. They can't understand why we would want to go surfing in that same sea.'

But Bainers and the Thurso crew will go surfing in conditions that would make the hardiest mariner flinch. Bainers' favourite board for Thurso East is an MMY 6′ 10″ rounded pintail shaped by Chris Harris, a man who he says has got designing boards for

Thurso 'absolutely wired'. Harris's boards, though, are sometimes used as a defence mechanism. 'In winter we'll get snow, rain and blocks of ice but the worst of the lot are the hailstones. They're the size of golfballs. When they come in you tread water and hold your board above your head. Like an umbrella.'

Bainers ran Thurso's surf school, though he was thinking of taking some time out for a trip to Australia at some stage and didn't anticipate keeping the school going in his absence. However, Thurso's surfers are also looked after by two surf shops: Stephen Donn's Surf 'n' Skate shop on the high street, and the Tempest Surf Shop, across the harbour from Thurso East itself. The Tempest shop is run by Rick Picken, a former St Ives and Sennen Cove lifeguard and surfer who set up on Thurso's harbour wall in autumn 2004. Picken was overrun throughout the O'Neill Highland Open, but said that business was good year-round, too: 'A year ago there were only two groms learning to surf but now there are over twenty. Surfing is taking off here, just like everywhere else. We get loads of travellers coming through – you'll see twenty different countries listed in my guest book.'

I was speaking to Picken outside his shop, which doubles as a café. It was a bright day, contest-free owing to a lull in the swell and relatively mild. Picken rushed off to serve some more customers, and I got talking to Ingrid Morrison, thirty, and Rosina Kerswell, twenty-five, who had driven some six hours for the Highland Open. They had been surfing further along the coast at Melvich but, while they were adamant that more and more women were taking to the water, neither expected to try their skills at Thurso East.

'I paddled out there once,' said Ingrid. 'But I paddled back in pretty damn quickly.'

Upon Picken's return I asked him if he thought Thurso would ever become as crowded as the breaks of Cornwall and Devon. After all, plenty of people had warned me that its line-up was sometimes as busy as Picken's café during the Highland Open. Picken didn't agree. 'No,' he said. 'It's too far, too cold, and too serious.'

Just how good, then, was Thurso's famous wave? Picken, who had travelled the world surfing (and, in the course of his travels, met Zed Layson), was forthright.

'Make no mistake, Thurso East is one of the world's great waves. It breaks at up to twenty feet and produces unbelievable right-hand walls and barrels. It's the kind of wave that very few people can surf well. But there's one man here who takes it on whatever the size. Whenever it's on, whatever time of year, he'll be there.'

That man is former Fraserburgh fisherman Chris Noble, whom I met on the third day of the contest at his house overlooking Thurso East. It tended to the threadbare and seemed to have more surfboards than furniture. Noble, who works for BT and is sponsored by surfwear companies including The Realm and Reef, went out of the contest on the first day, but was pleased to have had the chance to compete against professionals from around the world. He spoke softly, and his green-brown eyes bore the same faraway sheen as Hodel's. I asked him if he'd moved to Thurso purely so that he could centre his life around its waves. Noble, thirty-one, weighed the question as if aware that his answer, to non-believers, might sound more than mildly eccentric. 'Aye,' he said, after a pause, 'that'd be right.'

A short man with a wiry build and mousy-brown hair, with a scar on his chin showing through a few days' stubble, Noble once spent an entire February at sea, and he retains the aura of seasoned fisherman rather than stereotypical surfer. But surfing is very much his thing – even if when I asked him why this was so he seemed initially rather flummoxed.

'I don't know, it's just kinda cool, I suppose.'

Was that all?

'Well, I enjoy the feeling of speed. I enjoy challenging myself. My family has always had a kinship with the sea, which surfing gives me, too. But most of all I enjoy meeting so many people. Surfing has allowed me to travel, and I've been to places and met people that wouldn't have been possible if I wasn't a surfer. I've met people who've come here to surf from all over the world.'

Noble was involved, with Bainers (whom he described as 'the local'), in the newly formed Caithness Boardriders' Club, but felt that the town council could do more to promote surfing in the area. 'It's a great thing for kids to get into but there's not enough energy or support by the council. There are people here who don't want things to change but they are changing and people ought to accept that.' He seemed to have mixed feelings about the Highland Open. 'It's huge and it's great for the town but on a personal level I'm not relishing the attention. I'm not sure the contest thing is me. I started surfing in Fraserburgh when I was thirteen, decided then to make it my life, and I moved here six years ago for Thurso East. I surf natural foot and it breaks perfectly for me. Sure, you get blocks of ice going "clunk clunk" on your board in the winter – the ice floats down the frozen River Thurso and into the line-up – but we get seals, dolphins, sea otters and waves that are just perfect. All I want to do is surf those waves.'

The cold, for the likes of Noble and Bainers, did not matter, but top Brazilian pro Neco Padaratz was having difficulty acclimatizing. During the Highland Open the water temperature was seven degrees centigrade. After he had won his opening heat in 3–4 ft waves, Padaratz summed up his feelings thus: 'I've been doing the world tour for twenty years. This is coldest place I've ever surfed.' The heavily tattooed, muscular Brazilian – renowned for having survived a three and a half minute hold-down at big-wave spot Teahupoo in Tahiti – grinned before adding: 'Right now my lips are not really opening properly for me to speak. I think they're stuck.' Padaratz was also getting used to surfing in a thick winter wetsuit, boots, hood and gloves. 'It's all really strange,' he said, 'a whole new ballgame for me.'

At the beginning of the Highland Open the wave at Thurso East was only a notch or two away from being classic. At last, I got to see it being ridden – and by surfers of the repute of Padaratz and Hodel. It was Sam Lamiroy, however, who posted the highest score of the day on day one, with a superb ride resulting in a 9.4. The Tynemouth surfer – who was included in a *Sunday Times*

January 2007 supplement devoted to the great and the good who were shaping the success of the north-east – was strongly fancied to go all the way at the Thurso event, but success here eluded him. Lamiroy was knocked out midway through the Highland Open, but took his exit in his stride.

'I'm pleased we've had such cracking waves for the contest,' he said. 'I'm disappointed to go out, sure, but I didn't really make any mistakes. I was KOd by a Brazilian and the South Africans but, so far, I've still got the highest-scoring wave of the contest.'

Lamiroy's exit had come at Brims Ness, to which the event had moved following a lull in the swell at Thurso East. Brims Ness – which means 'surf point' in Nordic – is a few miles west of Thurso and sticks so far out to sea that it picks up any swell going. The pro surfers from overseas had been impressed by Thurso East during the first couple of days of the week-long contest, but were astonished by what 'the Brims bowl' had to offer. As Lamiroy put it: 'At Brims the surf comes out of nowhere. You think you're sitting in the right spot, then the waves appear and you realize you're in the wrong place. But if you catch the right wave at Brims, you'll be in one of the most insane barrels of your life.'

Lamiroy is an articulate man, a graduate of Plymouth University (where he studied Oceanography) and fluent in several languages. Born in Belgium, he grew up surfing in the north-east and has a large, redoubtable frame that seems tailor-made for big-wave surfing. He is at the vanguard of the contemporary push to tow-surf cold-water big waves in Britain and Ireland, and is twice a winner of the British Surfing Championships, most recently when O'Neill hosted the 2006 event in chunky 4–5 ft surf at the North Devon beach of Putsborough. The 30-year-old echoes the sentiments of English Surfing Federation coach Paul Jeffrey when discussing the state of surfing in Britain: 'When you see Russell Winter in the water next to the Hawaiians and the Brazilians, you can see that he's as good as them. But the support isn't there. We can't expect one person to influence an entire nation's sporting hopes. Surfing here is seen as a pursuit rather than a sport. In Australia kids are taught surfing, they're coached from an early age, they harness young talent. Why don't we do that? There's a romance and a grittiness to surfing here but there's no reason, with the conditions that we've got, that we shouldn't also have more professional surfers. But for that to happen there needs to be a nationwide embrace of surfing rather than pockets of localized activity. There should be a central academy, like the Lilleshall National Sports Centre for football.'

For Lamiroy, surfing is 'the overriding thing in my life. It permeates everything I do – where I live, how I interact with people, how I see the world.' Moreover, surfing is 'the moment that brings together many of the things that make us human – nature, subtle changes in your environment, your interaction with those things, your sense of balance and control of tiny fractions of movement.' Lamiroy agreed that surfing is addictive, but doubted that it is as harmful as other addictions: 'There might be someone who doesn't share your compulsion, but this is a healthy, good kind of addiction. And to succeed you have to have that kind of personality. Especially in this country. You have to have total and absolute dedication.'

That such dedication is a prerequisite was all too obvious at Brims Ness as the O'Neill Highland Open reached its final stages. The Brims Ness bowl, a right-hand reef break, was serving up majestic barrels but the cold – enhanced by a wicked southerly wind – was inescapable. Standing on the rocky beach was nothing less than freezing. Even veteran Hawaii-based cinematographer and waterman Larry Haynes, whose job it was to bob up and down in the line-up and film the action, was shivering. 'The cold gets a hold of you and won't let you go,' said Haynes, a man who has spent his life surfing Hawaii's massive waves and travelling the world to make surfing films. He sipped from a cup of soup as three surfers jostled for position before the one wearing a white identification vest leapt to his feet and tucked into another Brims barrel.

'Nice ride,' said Haynes.

He was watching Russell Winter. The man from Newquay was

on his way to one of the finest achievements by a British athlete in 2006.

It's day seven of the O'Neill Highland Open. The last day. The preceding couple of nights have been spent playing poker with Hodel and some of the other pros – Hank Gaskell (Hawaii), Dayvan Neve (Australia) and Royden Bryson (South Africa). We were joined by Ian Smith, a freelance photographer, as well as various people involved in organizing the event. The games took place in a large backroom of the Royal Hotel on Thurso's high street, where most of the surfing circus was staying. Just as in Porthcawl, lady luck hadn't been shining on me. But, according to St Ives lifeguard, ex-pro skateboarder and surfer Stef Harkon, things were going Russell Winter's way.

'He's been the best surfer of the event by far,' said Harkon, an ultra-fit man in his early forties who, along with Steve Jamieson from Sennen Cove, had been retained by O'Neill and co-sponsors Red Bull to take charge of water safety. 'You watch him tomorrow. If he surfs the way he has for the past week he's got every chance of winning this event.'

The morning after this conversation I am standing on the cliffs looking down at the Brims Ness bowl. I reflect on the relative ease with which Winter despatched Padaratz to reach the quarter-finals, but wonder if Harkon is right. Again the surf is excellent, again it is cold, again the wind is blasting out to sea from the south, but now, with all the remaining heats to be contested in the last day, the pressure is on. In contrast to the Rip Curl Boardmasters, it is pressure that will be withstood in the absence of a meaningful contingent of spectators. Looking around there are virtually no onlookers who are not, in some way, connected with the event (whether as competitors, organizers or media), and as I am pondering the dichotomy between the guaranteed crowds but imponderable surf of the Boardmasters, as against the Spartan atmosphere but undeniable kudos of the Highland Open, Harkon is walking to the water. He reaches the edge of the rocks, the place where the land meets the sea, as 6–8 ft faces implode on the reef just a few yeards ahead of him. He waits for an opportunity then jumps into the sea. Within minutes he is in the shifting Brims line-up, and soon he is dropping down the face of thunderous wave, stalling his board and disappearing fleetingly inside a barrel. Harkon takes three or four waves like this, wiping out badly on one, before returning to land and readying himself for contest duty. He has been surfing in waves that break in no more than 1 ft of water, and it is in these perilous conditions that Winter will have to prove himself.

Winter's is the first quarter-final of the day. He follows a similar path to Harkon's, to the edge of the exposed rocks, and dances lightly from toe to toe – rather as a boxer standing in his corner before a title fight – before paddling out. At twenty-nine, Winter is the most successful surfer yet to emerge from Europe. He is the only Briton, and the first European, to compete on the WCT, and now, with a victory in the Scottish leg of the BPSA already under his belt, he is the last Briton among a field comprised of American, Spanish, Brazilian, South African and Australian surfers. Over the past week I have only seen him in the water, for during contests Winter eschews almost any form of socializing, even with other surfers. He has been keeping himself to himself, staying in a caravan with his parents on a campsite outside Thurso. He is an intense, compactly built man whose entire being seems to be thrown into moves that are at once aggressive and flamboyant. His WCT stint was compromised by a serious injury, which, like Padaratz's near-death experience, was sustained at Teahupoo.

This year, though, Winter's determination to secure enough WQS points to make it back on to the WCT is palpable. He reaches the line-up with deceptive languor for his quarter-final against Australia's Kieren Perrow. The skies are blue, Bainers sits observing everything wearing a fisherman's all-in-one oilskin and dark glasses, the waves are perfect and Larry Haynes, in the water to record the denouement of the Highland Open, dives for the bottom as a wave collapses on his head. If it were not for the numbing wind, this could be a scene from Hawaii. Winter has no such comparisons on his mind: he is there to surf as well as he can, and, at this point in time, has obliterated anything other than surfing from his being. He slots into the slate-grey barrels with ease and surfs intelligently, waiting until the dying minutes before taking off and scoring so well that Perrow cannot catch him.

A similar story unfurls in the semi-final, in which Winter knocks out another big-name surfer, Australian Luke Munro. He is through to the final thanks to an array of snaps, floater re-entries and barrels, and, as a guaranteed top-four finisher, has booked himself an all-expenses return trip to Teahupoo courtesy of the O'Neill 'Mission', in which an elite group of surfers will judge each other as they ride the monster wave that injured Winter and so nearly killed Padaratz.

Winter takes to the freezing sea at Brims Ness for the last time to compete against Brazilian Bernardo Miranda for 2,000 WQS points and the $12,000 first prize. The wind by now is so strong that the crowd of onlookers is being blown over. In between rounds Harkon has swum into the roiling sea to retrieve one half of a broken board. I recall what he told me the previous night: 'At Brims, you need to take off as far back on the wave as you can.' Miranda and Winter paddle for position, with the Brazilian scoring first. Winter counters and then, midway through the final, a set wave comes through. Winter is so far back that I think there is no way he can make the wave. He might try but it will close out and nail him. Instead, though, he takes a couple of strokes and then leaps to his feet to slip into a barrel so deep that, for a second, he is invisible. He flies out of the green room punching the air in elation. The judges score the wave a perfect 10, and Winter's lead proves to be unassailable: fifteen minutes later he is duly crowned the inaugural O'Neill Highland Open winner. On dry land, the man who has largely kept his own counsel for the duration of the contest is ecstatic. 'I'm stoked. To bring home a win here is fantastic for me and for British surfing.' Among the first surfers to congratulate the man the commentator calls 'the British Bulldog' is Padaratz, just beaten to it by Sam Lamiroy. They, and the surf media, and everyone at the event, know that Winter's achievement in beating a field of the world's best surfers in heavy, cold Scottish waves cannot be overstated.

As the event winds down I find myself stamping my feet to keep warm, hoping that some hot soup might miraculously materialize. I cast a look towards the Old Man of Hoy and think of Alvarez feeding his own rat atop that slender and admonishing finger of God. And as I'm looking out to sea, across the raging Pentland Firth, I spot Lamiroy in the line-up, as ever *sans* hood and gloves. There are three other surfers in the sea with him. A set wave arrives. Lamiroy paddles for it and makes the drop, to find himself deep inside his own Brims barrel.

Robyn Davies, *sans* injury, at home.

22

SUNSHINE

Paul 'The Gill' Gill – the first man to surf Thurso East – wanted to be a surfer even before he had stood on a board. Now fifty-two, The Gill was born and bred in Liverpool and found himself living in Manchester as a teenager when his parents moved there. He gravitated to surfing because of a poster he once saw, perhaps of Australian waves breaking perfectly, being surfed by someone like Nat Young, or Mark Richards, or the latter's perennial bridesmaid, Cheyne Horan. The exact image on the poster is no longer clear to The Gill but it was enough to make him do everything possible to escape the industry and commerce of Manchester in favour of the sea. He spent hours as a teenager studying maps of the coastline of Britain and Ireland, educating himself in how and where and why waves break, and eventually procured an old pop-out board with a flowery deck. He would badger his parents, relatives, anyone to take him to North Wales, in particular Anglesey, which is where he rode his first wave.

As soon as he could drive The Gill was in the ocean every spare moment, often surfing with Bez Newton, who went on to write *The Natural*. The Gill read Carl Thomson's *Surfing in Great Britain* as well as *Surf Insight* and another seminal, and still extant, surf magazine, *Tube News*. He kept reading his maps and atlases and recalled a geology trip he'd made as a 15-year-old to northern Scotland. He remembered the waves he'd seen on that trip even as he moved to the Mumbles and went to art college in Swansea, even as he made a trip to France and even as he did a stint as a dishwasher in Newquay. The Gill told himself that he had to go back to northern Scotland, to Caithness, and when he got there he found himself looking upon 3–4 ft perfection at Thurso East in 1975. He paddled out, surfed the frigid reef, and never looked back.

The Gill began shaping boards in the early 1980s, and still does so today at the South Cornelly Industrial Estate in Porthcawl. He works with Albie Harris, an Aberavon surfer and father of Dan, a successful longboarder. He runs a B&B in the Mumbles, and surfs as much as ever.

The Gill is also sometimes known as 'the Oracle', a tribute to his encyclopaedic knowledge of surf breaks around the UK and Ireland and his ability to predict, with mathematical certainty, whether a particular break will have surf and how good that surf will be. If he possesses certitude in such matters, the man who continues to forsake warm and sun-blessed overseas surfing locales in favour of north-east England, Scotland and Ireland could not, when I finally met him, tell me whether I would ever find Robyn Davies.

'Robyn Sunshine Davies?' he asked. Outside the shaping room the rain continued to fall, and inside Albie Harris chuckled affectionately. 'A great surfer and a lovely girl,' he offered. 'That's her real name, you know.' The Gill, though, shook his head. 'I'm sorry,' he said, 'I haven't met her. I couldn't tell you.'

I met The Gill and Albie Harris on the last of the trips for this book. I had zig-zagged from north to south and almost everywhere had heard people talking of Paul Gill. Often, it seemed, our paths crossed by a matter of days, and somehow, for the duration of the O'Neill Highland Open, we managed to be in a small place like Thurso and miss each other. But I had to find him, and once I did his reputation as the Oracle prompted my Robyn Davies question. In truth, though, The Gill's answer was predictable. Robyn was a chimera, as elusive as a perfect point break in East Anglia.

Perhaps, though, not meeting Robyn was typical of surfing, whether in the UK and Ireland or Hawaii, France, Australia, Brazil – anywhere. Surfers search for perfect waves but even if, as is so rare and wonderful, they find them the search is only ever temporarily suspended. Alvarez might say that the rat comes back, nagging for another feed; Melville might cast the search in more grandiose terms, as if we all, unconsciously, cannot but accept the siren call of the sea. If so we are powerless in its grip, and whether we find what we are looking for or not makes no difference. If I'd met Robyn and asked for her take on the meaning of surfing, what then? She would no more have the answer than The Gill would be able to tell me what she'd be doing next Thursday.

These philosophical meanderings came to me as I walked down the sliproad in Porthleven that leads to the Ship Inn. I was there because, just as I had given up hope of meeting her, Robyn Davies had left me a message. The result was that we'd arranged to meet outside the Ship at 4.00 pm on a bright Saturday at the tail end of February. I arrived early and gazed at the ancient harbour, its waters churning with an unquiet sea as a south-westerly swell, aided and abetted by an onshore wind, reminded me of just how exposed Porthleven is. As I watched the ebb and flow of the sea I thought of the people I'd met over eighteen months of surf-related travel in the UK and Ireland. I remembered Alan Stokes, the David Beckham of British surfing, and his story of how he'd once broken an ankle while surfing Fistral early in the morning in the depths of winter. He'd landed an aerial and continued surfing for a second or two before looking down at his foot and realizing that the force of the manoeuvre had snapped his ankle. Stokes had paddled in and crawled up the deserted beach to find a telephone box, where he called his mother to come and rescue him. I thought of Tony Plant, out at the Cribbar in February, taking a hammering in search of the perfect shot of the perfect wave that he'd watched all his life. There was Nigel Semmens, one of the UK's first pro surfers, who, in his Ocean Magic shop in Newquay, avowed that he'd rather give up surfing than swap his cherished shortboards for a longboard, as well as insisting that Porthleven remained the best wave he'd ever surfed. This was a view shared by Jed Stone, another veteran of the Newquay scene. 'It was back in 1980,' said Jed, a mellow, tranquil man who has won three European Masters titles. 'I arrived to find massive, double-overhead waves breaking perfectly over the reef. There was another bloke there who didn't fancy it, but I persuaded him to paddle out. It was hairy once we were in the line-up, but my first wave was a nice little barrel and the second was a full-on, stand-up, screaming down-the-line wave, the best barrel I've ever had. I paddled back out and took another wave, and got nailed. It was the worst wipeout of my life. As fast as I was dropping down the face, the wave was rearing up. I took a beating.'

I thought of Stokes, Plant, Semmens, and Stone, and of the woman I'd met coming in from the cold surf of Strandhill in County Sligo, only to paddle straight back out again; of Jamie Knox and Castlegregory, of Aileens and the Cliffs of Ruin; of Linda Sharp, Vinnie, Cheggs and whales; of Pete Robinson with his Swell board on Brighton sea-front; of Tiki Tim, of Emily's in East Anglia, of the differing styles of *Pit Pilot* and *The Surfer's Path* and *Surf Insight*, of long lines of clean swell at Sennen Cove and howling westerlies in the Orkneys. I thought of the surrealism of the Severn Bore; of Dominique Munro-Kent teaching my boys to surf; of hitting pads with Sam Smart and conversations about jazz and surfing with the Bleakleys; of Chris Hines and his Eco Board, SAS and Finisterre and environmentalism, of Chops Lascelles, the Sport of Kings, PJ and Damien Hirst. I remembered a poor hand or two in Porthcawl, thought of how I'd scooped a pot in Thurso and wondered if Dave Daley's Vegas dreams had come true. I thought of Stef Harkon's barrels at Brims and of him blithely swimming into the Pentland Firth to retrieve a broken board, and wondered at what size Mark Durbano had by now surfed La Rocco Reef. And I thought of how, in 2006, Russell Winter had won the O'Neill Highland Open while Ben Skinner came home with a silver medal in surfing's Olympics, the World Surfing Games.

I was supposed to be waiting for Robyn but was desperate to

see the ocean. I found myself edging away from my long-awaited rendezvous to check what the reef at Porthleven was doing. I didn't need The Gill to tell me that it would be booming but blown out, but I had to see it. I wanted to see waves breaking, even if they were unruly and unsurfable. As I started up the sliproad I turned and saw a petite woman, dressed casually with her brown hair cut in a bob that was beset by the wind. We met, smiled and shook hands. She joined me and soon we were sitting on the cliff-top overlooking an unsurfable Porthleven reef. The salt spray from waves like thunder washed over us, and I learnt that Robyn had been badly injured for eighteen months after a car crash. She had surfed but twice in all that time, on both occasions only thanks to epidural injections to relieve severe pain in her back. She couldn't wait to surf again, and, at last, the prognosis was good.

'I went to a very dark place but in two weeks I should be in the water again,' she said, staring out to sea. 'I can't wait.' Her sorrow at not having been able to surf for so long was tangible. I told her of Linda Sharp's words – of how the Welsh woman had seen such exceptional talent in the younger Surrey-born girl who had moved to the Lizard peninsula in Cornwall when she was five. 'That's kind of her,' said Robyn. 'I remember coming fourth in the English Nationals when I was seventeen – that was when Linda and I first surfed together. Linda won the event. She was my inspiration. I saw her paddle for a wave, take the drop and just smack the lip. I had no idea that you could surf like that. She opened my eyes to what surfing really was.'

One of Robyn's two surf sessions in the eighteen months I'd travelled the UK and Ireland had occurred in California at the World Surfing Games. The epidural had worked for a while but then her back had completely seized up. Robyn had been all but immobile for weeks, but was delighted at the success of Skinner in winning a silver medal. 'He so nearly won gold, too,' she said, adding that with Russell Winter's win in Scotland, 2006 had been 'brilliant for British surfing'.

Again I thought of how miserable Robyn must have been

following her injury. What did it feel like, being away from surfing? Was it possible to put in words?

'It felt like my heart had been broken in two,' she said.

I looked once more at the Porthleven reef. A wave smashed on to the rocks and again the salt spray covered us. I thought of surfing in bright Cornish sunshine at Sennen Cove, and knew then that John McCarthy had put it best: surfing was the most blissful experience you can have on this planet, a taste of heaven. No more, and no less.

ACKNOWLEDGEMENTS

Thanks to everyone I met in the course of researching this book, but especially: Andy, Carla and Hannah Kerenza, for their hospitality; Elliot, Rich and Andy, for the formative maritime anarchy; Zed, for the boards; the Bleakley clan, for being so welcoming; Al Mackinnon, for always knowing what was what; Tony Plant, for Tony Plant; Simon Tucker, for a very long loan; Jamie Knox, for getting me windsurfing again; my Mum and Dad and brother Chris, for pioneering the under-rated windsurfing location of Budleigh Salterton in south-east Devon; Duncan Scott, who taught me why Only a Bore Surfer Knows the Feeling; Mark Durbano, for his great goodwill; Pete Robinson, for The Surfing Museum; the University of East Anglia, for skate heaven and, in a roundabout way, for Chris, Clive, Neil and Mark; Jesse Davies, for his good company among the Vikings; Sam Smart, for the boxing, and Stef Harkon, for surf-specific training; Cheggs, because a nicer bloke would be hard to find; Ed, for the board; the Lahinch crew, for their time; Tim Kevan, for some very fine books; Kirsten MacLeod, for a superb dissertation; Chris Power, Vince Medeiros, ADR and Steve Bough, for cast-iron advice, and Tom Anderson, for The Jolly Sailor, Herbie, Linda, Peter and poker.

Thanks also to Karen Walton and everyone at the BSA (www.britsurf.co.uk); to Dave Reid and the BPSA (www.bpsauktour.com); to everyone at the Hotel and Extreme

Academy, Watergate Bay (www.watergatebay.co.uk); to Jenny and www.visitscotland.com; to Inga and www.northlinkferries.co.uk; to Sarah at www.discoverireland.com; to James Rodd at www.sportsvision.co.uk; to Keeley and www.oneill.com; to James and www.ripcurl.com; to Tom, Ernie and everyone at www.finisterreuk.com; to Kate at www.flybe.com; and to Tynemouth council for its help.

As ever, my gratitude to my agent, David Milner, and to my editor, Andrew Gordon. My thanks also to Julia Silk, who copy-edited this book, and – for helping to spread the gospel of surfing in the national media – to Clare Hogan, Rose Wild and Tom Whitwell at *The Times* and Mark MacKenzie, Kate Simon and Simon Redfern at the *Independent on Sunday*.

I am grateful to the following photographers who contributed images, help and advice: Al Mackinnon, at www.almackinnon.com; Kirstin Prisk, at www.kirstinprisk.com; Greg Martin, at www.findyourwave.com; Tony Plant, at www.surftwisted.com; Mike Searle, at www.carvemag.com; Gary Knights; Jon Bowen, at www.localsurfer.co.uk; Neil Watson, of Surfeast Productions; Peter Britton, at www.peterbrittonphotography.co.uk; Paul Gill, at www.surfvisions.co.uk; John Carter; Roger Sharp, at www.slidemag.com; Alex Williams, at www.alexcam.co.uk, and Stuart Norton, at www.stunortonphotography.com

The following books were of great help in my travels: The *Stormrider* guides – see www.lowpressure.co.uk; *Surfing Britain* by Chris Nelson and Demi Taylor – see www.footprintbooks.com, and *Surf UK* by Alf Alderson, currently being updated – see www.fernhurstbooks.co.uk. The pioneering guidebook for British surfing is Carl Thomson's *Surfing in Great Britain* and another book of great appeal is *You Should Have Been Here Yesterday* by Rod Holmes and Doug Wilson, SeasEdge Publications, 1994. Jon Bowen's *Surfing Moods* (Halsgrove, 2006) admirably captures the joy of surfing in Devon and Cornwall while anyone doubting that surfing is a pursuit meriting serious scientific analysis need only read Tony Butt and Paul Russell's excellent *Surf Science* (Alison Hodge, 2002).

On celluloid, *The Endless Summer* remains the classic to inspire any surf trip, anywhere, but closer to home I would commend Mark Lumsden's *Cold Rush* (see www.liquidproductions.co.uk), Angus Dunlop's *The Elusive* (www.theelusive.com) and Donny Wright's *Longwave* (www.stillstoked.co.uk). Rod Sumpter's *Come Surf With Me* has some wonderful footage of early surfing in Britain and Ireland and is available from one of the leading surf forecasting websites, www.A1surf.com. There is a number of surf forecasting and general surfing websites devoted to the domestic scene but among the best are www.magicseaweed.com, www.surfcore.co.uk, www.surfhog.com, www.bloggsd.com, www.ecosurfproject.org, www.coldswell.com, www.thesurfingmuseum.co.uk, www.coldwatersoul.co.uk and www.sas.org.uk.

The British and Irish surfing community is well-represented in magazine form and the following publications, read over the years or, in some cases, since their more recent arrival, were an ongoing inspiration: *Carve; Wavelength; The Surfer's Path; Huck; Drift; The Surfer's Journal; Slide; Pit Pilot; Surfer; Surfing; SurfGirl; ThreeSixty; Stranger; Tonnau; Fins; Freeflow; Windsurf* and *Boards*.

There's a lot out there, on our Atlantic, North Sea and English Channel coastline; more than you might think. Indeed, if I'd tried to talk to everyone involved in British and Irish surfing I'd never have finished this book. I'll be writing some more about the surfing scene on our admittedly sometimes rather chilly doorstep at www.timesonline.co.uk/surfnation, but meanwhile: keep looking, and keep surfing.

GLOSSARY

A-Frame – a clean wave with distinct shoulders on either side, meaning that it can be ridden by one surfer going frontside, the other backside, at the same time.

Aerial – a manoeuvre by which a surfer propels his or her board above the wave

Alaia – a surfboard made of wood used by the Hawaiians in the late 19th century

Aloha – Hawaiian word meaning, variously, hello, goodbye, peace, goodwill

Artificial Reef – an underwater, man-made structure that – all things being equal – will cause waves to break with predictable form where otherwise they would not (cf. the long-debated and awaited Boscombe Reef in Bournemouth)

ASP – Association of Surfing Professionals

Backside – surfing with your back to the wave

Barrel – a hollow wave that allows 'tube time'

Beachbreak – a sand bottom break

Blank – a foam block from which a surfboard is made

Blown out – surf destroyed by howling onshore wind (one of the first terms learnt by British and Irish surfers)

Bottom turn – turning the board at the foot of the wave: the crucial manoeuvre to set up the rest of the ride

Charger – a surfer who gives it everything whatever the conditions (cf. Robyn Davies, John McCarthy)

Close-out – a wave that breaks in one motion, without peeling, rendering it unsurfable

Corduroy – surf that is strong and distinct; lined up like 'corduroy' as it approaches

Core – an abbreviation of 'hardcore' to denote a surfer who surfs throughout the year, in any conditions (cf. many British and Irish surfers)

Cutback – to turn back to the curl (the breaking part of the wave)

Dawn patrol – to surf at first light, often to avoid the crowds

Drop in – the cardinal sin of surfing: to catch a wave on the shoulder when someone else is already up and riding, deeper on the face (cf. Andy Martin's *Stealing the Wave)*

Duck dive – the means by which a surfer on a shortboard or a mini-mal pushes the board underneath incoming waves to reach the line-up

Face – the unbroken part of the wave: that which the surfer rides

Falls – the pitching part of the wave (see 'over the falls')

Filth, filthy – something very good

Firing – surf that is filthy or 'going off, pumping, cranking'

Floater – off-the-lip to re-entry across the white water; like being off-piste

Freight train – extremely fast and hollow wave (cf. Freights, in Barbados)

Frontside – to surf with one's front to the wave

Geek – an inexperienced surfer

Glassy – clean, perfect swell with no wind; note also 'glass-off' – when the water is smooth as glass

Glide – an epiphanic moment in surfing when board, wave and surfer come together: the surfer, then, has 'the glide' (cf. Allan Weisbecker's *In Search of Captain Zero)*

Gnarly – horrible and intimidating surf, usually sizeable

Goat boat – a waveski

Goofy foot – a surfer who rides with his right foot forward

Green room – inside the tube, where the surfer is covered by the pitching lip

Grom/grommet – a young surfer, often given to hanging around surf shops when not surfing

Gun – a long, narrow and pointed gun for seriously big surf

Hang Ten – to hang all ten toes off the nose of the board, part of the art of longboarding

Hold down – the experience of being held under water in big surf

Hollow – a concave, curling wave, often one offering a barrel, tube or the green room

Impact zone – where the waves are breaking. Not a good place to be

Kick out – to exit a wave in control and gracefully

Killer – something very good

Kook – beginner or inexperienced surfer

Kook out – the opposite of kick out

Leash – the cord (of semi-elastic urethane) that attaches a surfer's ankle to the board

Left or left-hander – a wave breaking to the surfer's left as he looks to the beach

Line-up – the place where surfers wait for waves; once they are there, they line up their position with a point on the shore

Lip – the pitching crest of a wave

Locals – those who live at and always surf a particular spot

Log – a longboard; a board over 9 ft in length

Longboard – a board over 9 ft. Their size makes them easier to paddle into waves

Malibu – a legendary surf spot in California and, outside the US, the term often used to describe a longboard

Mini-mal – a board around 7′ 6″ in length which is a hybrid of a longboard and a shortboard. Versatile and popular among many intermediate surfers

Natural/natural footer – a surfer who rides with his left leg forward

North Shore – the area on the north side of the Hawaiian island of Oahu; surfing's mecca, the home to many of the world's best breaks

Off-the-lip – to snap the board hard against the lip of a breaking wave and turn 180 degrees back down onto the wave face

Offshore – when the wind blows from the land out to sea, often helping create perfect surfing conditions

Old school – a dyed-in-the-wool approach to surfing, skateboarding and the like

Olo – a surfboard made of Koa or wiliwili wood, used by Hawaiian royalty in the late nineteenth century

Onshore – when the wind is blowing from the sea on to the land, rendering the surf blown-out

Outside – beyond the breaking waves. Surfers will shout 'outside!' meaning paddle for the outside when a large set is approaching

Over the falls – the hideous experience of being pitched from top to the bottom of the wave as the lip breaks

Peak – the middle and highest part of an incoming wave, which defines which way a surfer will ride (to the right or left)

Pit – the hollow part beneath the pitching lip of a wave

Point break – where waves wrap around an exposed piece of land creating excellent, predictable waves

Prone out – to ride a wave to the shore on one's belly

Quiver – a surfer's selection of surfboards

Rag dolled – to be nailed, drilled, destroyed by a wave

Rail – the edge of a surfboard

Redonculous – a word apparently meaning 'very, very good' that no one has ever heard

Reef break – waves that break over an underwater reef (e.g. of coral) or series of rocks. Often dangerous (cf. Pipeline, Porthleven, Aileens)

Re-entry – to return to the wave face having executed a floater, off-the-lip, aerial or other such move

Regular foot – same as natural foot

Right or right-hander – a wave breaking to the surfer's right as he looks to the beach

Rip (1) – to shred the wave, to ride it to the best of one's ability (term deployed for good surfers riding at their best)

Rip (2) – current that flows out to sea, a characteristic of many UK beachbreaks. Take care and ask the lifeguards

Rocker – the curvature along the bottom of a surfboard from nose to tail. The greater rocker the better for turning but the more difficult to paddle into waves

Roundhouse cutback – stylish move whereby the surfer carves in a wide arc back to the breaking curl

Set – a group of approaching waves

Sex wax – most famous brand of surfboard wax, necessary to give grip

Shortboard – used for high performance surfing and between 5′ and 7′ 6″. Not for beginners

Shoulder – part of the wave some distance from the peak; still rideable, but only just and often with the likelihood of dropping in on someone

Sick – something very, very, very good

Soul surfer – difficult to define but generally speaking someone who lives for surfing and embodies the surfing stoke to the max

Sponge – a bodyboard

Stoked – to be ecstatic after a surfing experience

Stringer – strip or strips of wood running down the length of a board

Surfari – surf trip

Takeoff – when the surfer catches a wave just before it breaks and starts his ride

Tanker – a large longboard

Thruster – a surfboard with three fins

Trim – to adjust one's position and achieve maximum planing speed for the board

Tube – cylindrical wave into which surfers disappear (cf. Russell Winter at the O'Neill Highland Open)

Walking the board – to walk up and down the board, a move cherished by longboarders

WCT – World Championship Tour

WQS – World Qualifying Series

Zoo – a crowded line-up